MANCHESTER

For Elaine, Jonathan and Matthew
and in loving memory of my parents,
Ellen (1970–1991) and Charles (1908–1992)
and my brother, Ronald (1933–1993)

Manchester

Third edition

Alan Kidd

Illustrated from the archives
and with contemporary photographs by
Ian Beesley

Edinburgh University Press

First edition © Alan Kidd, 1993
Second edition © Alan Kidd, 1996
Third edition © Alan Kidd, 2002
Ian Beesley's photographs © Ian Beesley

Edinburgh University Press Ltd
22 George Square, Edinburgh

Typeset in Janson Text
by Carnegie Publishing Ltd, Chatsworth Road, Lancaster, and
printed and bound in Great Britain by The Cromwell Press

A CIP Record for this book is available from the British Library

ISBN 0 7486 1552 2 (paperback)

Contents

Historical Editor's Foreword

The books in this series are designed and written with a broad readership in mind: local people interested to know how the character of their town has been shaped by major historical forces and the energies of their predecessors; newcomers and visitors curious to acquire a historical introduction to their new surroundings; general readers wishing to see how the sweeps of national and international history have manifested themselves in particular urban communities; and the scholar seeking to understand urbanisation by comparing and contrasting local experiences.

We live, most of us, in intensely urban environments. These are the products largely of the last two centuries of historical development, although the roots of many towns, of course, go back deep into the past. In recent years there has been considerable historical research of a high standard into this urban history. Narrative and descriptive accounts of the history of towns and cities can now be replaced by studies such as the TOWN AND CITY HISTORIES which investigate, analyse and, above all, explain the economic, political, social and cultural processes and consequences of urbanisation.

Writers for this series consider the changing economic foundations of their town or city and the way change has affected its physical shape, built environment, employment opportunities and urban character. The nature and interests of those who wielded power locally and the structure and functions of local government in different periods are also examined, since locally exercised authority could determine much about the fortunes and quality of urban life. Particular emphasis is placed on the changing life experiences of ordinary men, women and children – their homes, education, occupations, social relations, living standards and leisure activities. Towns and cities control and respond to the values, aspirations and actions of their residents. The books in this series therefore explore social behaviour as well as the economic and political history of those who lived in and helped make the towns and cities of today.

Stephen Constantine
University of Lancaster

Preface and Acknowledgements

A study of an historically important city like Manchester needs no justification, but it may seem curious to some that this is a history of Manchester alone and not also of its close neighbour Salford. In fact, at many points in the text there is an overlap in the treatment of the 'twin cities'; the municipal and parliamentary boundaries have had little reality in terms of industry and employment, and everyday patterns of living and working have had a great deal in common. However, a compelling reason for treating Manchester and Salford separately is their quite distinct political identities and cultural traditions. Each has a justified pride in its past. Each has a history worthy of separate recording. It would have done justice to neither to subsume both in a joint study, and been a denial of their individuality to regard them as a single city. It is worth noting that in some histories statistics for Manchester and Salford are combined. Geography may seem to justify this, but their economic patterns were not identical and in this study combined figures have generally been eschewed.

In writing this history I have benefited greatly from the valuable local history collections in the libraries of the Manchester region, especially the Local Studies Unit of the Manchester Central Reference Library and the Local Collection of the library of the Manchester Metropolitan University. The staffs of both have been consistently helpful. Most of the archive illustrations included in this history appear by kind permission of Chris E. Makepeace: my publisher and I are grateful both to him and to Ian Beesley who has provided the modern photographs.

Anyone who sets out to write a general history risks treading on several toes; one cannot have specialist knowledge in every area. I have been fortunate in the three people who have given detailed comments on the work in progress: Stephen Constantine, who is in my mind a model editor; my colleague, Terry Wyke, whose encyclopaedic knowledge of the city's history is legendary among those who know him; and my wife, Elaine, whose unfailing support and critical honesty were welcome in equal measure. Each has saved me from many errors, those that remain are entirely my own responsibility.

Alan Kidd
Manchester, October 1992

Preface to the Third Edition

It is now almost ten years since the first edition of this history was published. In that time Manchester has undergone a dramatic transformation. Confronted with industrial decline, the city has engineered a recovery through a physical and cultural 'renaissance' more remarkable than that found in any other UK city. It is a timely moment for a historian to make a fresh assessment of Manchester's future prospects in the context of its past achievements. Consequently this edition includes an entirely new chapter on the developments of the last ten years or so. I am indebted to Terry Wyke for his advice in the writing of this chapter. In addition, I have taken the opportunity to update the earlier chapters in the light of recent historial writing. I have included a guide to the latest research as an addition to the bibliography to be found at the end of the book. Further evidence of recent writing on the city can be found in the revised footnote references to most chapters.

Manchester,
January 2002

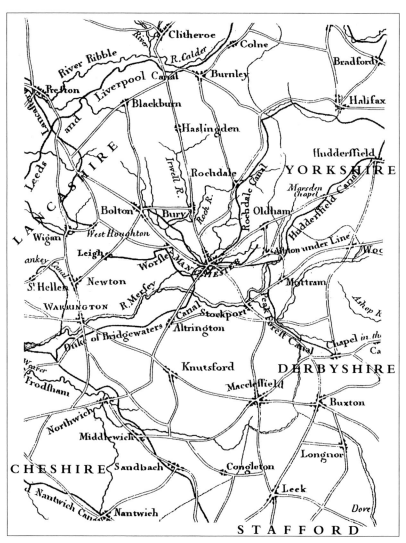

A map to show Manchester and surrounding towns, adapted from John Aiken, *A Description of the Country from Thirty to Forty Miles Round Manchester* (1795).

CHAPTER I

Before the Industrial Revolution

Every town and city has its story, but few have a history which belongs to the world. Although Manchester has been intermittently inhabited for almost two thousand years, a process beginning just over two centuries ago was to put this hitherto remote Lancashire commercial and manufacturing town on the international map. Manchester was arguably the first modern city. Changes wrought by the industrial revolution caused unprecedented urban growth, ushered in new ways of living and working and generated new ideas of economy and society. Manchester's history is more than just the story of a town it is a contribution to the history of the modern world.

Manchester stands just south-west of the foothills of the Pennines. To the south lies the Cheshire plain. This undulating glacial landscape long ago carved out the natural defences and provided the navigable rivers which attracted the earliest settlers. The casual visitor to the modern city of Manchester could, however, be excused for failing to notice that the city centre occupies the land between the confluence of one large river, the Irwell, with two smaller streams, the Irk and the Medlock. In recent times the natural geography of the place has been obscured by railways, bridges, buildings and roads. In the eighteenth century, before the industrial revolution, the sandstone bluff on which the town was built was much more discernible, and surrounding fields were visible instead of the modern urban sprawl.

But there have been two 'Manchesters' in the past. The eighteenth-century town was a development from the medieval settlement on the high ground above the confluence of the Irwell and the Irk, the area around the present-day cathedral. By contrast, the earlier Roman fort and settlement had been further south. The 'breast-like hill' which gave the town its Roman name, Mamucium, was situated where the Medlock flows into the Irwell in what is now Castlefield. Thus the modern visitor who passes along Deansgate from one end to the other is following a thoroughfare linking Roman Mamucium to medieval Manchester.[1]

Roman Manchester

Mamucium was a frontier fort and settlement of the Roman Empire. It was strategically placed at a meeting-point between the east-west route linking the legionary bases at Eboracum (York) and Deva (Chester) with another vital route striking north along the western rim of the Pennines to Luguvalium (Carlisle). Much of the area stretching from the Peak district to Hadrian's Wall was the homeland of a loosely confederated Celtic tribe which the Romans called the Brigantes. The Manchester region may have been the home of a tribal sub-group, the Setantii.

First conquered in the mid-70s A.D., Brigantian territory was always under direct military rule. Thus its forts were vital to the control of the region. The site for Mamucium was personally chosen by Britain's new governor, Agricola, and earliest Roman levels excavated by archaeologists date from about A.D. 77–8. The first fort on the site was square in plan covering an area of about three acres and designed to hold a 480-man infantry unit. This original fort of stockpiled timber with defensive turf ramparts was later expanded and subsequently replaced by a larger stone construction in the third century. Military occupation of the site lasted until the Romans left Britain early in the fifth century.

Although the Brigantes were never fully integrated into the Roman Empire and the military function of Mamucium remained paramount a civil settlement or *vicus* grew up outside the fortress walls. This was the first Manchester. It provided facilities for the troops and housed small industrial workshops. Thus, to the north of the Roman fort, rude timber-frame houses faced the occasional more substantial two-storey structure overlooking surrounding market gardens. Iron-working furnaces abutted storehouses, shops and brothels. The area to the south and west was marshy and swamped. The *vicus* did not survive the Romans' departure from Britain. The stone walls of the fortress remained an abandoned ruin for hundreds of years until plundered for building materials between the tenth and the twelfth centuries. All the archaeological evidence suggests that in the centuries following the demise of Mamucium there was no town of Manchester and settlement of the area was rural rather than urban.

Medieval Manchester

Manchester reappears in the historical record in a brief reference in the Anglo-Saxon Chronicle under the year 919. There is also some archaeological evidence suggesting settlement during the tenth century, although the 'Angel Stone', now in the cathedral and said to date from that period, is probably a later survival. The place may have been a fortified outpost against Viking incursions. It is, therefore, possible that the origins of the medieval town of Manchester lie in the period prior to the Norman Conquest of 1066. As it stands, however, the evidence is inconclusive. One thing is sure. The post-Conquest settlement was

Market Place. The heart of Manchester through to the early nineteenth century when this print was published. One of John Ralston's 'Views of the Ancient Buildings of Manchester'.

upstream of the Roman fort, on the site today occupied by Chetham's College and Manchester Cathedral.[2]

Medieval Manchester was not an important town. The most prominent places in Lancashire were the Royal Boroughs of Preston, Lancaster, Liverpool and Wigan. Manchester, by comparison, was not to enjoy independent status, with borough corporation and parliamentary representation, until the nineteenth century. It was a small market town with an annual fair. For administrative purposes, Manchester was originally part of the extensive Salford Hundred created after the Norman Conquest. Thus was Manchester subordinated to Salford. But this did not last for long. The Salford Hundred had been part of the territories granted by a grateful William the Conqueror to Roger de Poitevin who had been with him at the Battle of Hastings. This Norman earl likewise divided his newly acquired lands into a number of feofdoms including what was to become the barony of Manchester. Thus the administrative separation of Manchester from Salford was achieved and their paths were hitherto divided. The first baron of Manchester was Albert de Gresle (Grelley) whose family ruled the manor of Manchester for two centuries. Thereafter it changed hands several times before coming to rest, in the 1590s, with the Mosleys who held the manor till the new Corporation of Manchester purchased it in 1846. By contrast, Salford came to the Crown in 1399 as part of the Duchy of Lancaster. Thus today the Queen is both Duke of Lancaster and lord of the manor of Salford.

Few people realise that Manchester once had a castle. This is not

Chetham's College, from a print of 1836. Built in the fifteenth century as a college for priests, Chetham's opened as a school and free library in 1653. It is now Chetham's School of Music. Although the River Irk has been culverted, the building can still be seen from this vantage point.

surprising since it was of no political or military importance. It probably stood where Chetham's College stands today, on flat land overlooking the Irwell and the Irk. It is unlikely ever to have been more than a timber structure with a wooden palisade. By the late thirteenth century the Grelleys had replaced it with a fortified manor house. From here, as lords of the manor, they let out land to free and villein tenants who, in return, worked on the demesne land at required times. The lord also owned the only mill, by the Irk at Long Millgate, at which all tenants had to grind their corn. But the lord of the manor of Manchester also benefited from the growing number of his tenants who were exempt from compulsory labour services. These were the townsmen or burgesses.

Medieval Manchester grew up around the manor house and the parish church of St Mary. At one end was Long Millgate, the main access from the north, tracing the course of the Irk, at the other, Market Place (now destroyed) from which developed Market Stead Lane (Market Street), and finally Deansgate, the route to Chester and the south. The town developed in a series of plots of land either leased directly from the lord or by burgage tenure. In addition to houses, plots might contain workshops and open spaces such as yards and gardens.

It grew into a market town but never escaped the clutches of the lord of the manor. Nonetheless, the right to an annual fair was obtained in 1223, and the town was important enough to be granted a charter in 1301 which was to provide for its government until the nineteenth century.

The annual fair, traditionally held on Acresfield, arable land adjacent to the town, part of which space now forms St Ann's Square, was the first to be founded in the Salford Hundred and only the fourth in south Lancashire. This and the customary Saturday market signify the town's trading function. Manchester was not, however, a centre of craft production and there is no direct evidence of the existence of craft guilds.

Manchester may have been a small and unimportant town, but the medieval parish of Manchester was extensive and wealthy. It covered about sixty square miles, between the parish of Prestwich-cum-Oldham in the north, Ashton-under-Lyne and the River Tame to the east, with Flixton and Eccles in the west and the River Mersey from Stockport to Urmston to the south. When St Mary's was made collegiate in 1421, Thomas de la Warre, lord of the manor, granted the site of his manor house and other lands to build and support a college of priests. Although dissolved in 1547, it was later refounded and the warden from 1596 to 1608 was John Dee, polymath and adviser to Queen Elizabeth I. The building was acquired by Humphrey Chetham in 1653 and converted into a residential school (Chetham's Hospital) and free public library (Chetham's Library).

Fifteenth to Eighteenth Centuries

Between the fifteenth and the eighteenth centuries Manchester was to develop from the unimportant township of the medieval era into the regional capital of south-east Lancashire. Its new importance had nothing to do with politics or local government, indeed its manorial administration endured as an anachronism into the industrial era. Manchester's rise had everything to do with its economy. For at least two centuries before the industrial revolution and the mechanisation of cotton production, Manchester had been a cloth town which combined manufacture with trade. Its population rose from an estimated 2,300 in 1543 to around 43,000 in 1773.[3] The greatest period of growth came in the century following 1660 when the town's population more than quadrupled in size. Studies of the sixteenth century make it clear that Manchester's regional preeminence was established early.[4]

The origins of cloth production in the town remain obscure but it is certain that Elizabethan Manchester was already a manufacturing as well as a market centre for woollens and linen. Raw materials were imported from as far afield as Ireland (linen yarn) and goods sold throughout the provinces and on the London markets. Although this trade increased the wealth of Manchester merchants and attracted migrant workers, it did not make the town of national significance. The diversity of Manchester's economy made it the most prosperous place in sixteenth-century Lancashire, but the county itself was among

the poorest and most backward in the land. It was the introduction of
new manufactures in the early seventeenth century which proved a
portent of future greatness and which, ultimately, was to raise Manchester to commercial preeminence and to transform the economic
fortunes of the county. Around 1600 began the momentous rise of the
Lancashire cotton industry.

Cotton was first introduced to the region through the manufacture
of fustian cloth, a mixture of linen and cotton. Its production spread
rapidly throughout south-east Lancashire, notably in the Bolton, Blackburn and Oldham areas as well as in the villages of the parish of
Manchester, where the proportion of the population employed in manufacture may have exceeded the numbers in agriculture as early as 1650.
By the later seventeenth century, Manchester was one of a string of
newly expanding inland towns situated in rural-industrial regions, each
catering for a specialised product. Birmingham was already a centre of
metal manufacturing, Nottingham and Leicester were noted for their
hosiery and Leeds for its woollen textiles; with Manchester it was
fustians and linen. These middle-ranking towns of the seventeenth
century were the future industrial giants of the nineteenth century.
Why was Manchester such an economic success?

The precise reasons for Manchester's growing importance are
unclear. No more than there is a clear consensus on why the south-east
Lancashire cotton industry became the cradle of the industrial revolution.[5] The town had always enjoyed some natural advantages from its
location at the confluence of several rivers and proximity to Liverpool
for imports of raw material. Manchester also enjoyed freedom from the
traditions of the past. The absence of a corporation and of craft guilds
is usually regarded as a positive contribution to Manchester's rising
fortunes. It was a non-corporate town in which the interests of newcomers were not sacrificed to the privileges of freemen. The lack of
restrictions also enabled the linen industry to adapt quickly to the
introduction of cotton. But some incorporated towns expanded too
(Leeds and Nottingham are examples) and in the process generally
abandoned guild restrictions. There may be more to the general point
that once a town had developed a specialised role in terms of production
and marketing, this initial advantage was reinforced by the arrival of
an appropriately skilled population, the growth of a reputation for a
particular product and the development of a merchandising network.[6]
In Manchester's case the trading links already established with London
during the sixteenth century facilitated the export of the new fustian
fabrics. From the early Tudor period the town had become famous for
its distribution of the so-called 'Manchester Cottons' (in fact a variety
of woollen cloth manufactured in the surrounding area) and population
growth had as much to do with an expanding workshop sector as with
increasing commercial functions. When the market for cotton expanded

Wellington Inn, Old Shambles. Once in Market Place, this timber-frame building (which survives today in a new location near the Cathedral) is a reminder of Manchester's pre-industrial architecture. (*Photograph: Manchester Central Library*)

in the eighteenth century, Manchester was well poised to exploit its potential for wealth creation.

Manchester remained the regional centre of the woollen and linen industries in the seventeenth century, and was notable for its smallware manufacture (ribbons, tapes and buttons etc.) and silk weaving, but it was the trade in cotton products which took off. By the 1690s cotton was being added to established linen lines to produce cotton-linen checked and striped cloths to meet a growing domestic market. The relative importance of cotton cloth amongst the other textiles manufactured in the region continued to advance during the first half of the eighteenth century. By 1750 pure cottons were already being produced and Manchester was in decline as a centre of the woollen industry. The future was hitched to cotton.

During the eighteenth century Manchester became a town of national significance, although its antiquated system of local government attracted attention: 'the greatest mere village in England' as Defoe called it.[7] Its business community flourished, dominated by great merchants and merchant manufacturers who increasingly controlled the 'putting-out' system or domestic industry by which most cloth was produced. Independent weavers who owned their own homes and dealt with the masters

Long Millgate. Until the nineteenth century this narrow thoroughfare was the main road into Manchester from the north. The picture dates from the 1870s and shows the new Manchester Grammar School building towering in the background (this now belongs to Chetham's School of Music).

on equal terms were a dying breed. Most workers in the Lancashire textile industry were inured to wage labour even before the advent of the factory. Manchester merchants were the effective employers of their cottage workers: putting out the raw material to weavers, cutters, dyers, bleachers and printers. Some linen and check manufacture was on a workshop basis.

Great fortunes were made in Manchester well before the industrial revolution. By the early eighteenth century, trade and manufacture had produced an elite of successful business families. For example, James

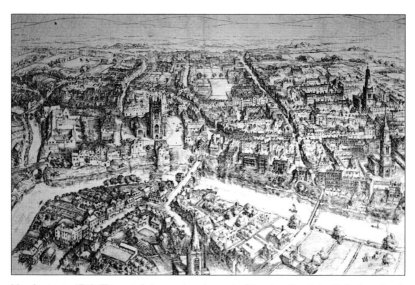

Manchester in 1760. This artist's impression shows the River Irwell and the Collegiate church in the foreground with the narrowness of Market Street rising from the bustle of Market Place to open fields at Piccadilly on the outskirts of town.

Bayley (1674–1753) was a prominent Manchester merchant whose father had been a silk weaver in the town. His eldest son converted the family inheritance into a country estate but the younger sons stayed in trade and their sons in turn were check manufacturers and cotton merchants. The strength of the Manchester business community prior to industrialisation is indicated by the willingness of gentry families to pay premiums of up to £500 for their younger sons to become apprentices in Manchester mercantile houses.[8]

By the second half of the eighteenth century, Manchester had become a provincial centre of the first rank, already attracting interest for its urban growth, commercial life and transport innovations. Roads, packhorse routes and canals converged on Manchester markets. The Irwell and Mersey Navigation was completed by 1736, thus establishing a navigable water route to Liverpool. In 1729 Sir Oswald Mosley had built the first Exchange. Urban growth proceeded apace. By 1783 James Ogden could observe that: 'The large and populous town of Manchester has now excited the attention and curiosity of strangers, on account of its extensive trade and the rapid increase of its buildings, with the enlargement of its streets'.[9]

Manchester had arrived, and this before a single factory had been built. But if the previous two centuries had served to put Manchester on the national platform, the events of the seventy years between 1780 and 1850 were to push it firmly to the centre of the stage. From being an object of curiosity, Manchester and the industrial system it appeared to epitomise were to become almost a national obsession. The history of Manchester up to 1780 is but a prelude to the momentous happenings of the industrial age which followed.

References

1. For a useful introduction to Roman Manchester see S. Bryant *et al.*, *The Archaeological History of Greater Manchester, Vol. III, Roman Manchester: A Frontier Settlement*, Greater Manchester Archaeological Unit, Manchester, 1987.

2. For a survey of Manchester from the Anglo-Saxon period to the end of the Middle Ages see M. Morris, *The Archaeological History of Greater Manchester, Vol. 1, Medieval Manchester*, Greater Manchester Archaeological Unit, Manchester, 1983.

3. T. S. Willan, *Elizabethan Manchester*, Chetham Society, Manchester, 1980, p. 38; A. P. Wadsworth and J. de Lacy Mann, *The Cotton Trade and Industrial Lancashire, 1600–1780*, Manchester University Press, 1931, p. 510.

4. Willan, *Elizabethan Manchester* and N. Lowe, *The Lancashire Textile Industry in the Sixteenth Century*, Chetham Society, Manchester, 1972.

5. The classic account of this period is Wadsworth and Mann, *Cotton Trade and Industrial Lancashire 1600–1780*, Manchester University Press, 1931. For more recent assessments of the issues see J. Walton, 'Proto-industrialisation and the first industrial revolution: the case of Lancashire' in P. Hudson (ed.), *Regions and Industries: A Perspective on the Industrial Revolution in Britain*, Cambridge University Press, 1989 and G. Timmins, *Made in Lancashire: A History of Regional Industrialisation*, Manchester University Press, 1998, Part I.

6. For this point see P. Corfield, 'Economic growth and change in seventeenth-century English towns' in C. Phythian-Adams *et al.*, *The Traditional Community under Stress*, Open University, Milton Keynes, 1977.

7. D. Defoe, *A Tour Through the Whole Island of Great Britain, 1724–6*, Penguin edn, Harmondsworth, 1971, p. 544.

8. J. Aiken, *A Description of the Country from Thirty to Forty Miles Round Manchester* (1795), David and Charles, Newton Abbot, 1968, p. 184.

9. J. Ogden, *A Description of Manchester* (1783), Library Association, Bath, 1968, p. 3.

Part I

First Industrial City: 1780–1850

CHAPTER 2

Manchester, Cotton
and the Industrial Revolution

The Manchester of the 1780s was already attracting the notice of outsiders as a centre of wealth-creation and urban growth. But this was as nothing compared to the attention it was to receive some six decades later. By then, over half a century of revolutionary change had made Manchester the 'shock city' of its age.[1] It was the shock of the new which assaulted the senses and stimulated the imaginations of contemporaries. Manchester attracted visitors from home and abroad seeking the sights and sounds of a new way of living. Some were appalled, others excited, still others saw in its newness a historical development of epoch-making proportions. It seemed as if all roads led to Manchester. Why was this?

In the first place, it took until the 1840s for the nation to absorb the fact that there had been an industrial revolution in northern England. From the late eighteenth century, the machine manufacture of cotton had made the Manchester region (south-east Lancashire and parts of northern Cheshire) a centre of sustained economic growth, the like of which the world had never seen before. Cotton was central to British industrialisation and cotton meant Manchester and its region. As early as the 1790s, 70% of the British cotton industry was concentrated in the cotton district of Lancashire and Cheshire; by 1835 the figure had risen even further to 90%. How do we explain this success? Crucial was the existing combination of textile manufacturing skills in the putting-out system coupled with financial and commercial networks that had grown up over the previous century. To this can be added Manchester's long experience in marketing and distribution and the proximity of Liverpool for imports of raw cotton. Demand for cotton cloth continued to rise and the economic attraction of mechanised production acted as a spur to human ingenuity. Crucially, Lancashire producers adopted the new technology of the machine age earlier than in other cotton regions (East Midlands, North Wales, Ulster and Lowland Scotland). Moreover, water-powered production had encouraged geographical diversity but the transition to steam power from the 1780s onwards ensured the concentration of production in the towns of Textile Lancashire. From the outset Manchester was the commercial hub of the region. Transport developments during the canal era and later the railway age strengthened its position. Finally, as we shall see, the local economy was more complex than at first sight. Whilst cotton was dominant, Manchester itself was strong in other industries vital to cotton's growth such as machine manufacture and repair and the chemical industry.

A second reason for Manchester's prominence was the enormous urban growth revealed by the Census of 1841, which made contemporaries accept that theirs was the 'age of great cities'. It was not just the rising national population figures which impressed contemporaries but their concentration in large towns, especially certain provincial centres which were growing at an unprecedented rate. Whilst between 1801 and 1841 the population of London had doubled, that of Manchester had more than trebled and by 1851 was over four times larger than fifty years before. Manchester was not alone in this; among the larger towns Liverpool had also multiplied fourfold, and Bradford's population was eight times greater than in 1801. But there was a difference of scale. Manchester and Liverpool were three times the size of Bradford; outside London they were the biggest towns in England. The environmental and social problems created by rapid urban growth were most marked in the biggest centres and, for a while, Manchester became a symbol for the nation of twin developments. It combined massive urban growth with factory production and acquired almost mythical status as the emblem of a new order of things.

Population of Manchester 1801–1851
(Based on the municipal boundaries of 1838)

1801	76,788
1811	91,136
1821	129,035
1831	187,022
1841	242,983
1851	316,213

A third cause of the huge international interest in all things Mancunian was the sense that Manchester represented new social classes and unleashed political forces: trade unionism, Chartism and socialism. Working-class politics demanded democracy and appeared to threaten property. If it was to be contained, it had to be understood, and Manchester seemed to hold the key to this knowledge. Finally, the Manchester middle class was, by 1850, a force to be reckoned with in national politics. Manchester entered the political arena as the voice of the provinces against London, the proud possessor of a new economic creed, free trade, and the home of the powerful political lobby which

Cotton mills, Ancoats. Although altered during the nineteenth century, the McConnel & Kennedy and Murray mills are a vivid reminder of the early years of the industrial revolution in Manchester. (*Photograph: Ian Beesley*)

had helped to forge this creed into national policy, the Anti-Corn Law League. On each of these counts, Manchester could not be ignored. Events had forced it centre-stage.

Subsequent chapters will consider Manchester's place in the social and political history of the early industrial era. It is the purpose of this chapter to examine the town's symbolic image as the industrial capital of cotton. It is a familiar and enduring image, but is it an entirely accurate one?

A Factory Town?

Associate the words industrial revolution and cotton and they conjure up scenes of grimy northern factory-scapes. A forest of arrogant chimneys belching smoke. Grim factory towns throbbing to the pulse of steam engines. Multi-storey cotton mills employing thousands of men, women and children in long hours of monotonous toil. The mills might be anywhere in south-east Lancashire but in the popular imagination they are most often in Manchester. The Lowry print on the living room wall may be a Salford scene but since it portrays industrialism, to the average eye, it must be Manchester. It was ever thus. To the nineteenth

century, contemporary Manchester was 'Cottonopolis', the very essence
of industrialism, the first factory town. How accurate are such im-
pressions?

What was Manchester? Many contemporaries saw it as the archetypal
manufacturing town, the model of all the other Lancashire mill towns,
themselves sometimes referred to as 'Little Manchesters'. But if we are
to take this as our starting point we will be misled, for Manchester was
never merely a mill town. As we have already seen, for centuries it had
offered marketing facilities for linens and woollens, and during the
eighteenth century had become the regional market centre for cotton
mixtures. Thus before the first factory was erected in the 1780s,
Manchester was already known for its warehouses. The warehouse
continued to play a vital role in its economic life. Despite its undoubted
contribution to the growth of factory production, Manchester may more
appropriately be described as a 'warehouse town'. What does this mean?

First of all, it does not mean there were no factories. Whereas a
stranger approaching the town in 1783 would have noticed the chimney
of only one large mill, that owned by the famous Richard Arkwright
on Miller Street near Shudehill,[2] by 1816 there were 86 steam-powered
spinning factories in Manchester and Salford. Around this time the
main factory district was that focused on Ancoats but also including
New Cross, Beswick and Holt Town. Here could be found the huge
factories of McConnel & Kennedy and the Murray brothers as well as
the greatest density of working-class housing. There was also a clutch
of mills along Oxford Road by the River Medlock, including those of
Hugh Hornby Birley and Robert Owen. During the 1820s, more
factories were built in Ancoats and along the Medlock, and new industrial zones developed alongside the Rochdale and Ashton canals to the
east and astride the Irk Valley to the north of the town. As the River
Irwell wound its way through Salford it brought industry in its wake.
The increasing complexity of the local canal network, and the advent
of a rail network after the Liverpool to Manchester line was opened
in 1830, further added to the industrial belt.

But visitors who saw only this side of Manchester life missed something
very important. Never more than a few streets away was the main
warehouse district. As the demand for commercial premises grew so the
warehouses spread from King Street and St Ann's Square in the 1780s
to the Cannon Street, High Street and Market Street area by the 1800s;
thence they moved to the region of Mosley Street by the second quarter
of the nineteenth century and later to Portland Street and Princess
Street. Here lay the commercial heart of the city. On Cannon Street
alone, in 1815, there were 57 warehouses occupied by 106 separate
firms. But the importance of the warehouse to the local economy is
most tellingly revealed by the striking imbalance of investment between
the warehouse and factory sectors of the 'first factory town'.

Total capital investment in factories was considerably less than in warehouses. Warehouses absorbed over 48% of property asset investment by 1815 as opposed to a mere 6% in factories. Even public houses and inns attracted a larger proportion at almost 9%. This does not allow for machinery or the power to drive it. But even assuming a doubling of the value of the fixed assets of factory plant and buildings, the dominance of warehouse investment remains clear. Investment in cotton mills increased, especially as weaving was mechanised in the 1820s, but Manchester's business structure still leaned heavily towards its commercial sector. Whilst the proportion of all capital tied up in cotton factories had increased to some 12% by 1825 that invested in warehouses remained much higher at nearly 43%.[3] Industrial Manchester was not a factory town which became a commercial centre; from the beginnings of industrialisation it had been a warehouse town with factories.

Indeed, Manchester's symbolic role as the focus of the factory system may be best understood in terms of labour rather than capital. Workers flocked to the mills. In 1815 Manchester's cotton factories employed approximately 11,500 men, women and children. By the time of the 1841 Census, there were 19,561 working in all branches of cotton manufacture in Manchester. This was a huge workforce. In size it approached the total for the combined cotton workforces of Oldham, Blackburn and Ashton-under-Lyne (21,615). But these figures can be misleading. Although cotton manufacture was a major source of work in Manchester, it did not dominate the local labour market as was the case in the surrounding mill towns. As a proportion of total occupied persons in 1841 cotton employed 18% of Manchester's labour force, compared with the respective figures of 50% in Ashton, 40% in Oldham, and 40% in Blackburn. These were the mill towns proper.[4]

The different occupational pattern in Manchester is indicated by a further statistic. It is well known that women formed a majority of the cotton workforce. Predominantly young and single they were the Lancashire mill lasses of legend. In 1841 there were 11,427 women working in Manchester's cotton mills and workshops (out of a total female labour force of 37,779). But this figure was exceeded by the combined total of domestic servants (9,961) and dressmakers/milliners (2,251). Mancunians certainly heard the clatter of clogs on cobbles but what they could not so easily discern was the gentler sound of the chamber maid's footfall on the back stairs. Amongst the men, whilst over 8,000 could be found working in the mills, approaching 6,000 were to be found in the commercial district as warehousemen, porters and clerks. Manchester was a city with a wide range of employments and its social structure cannot be simplified to mill master and mill hand.

Contemporary maps, such as *Bancks & Co.'s Plan of Manchester and Salford* of 1831, reveal a complex pattern of buildings. Although there were several workshops and mills in and around the central area, such as the huge Newton Street Cotton Mills near Stevenson Square, most industry was confined to what was then the periphery, adjacent to the main transport arteries (in 1831 the canals, later the railways). Thus the Medlock industrial belt along Oxford Road grew up in close proximity to the river and the Rochdale Canal. Here, gasworks, canal wharves, timber yards, saw-mills, foundries, ironworks and cotton mills dominated a district entirely given over to manufacturing, and relieved only by pockets of back-to-back houses and courts. By contrast, the streets of the city centre were dominated by public buildings, offices, warehouses, shops and hotels.[5]

But it was the novelty of the factory which most impressed contemporaries and monopolised their attention. Factories were functional buildings with only limited attention to architectural aesthetics: rectangular multi-storey blocks or a series of two-storey buildings round a yard. They were a visible manifestation of the coming economic order. Moreover, their influence was pervasive in other ways. Steam-powered manufactories dominated their environment in a manner unprecedented for any previous type of building. The smoking chimneys which encircled Manchester breathed their foul fog over the entire city, clouding the sky and covering buildings with the distinctive soot which was to characterise the urban industrial environment for over 150 years. As well as industrial pollution, the sheer size and shape of some of these grimy leviathans of industry were inescapable, set as they often were amongst street upon street of terraced housing. The Manchester novelist Elizabeth Gaskell described the view from the train arriving in her fictional Milton (Manchester) in the 1840s:

> they were whirled over long, straight hopeless streets of regular built houses all small and of brick. Here and there a great oblong many-windowed factory stood up, like a hen among her chickens.[6]

Numerous other commentators, from Frederick Engels to Benjamin Disraeli, conveyed a similar impression of a factory-dominated landscape and, more misleadingly, a factory-dominated society.[7]

In the second quarter of the nineteenth century it seemed to contemporaries that factory size was increasing as capital became concentrated in fewer and fewer hands. Richard Cobden wrote of 'the huge factories of the cotton district, with three thousand hands under one capitalist'. Such views gained currency. The French visitor Alexis de Tocqueville saw in Manchester 'a few great capitalists, thousands of poor workmen and little middle class'.[8] Thus was emerging a powerful myth about the first industrial city: the supposed dominance of a handful of great cotton masters employing thousands in each mill. In fact the cotton lords of legend were thinner on the ground than might be imagined.

Interior of a mule spinning factory.

Firms were not growing bigger and the small firm was not being squeezed out as contemporaries had feared. In fact the opposite was happening. Between 1815 and 1841 the share of larger cotton firms in Manchester's total labour force actually fell from 44% to 32%. Manchester firms were larger on average than those in the surrounding mill towns but even here, in 1841, the average primary producer employed only 260 hands and a quarter of all firms gave work to under a hundred.[9] There were giant firms, but only a handful employed over 1,000 each and these were not new creations. The largest in 1833 were the fine spinners McConnel & Kennedy, with 1,545 employees. Established in 1797, they had moved to their newly-built eight-storey mill in Union Street, Ancoats, in 1818. Fireproofed and lit by gas, it was one of the sights of Manchester. But it was not typical. In any case, large factories did not necessarily mean giant firms. It is a mistake to see the factory and the firm as synonymous. A single mill might house up to ten or more small businesses; in 1815 around two-thirds of firms shared factory space with others.

All this does not deny the importance of the factory to the industrial revolution. Simply to say that Manchester's contribution to that process was not confined to the steam-powered mechanisation of cotton production. Manchester's rapid industrialisation served to secure its economic importance, but in the end this owed more to its role as a centre of commerce and finance than to its manufacturing sector. It was Manchester's trade with the world that counted.

Manchester's nineteenth-century commercial pre-eminence depended upon the phenomenal growth in the production of cotton cloth during the industrial era. Precise data is not available but a few figures will suggest the scale of expansion. National consumption of raw cotton increased from 5m. lbs in 1781 to an annual average of 82m. lbs by 1818–21 and 937m. lbs by 1856–60. Manchester was the chief beneficiary of this industrial growth and, whilst Liverpool was the marketing centre for the import of raw cotton, Manchester became the world's central market for the sale of cotton products. This is why its commercial streets were lined with warehouses.

The warehouse was more than a place of storage; it was also a venue for the display and sale of goods. The spread of the warehouse sector was a constant element in the evolution of the built environment of Manchester from the 1780s to the second half of the nineteenth century. Counting the number of individual warehouses is not an accurate guide to commercial expansion because of the subdivision of premises into several units. Taking the latter as a yardstick, it has been estimated that by 1807 there were already 1,182 warehouse units in the town, a figure which rose to 1,819 by 1825. Of the 57 warehouses on Cannon Street in 1815, 31 were wholly occupied by a single firm whilst the others were subdivided into separate units. There may have been a trend towards multi-occupancy as time wore on.[10]

In the early nineteenth century, merchants still had a role in the production of cloth. Although Edmund Cartwright had invented a powerloom as early as 1785, it was not successfully applied until the mid-1820s (it actually took until the 1840s before the handloom was finally overtaken by the powerloom). Meanwhile, the expansion of mechanised spinning served to stimulate the existing 'putting-out' system of weaving. The master-weavers dominated the trade with a string of handloom weavers under their control to whom they distributed the cotton yarn. The larger Manchester master-weavers employed their own 'putters-out as managers but smaller masters directly employed handloom weavers generally working in their own homes but sometimes on warehouse premises under the supervision of the master. Thus the warehouse might also be a workshop. This system of production had preceded the mechanisation of spinning and survived until the mechanisation of weaving itself. The masters rented or owned warehouse space in which to display the finished cloth for sale. These men were 'merchant-manufacturers', sharing the warehouses with dealers pure and simple.

The town's growth as a marketing and warehouse centre in the eighteenth century had displaced rival cloth markets in the smaller textile towns. Whereas as late as 1760 the merchants of Bolton might still be trading from their hometown warehouses, by 1780 they had chiefly transferred to the Manchester market. Thus on the major market days, out of town manufacturers met drapers and merchants on the streets around the Cotton Exchange, in the many surrounding inns, in

Heywood's Bank on St Ann's Square, now a branch of the Royal Bank of Scotland.
(*Photograph: Ian Beesley*)

their own warehouses, or in temporary salerooms hired for the occasion. Interesting sales techniques were used to attract customers. Men known as 'hookers in' were employed to solicit custom when stage coaches arrived at the various inns and coaching houses. Lists of likely customers were also obtained from the way-bills of coaches recently arrived. Such practices were rendered obsolete by the advent of the railway, and instead firms employed commercial travellers, each supplied with an array of samples to show prospective customers. Cheaper postage and the introduction of the telegraph further refined sales techniques as the century progressed.

The warehouse sale itself could be a frenzied affair. As a young man, Samuel Bamford, the Middleton radical, was a warehouse assistant on Cannon Street. In his autobiography he describes a market day sale of around 1810. The doors of the warehouse were opened at seven in the morning. Bamford's job was to carry pieces of cloth, 20 at a time, on his shoulders up to the first-storey sales room, throwing them down on a clean white cloth which covered the floor.

A scramble then commenced among the buyers, which should get the most pieces; sometimes they met me at the sale door and tore them off my back; and many a good coat have I seen slit up, or left with the laps dangling, after a struggle of that sort.[11]

Manchester's commercial roots were the springboard for its nine-teenth-century status as the first industrial city. The regional preeminence acquired through centuries of trading was translated into national and then international significance. From the earliest days of industrialisation, the town's influence lay in its dominance of the export market. As early as the 1790s, Manchester was fast displacing London as a centre of overseas trade in cotton cloth. It attracted a dynamic and increasingly cosmopolitan merchant community eager to exploit the town's proximity to the new centres of production. The demand for warehouse space soon spread far beyond the Lancashire region, and foreign merchants mingled with regional drapers and dealers in the busy warehouse district. In 1799 the famous Rothschild family of Frankfurt first opened business in England when Nathan Meyer Rothschild acquired a Manchester warehouse. According to one contemporary the town had already 'assumed the style and manners of one of the com-mercial capitals of Europe'.[12] The town's financial significance grew to consolidate its commercial position. Banking and insurance facilities developed, from 1826 with the opening in Manchester of the first provincial branch of the Bank of England to 1872 when the first clearing house in the provinces was established in the city. Manchester banks established branches in the cotton towns, and later mergers with London firms produced national banks. Manchester developed a finan-cial infrastructure appropriate to its status as mercantile metropolis.

Cottonopolis?

The overworked sobriquet 'Cottonopolis', if it focuses on the factory, therefore masks Manchester's real economic character. Moreover, even within textiles Manchester was important in areas other than the pro-duction and sale of cotton cloth. The regional manufacture of smallwares remained concentrated in Manchester as had been the case since the seventeenth century, and the town was also the main centre of the silk industry in south-east Lancashire. Moreover, the value of cotton to the Manchester economy can serve to obscure the significance of develop-ments in other industrial sectors, especially the metal and engineering trades and the chemical industry. Events in these areas began as a spin-off from cotton, but soon developed their own momentum.

Cotton spinning itself was dependent upon developments in machine technology and was a constant stimulus to machine manufacture. In fact some of Manchester's earliest cotton spinners began as machine makers and engineers; McConnel & Kennedy, the Murray brothers,

The Irwell from Blackfriars Bridge, c. 1860. The Cathedral tower is being rebuilt.

Robert Owen, Peter Ewart and others fall into this category. In the early stages a major capital outlay in cotton spinning would be the machinery. Thus existing machine makers had a logical entry-point into the cotton trade. As the latter became more profitable it made sense to devote all available factory space to spinning and to purchase machines instead. McConnel & Kennedy ceased their machine business around 1800. So the specialist machine firm became more common. At this time, in addition to millwrighting and machine-making businesses, iron-founding and forging firms carried on a more general engineering. These included the firms of Peel & Williams of the Soho Foundry in Ancoats and Galloways of Great Bridgewater Street. These were pioneers in the field later dominated by such important figures as Richard Roberts, William Fairbairn, James Nasmyth and Joseph Whitworth.

Manchester was, therefore, at the centre not only of the revolution in the cotton industry but also the parallel revolution in engineering. Manchester engineers made technological innovations vital to industrialisation such as Nasmyth's steam hammer and Whitworth's standardised screw threads. In particular, Manchester became the centre of the British machine-tool industry, and local firms like Nasmyth's, Whitworth's and Sharp Roberts were paramount in the field of precision engineering. Manchester engineering was of international significance. An interesting example is the business of William Fairbairn. Beginning in a small workshop in High Street in 1817, Fairbairn's partnership with James Lillie grew until by 1830 they employed 300 in their Canal Street iron works in Ancoats. They undertook all the iron work in the

construction of mills. In the 1830s (after his partnership with Lillie was
dissolved) Fairbairn branched out into iron shipbuilding, establishing a
second works on the Thames at Millwall. His Manchester business
expanded into a variety of engineering endeavours, as this glowing
account of a visit to Canal Street in 1839 suggests.

> In this establishment the heaviest description of machinery is manu-
> factured, including steam engines, water wheels, locomotive engines
> and mill gearing. There are from 550 to 600 hands employed ...
> and a walk through the extensive premises ... affords a specimen
> of industry, and an example of practical science, which can scarcely
> be surpassed.[13]

Fairbairn's developed a large export trade. The firm also did iron
construction work in Turkey, Russia and Sweden as well as the supreme
example of their mill work in England, the steam-powered woollen
mills built for Titus Salt at Saltaire near Bradford in the early 1850s.
Add to this the role of Fairbairn as a process inventor and research
scientist, his numerous engineering treatises for which he was awarded
a Royal Society gold medal in 1860, his international reputation as a
'practical scientist' and in this individual alone we have enough to
suggest the inadequacy of a picture of 'Cottonopolis' which confines
itself to the cotton trade. Fairbairn's is but one example of a vital
element in Manchester's industrial history; the engineering sector.

Intimately linked to the rise of cotton were the chemical and finishing
trades. After all, the rapidly expanding output of yarn and cloth had
to be bleached, dyed and printed. Chemical innovation went hand in
hand with increased production. The demand of the finishing trades
for chemicals, especially alkalis for bleaching, led to the development
of chlorine bleaching in the early 1800s. As early as 1783, the newly
founded Manchester College of Arts and Sciences placed special emphasis on chemistry in its proposed courses, because of its application 'to
so many of the arts on which our manufactures depend'.[14] During the
first half of the nineteenth century, the town saw the emergence of
several large firms in the chemical and finishing trades. Thomas Hoyle
operated the biggest dye works in Manchester in 1815 and also ran a
large print warehouse; William Newton, William Oliver, Jonathon
Whitelegg and Rothwell & Harrison owned some of the largest works
of their type in the world.

Canal, Road and Rail

The 'transport revolution' of the eighteenth and nineteenth centuries
played a vital part in the transformation of the once backward North
West into the most energetic industrial region of the country. Its

essential elements are well known. The Duke of Bridgewater's Canal, the first stage of which was completed in 1762 to carry coal to Manchester from Worsley and which was extended across north Cheshire to Runcorn in 1776 thus halving the costs of the transport of raw cotton from Liverpool, pioneered a process which ended in industrial Manchester being at the core of a complex of navigable waterways. The Liverpool to Manchester Railway was opened in 1830 as the first passenger service in the world, although its economic impact as a new form of transporting goods took longer than might be imagined. Not till 1850 did the railway lines of the Manchester region capture a majority share of the freight traffic from canals.

By 1821 there were three navigable routes from Liverpool to Manchester: the Mersey and Irwell Navigation of 1736, the Bridgewater Canal and the Leeds and Liverpool Canal (the branch linking it to the Bridgewater at Leigh was completed in 1821). The largest bulk traffic was in coal, grain and construction materials (timber and stone) with a smaller business in textiles. The Rochdale Canal, the first of the trans-Pennine waterways, had been completed in 1804 and a short cross-city section linked it to the Bridgewater Canal at Castlefield. The Ashton Canal joined the Rochdale Canal near London Road. The canals turned Manchester into an inland port, with wharves and quays and the constant bustle of horse-wagons and narrow boats at the Castlefield and Ashton canal basins. Before the railways came large sites with water frontage were at a premium. The waterways were a major stimulant to industrialisation. But there should not be a simple sequence of chronological displacement (roads replaced by canals, themselves replaced by railways), at least not in the case of Manchester. Road transportation continued to be of importance to Manchester's industry well into the nineteenth century. Even one third of the town's requirements of a bulk item like coal was carried by road as late as 1836. Moreover, in cotton itself there seems to have been a preference for road transport in some quarters on the grounds of speed and reliability of delivery time rather than cost.

The remarkable records of the McConnel & Kennedy mills provide evidence of such a preference. Given their location near central Manchester and their dependence on Liverpool for the supply of raw cotton after about 1810, one might have expected this company to use one of the two lines of water communication available at that time. Their records show, however, that they made more use of road carriers. The substantial edge which canals possessed in per mile rates suffered considerably from the costs, in time and money, of carting at origin and destination. McConnel & Kennedy imposed penalty clauses for late delivery in their contracts with hauliers. The convenience and reliability of road haulage over fixed routes of communication which today often gives it the edge over railways could also give a competitive advantage over canals in an earlier age.

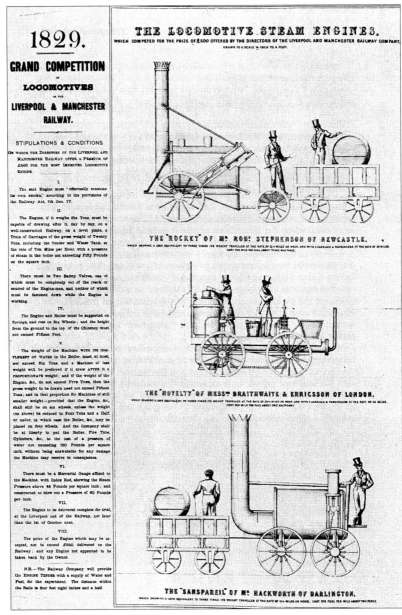

The Rainhill Trials to choose the locomotive for the Liverpool and Manchester Railway. Stephenson's *Rocket* was the successful entry.

The 'Railway Age' can be said to have begun in Manchester. Although the Stockton to Darlington line of 1825 was the first to use a locomotive for coal-trains, its passenger service was pulled by horses. It was left to the Liverpool and Manchester Railway to demonstrate the potential of this new form of transport. The project was underwritten by Liverpool money. In 1829 only 2% of the shares in the new company were held in Manchester, whilst 50% were in Liverpudlian hands. It was Liverpool merchants who had invited George Stephenson to draw up plans for a railway line between the two cities (although in the event it was his son, Robert, who supervised the construction). Liverpool businessmen quite correctly assumed the railway would enable them to obtain a virtual monopoly over imports of raw cotton, a proportion of which had previously come direct to Manchester traders. But Manchester also had much to gain from the new form of transport. The creation of a regional rail network in the decades following the opening of Liverpool Road Station in 1830 undoubtedly strengthened Manchester's commercial predominance in the cotton district of Lancashire. By 1850 London Road (now Piccadilly) and Victoria Stations saw the beginnings of railway warehouse and office developments which, after 1850, were to swallow up entire areas of the city. The railway made it much easier for out of town producers and buyers to visit the main market and therefore made access to warehouse space even more essential. It also cut transit times considerably. Finally, as we shall see, it also made it much easier to get out of Manchester, at least for those who could afford to live at a distance from their place of business.

The Liverpool and Manchester Railway was opened with great ceremony on 15 September 1830 in the presence of the Prime Minister, the Duke of Wellington. The famous Rainhill Trials of the previous October had proved the Stephensons' *Rocket* to be the best locomotive and the inauguration of the world's first passenger steam-railway was an occasion which ushered in a new era of transport history. It was also the occasion of the world's first railway accident. William Huskisson, Tory MP for Liverpool and President of the Board of Trade, stumbled from a stationary carriage onto the track on a narrow embankment where the only standing room was between the two lines of railroad. Alarmed at the sight of the oncoming locomotive he panicked, fell into its path and was killed. Despite this ominous beginning the Liverpool and Manchester Railway proved to be a profitable concern. Its passenger service became extremely popular, soon carrying twice as many as the coaches had conveyed before the line was opened and revealing that the railway would be more than a means of goods transportation. The Company's shares soon doubled in value, and in its wake railway investment boomed in the 1830s and even more so during the so-called 'Railway Mania' of the 1840s. The Liverpool and Manchester Railway had opened up a new world.

An Economic Marvel in an Age of Great Cities

The seventy years to 1850 in Britain witnessed the world's first industrial revolution. They were dynamic years of economic and urban growth. By 1850 places like Birmingham and Glasgow were producing a great deal more than they had in 1780, but only Manchester made contemporaries speak of an industrial revolution. In Manchester and the cotton district of Lancashire and Cheshire had taken place not only an economic but also a social transformation. New social forces had been conjured up by industry in the age of the factory, and Manchester was the symbol of new ways of working and living. The factories aroused tremendous interest and the numerous visitors who wrote about them and the city which housed them contributed to myths about Manchester which this chapter has attempted to correct.

Manchester had grown from the 'boom town' of the 1790s, when the chance of gain attracted newcomers from far and wide as new red-brick factories with their towering chimneys rose above the roofs of other buildings and the demand for warehouse space transformed quiet residential streets into a busy commercial quarter, to the massive urban sprawl of the 1840s, the first city of the industrial revolution. Demographic growth was dramatic. Each decade between 1811 and 1851 had witnessed an increase in the number of inhabitants of 30% or more with the most striking advance taking place between 1811 and 1831, when the town's population more than doubled in twenty years. Cotton was the driving force of this expansion. Indeed, banks and financial services, transport and communications, urban growth and a more complex labour market all flowed from this miracle product of mechanised manufacture. Yet Manchester was a market first and a centre of industry second. Cotton was an engine of economic growth in the industrial revolution and it was Manchester which provided the commercial infrastructure essential for the success of the venture.

There were high profit margins and great fortunes to be made in the Manchester of the early industrial revolution, although fiercer competition between firms by the mid-1820s may have spread the profits more thinly. Despite commercial crises in 1826, 1836 and 1847, and the economic fluctuations of the trade cycle, there were few periods in which the Manchester cotton trade was less than lucrative. Furthermore, as the town grew, so its economic base diversified. Cotton manufacture spawned an engineering industry which grew to dominate national production in certain areas. The need for steam-powered factories engendered a transport revolution which began with canals and extended to railways, although as we have seen we must not assume that road haulage was immediately eclipsed. The transport revolution confirmed Manchester's supremacy and was a key factor in its continued economic growth. The city became the focus of a network of industrial communications in which all canals and railways seemed to lead to Manchester.

Manchester entered the second half of the nineteenth century with a global reputation: an economic marvel in an age of great cities. Manchester was proud to proclaim its pre-eminence over all other provincial cities and its rivalry for economic leadership with London. This, however, was the pinnacle of its achievement. After 1850 other cities and other industries caught up and Manchester's comparative importance gradually declined. Moreover, the town's economic rise had been accompanied by the social costs of success. Massive urban growth brought enormous problems of organisation, provision of amenities and maintenance of public order. In particular, the environmental consequences of dramatic and continuous growth for over fifty years were on the debit side of the balance sheet of industrialisation. During the first half of the nineteenth century Manchester was one of the most overcrowded and unhealthy places in the whole of England.

References

1. A. Briggs, *Victorian Cities*, Penguin, Harmondsworth, 1963, p. 56. This book includes an excellent chapter on Manchester.

2. Shown on Green's map of 1794 and Laurent's map of 1795 as Simpson's Mill after its new owner and Arkwright's former manager, John Simpson. See C. Laurent, *A Topographical Plan of Manchester and Salford* (1795), Historical Discovery, Crewe, 1992. For the industrial archaeology of Manchester's factories, see M. Williams with D. A. Farnie, *The Cotton Mills in Greater Manchester*, Preston, 1992.

3. R. Lloyd-Jones and M. J. Lewis, *Manchester and the Age of the Factory*, Croom Helm, London, 1988, pp. 30, 105. This book is an important contribution to economic history and should revise our view of the business structure of Manchester during the industrial revolution.

4. Howe divides the towns of the cotton district into those which were 'textile dependent', Ashton, Oldham, Blackburn, Preston, Bolton, Bury and Rochdale, and those with more diversified economies, Wigan, Warrington, Lancaster, Salford and Manchester. A. Howe, *The Cotton Masters 1830–1860*, Oxford University Press, 1984, p. 46.

5. See *Bancks & Co.'s Plan of Manchester and Salford* (1831), Neil Richardson, Swinton, 1982.

6. E. Gaskell, *North and South* (1855), Penguin edn, Harmondsworth, 1970, pp. 96–7.

7. For a selection of visitors' opinions of Manchester see, L. D. Bradshaw (ed.), *Visitors to Manchester: A Selection of British and Foreign Visitors' Descriptions of Manchester from c. 1538 to 1865*, Neil Richardson, Swinton, 1987.

8. Cobden's remark is in a letter to Samuel Smiles in 1841, see S. Smiles, *The Autobiography of Samuel Smiles*, John Murray, London, 1905, p. 112; for de Tocqueville's observation made during a visit in 1835 see, A. de Tocqueville,

Journeys to England and Ireland, trans. G. Lawrence and K. P. Mayer, Faber and Faber, London, 1958, p. 104.

9. R. Lloyd-Jones and M. J. Lewis, 'The size of firms in the cotton industry: Manchester 1815 to 1841', *Economic History Review*, XXXIII (1980), p. 76; V. A. C. Gatrell, 'Labour, power and the size of firms in Lancashire Cotton in the second quarter of the nineteenth century,' *Economic History Review*, XXX (1977), p. 125.

10. Lloyd-Jones and Lewis, *Age of the Factory*, pp. 90, 108, 109.

11. S. Bamford, *Autobiography, Vol. I, Early Days* (1849), Frank Cass, London, 1967, p. 278.

12. J. Aiken, *A Description of the Country from Thirty to Forty Miles Round Manchester* (1795), David and Charles, Newton Abbot, 1968, p. 184.

13. *Manchester As It Is* (Love and Barton, 1839), E. J. Morten, Manchester, 1971, p. 210.

14. Quoted in A. E. Musson and F. Robinson, *Science and Technology in the Industrial Revolution*, Manchester University Press, 1969, p. 242.

CHAPTER 3

Living in the First Industrial City

Manchester was the greatest of the trading cities created by the industrial revolution. Its economic energy and novel social patterns led contemporaries to regard it as a model of urban development: a mirror of the future. But the image in the glass was blurred. Manchester's economic miracle, which made it seem heroic to some, was overlaid by living conditions which offered instead the prospect of social catastrophe. Benjamin Disraeli felt able to make comparisons with the Classical World claiming that industrial Manchester was 'as great a human exploit as Athens'. But such optimism was qualified. Manchester generated great wealth but also great squalor. In the words of Alexis de Tocqueville, from Manchester:

> the greatest stream of human industry flows out to fertilise the whole world. From this filthy sewer pure gold flows. Here humanity attains its most complete development and its most brutish; here civilisation works its miracles, and civilised man is turned back into savage.[1]

If urban living was the pattern of the future then early industrial Manchester seemed to be its herald. The town's population soared as it became a magnet for migrants. As with the industrialisation process itself, urban growth was unplanned. And those who did have an influence on its development were chiefly the rich and the powerful. Urban growth can be measured by means other than population figures. Between 1773 and 1821 the total number of houses in Manchester rose from 3,446 to 17,257. Whilst population density increased, the town expanded physically. But only a small proportion of the population was responsible for the major part of this urban growth. By 1850 the built-up area of 'Greater Manchester' covered about seven square miles. Of this over one-half was occupied by prosperous suburbs and only one-fifth by artisan housing. It was the wealthy middle class who did most to determine the shape of Manchester. It was they who created its built environment.

Patterns on the Ground

The Manchester of 1780 was modest in size. Though it had developed (southwards along Deansgate and eastwards along Market Street) from

Workers' cottages in Bradley Street, dating from the 1780s and virtually rebuilt since this picture. Manchester's only surviving examples of one-up, one-down dwellings. (*Reproduced by kind permission of the Manchester Early Buildings Research Group*)

the medieval layout of short winding streets surrounding the Collegiate Church, it remained a formless jumble of buildings. There was little in the way of a warehouse district and no retail area or residential suburbs. There was little separation of workplace from residence. Bankers worked from their homes, merchants lived in a few domesticated rooms in their warehouses. Several leading citizens did have country houses, usually only a mile or two out of town, but used their town houses for the conduct of business. The homes of the poor sat cheek by jowl with the residences of the rich. But the wealth generated by the cotton trade would not allow such a situation to continue.

Land values increased with the prosperity of trade and the later decades of the eighteenth century witnessed the beginnings of the seventy year 'building boom' which was physically to construct the first industrial city. This began modestly enough with the creation of residential districts on the edge of the existing town in gridiron patterns of broad streets with the occasional square, sometimes with a church at the centre. Despite the intervening changes this pattern of streets and squares characterises those districts down to today. The Quay Street/St John's estate, the Aytoun/Sackville Street area and the region of Stevenson Square were each laid out in the late eighteenth century. The broad thoroughfares of these estates were not solely for gentlemen's residences. The narrower back streets sometimes contained workers' cottages or even workshops built onto the rear of the smart Georgian terraces. For example, workers' cottages were built in 1787 on land belonging to Sir Ashton Lever of Alkrington in Bradley Street behind 69–73 Lever Street (see photograph on page 32). These new estates were more homogeneous in character than the rambling streets of the 'Old Town'. They were accompanied by the beginnings of 'zoning' according to function as a distinct commercial district and later industrial zones emerged.

Residential patterns followed the town's business development. In effect this was zoning by class. As industrialism proceeded, the middle class sought to escape from the city centre. In the late eighteenth century this could still be achieved by lining Mosley and Princess Streets with plush Georgian terraces for the well-to-do, and Quay Street/ St John's was a fashionable area. Some took to more rural surroundings at Ardwick Green, Manchester's first suburb, or on the Crescent in Salford. Travel time largely determined place of residence. Good roads made distance less of a problem: Ardwick Green and the Crescent were served by turnpike trusts. As the railway came the rich could live even further afield. The spread of the Medlock industrial belt by the 1820s had made Mosley Street much less fashionable and denied such status entirely to an Oxford Road development like Grosvenor Square (All Saints).

As Mosley Street residents moved out, warehouses and banks moved in. In 1839 Richard Cobden built the first of Manchester's notable palazzo-inspired warehouses at what is now 16 Mosley Street. Earlier, in 1836, the Manchester and Salford Bank had erected new premises (10 Mosley Street) in what was becoming the commercial heart of the town. By 1850 the 'breezy heights' of Cheetham Hill and Higher Broughton or the seclusion of Buile Hill, Pendleton, were better prospects for the very rich. The larger mass of the middle class populated suburban terraces and villas astride the routes north in the direction of Bury and south along the line of Oxford Road. Dormitory villages at Withington and Didsbury were served by omnibus services from the 1820s. The railway further stimulated this pattern, but its chief impact came after 1850.

Meanwhile the working class occupied the town's inner residential belt, the meanest streets, generally within a short walk from work. Street upon street of densely-packed housing rapidly covered the open spaces between the mills and workshops of Ancoats, Chorlton-on-Medlock and Holt Town to the south and east, Irk Town and New Town to the north, and Salford to the west across the Irwell. Most of this housing was constructed by the speculative builder with little capital, himself recently risen from the working class. These 'jerry builders' usually did not work to any building standards and were often desperately inefficient. Some working-class districts grew to the proportions of a medium-sized town. Hulme, which was still mostly fields as late as 1831, was developed for artisan dwellings and had a population of

53,000 by 1851. But population growth is only half the story. The pattern of living in the first industrial city separated class from class. The effect of this spatial segregation was to create a residential pattern of concentric circles (first described in 1844 by Frederick Engels in *The Condition of the Working Class in England*). At the core, where the spread of the commercial district contributed greatly to overcrowding, lived the very poorest in some of the nation's worst housing, surrounded by a solid mass of working-class terraces and at the periphery a ring of middle-class suburban villas.

The Quality of Life

The quality of life is determined by many things: income, prices and rents, employment prospects, working conditions, housing and health, leisure facilities and community relations. Industrial growth generated great wealth and diffused it more widely, but it also occasioned great poverty. Migrants came to Manchester in search of a better life. They did not always find it. From the first, rural migrants from Lancashire and Cheshire were attracted by the higher wages of industrialism. Later came Irish migrants fleeing the horrors of the Great Famine. Plentiful work for the young of both sexes encouraged early marriage and an increased birth rate. It was these factors which fed the startling growth of Manchester's population. It was not due to any reduction in the death rate, which became notoriously high. It has already been suggested that Manchester's complex economy made it much more than a mill town. Thus the quality of life in early nineteenth-century Manchester is a question of the impact of urban growth rather than of the factory system alone.

Urban wages may have been higher than their rural equivalents, but they were not always secure and there was a wider range of incomes. Rates of pay varied considerably even within the cotton industry. Even the reputedly high wages of the 'aristocrats' of labour, the mule-spinners, would fluctuate with booms and slumps in trade and may have gone into a decline with the technical innovations in mule-spinning of the 1830s. Manchester mule-spinners might earn in excess of 25 shillings (£1.25) a week, but most were left with around 16 shillings (80p) after paying their assistants or 'piecers'. If the latter were relatives this would boost family income. Indeed, the employment of women and children was a feature of the Lancashire cotton industry (although subject to restriction by factory legislation in the 1830s and 1840s). For example, women monopolised work in the card-room, where raw cotton fibres were prepared for spinning, and children worked as 'piecers', crawling under the spinning mules to 'piece' or mend broken threads. Carders earned around nine shillings (45p) a week and piecers between three shillings (15p) and eight shillings (40p) depending on age and experience. The average working week in the cotton mills of the early 1830s was 69 hours.

Rates of pay outside the cotton mills varied even more although, as in the mills, adult male wages might often be added to by the incomes of other family members and even the contributions of lodgers. By the 1830s amongst the poorest workers in Manchester were the handloom weavers, squeezed by the advent of powered weaving. The *Report of the Select Committee on Handloom Weavers* in 1835 gave the average wages of Manchester weavers as five shillings (25p) to seven shillings and sixpence (37p) a week. Some were even worse off. The *Manchester Guardian* of 30 January 1830, in a survey of 41 weavers' families in the New Town district, estimated the average income per head at two shillings and 11 pence (15p) or fivepence (2p) a day. Powerloom weavers in the late 1820s were said to earn up to 12 shillings (60p) a week. Skills which could not be automated included many in the building trade. A bricklayer's wages were around 27 shillings (£1.35) at their summer peak. His labourer might be paid 18 shillings (90p). Other unskilled jobs, like street labourer or carter, might bring up to 16 shillings (80p), but often less. Such occupations were generally casual in nature and left individuals and families dependent on irregular and insecure incomes. Surprisingly, the constable in Manchester's new police force, patrolling the working-class districts, was not highly paid at around £1 for a 70-hour week, but at least his job was secure.

Information about money wages may mislead without comparable statistics on rents and prices. Rents in Manchester, as in most provincial towns, may have been half London figures. The better-paid worker could afford a weekly rent of around six shillings (30p) for a 'through' house (not 'back-to-back'). More humble rooms or cellar dwellings might cost two to three shillings (10p to 15p) a week. There is evidence that Manchester's food supply had become more varied and abundant by the 1820s with food prices much lower than during the Napoleonic Wars, although still higher in Manchester than elsewhere in the cotton district. For those with good incomes, buying from the town's innumerable local shops (over 1,500 retail outlets for non-perishable foodstuffs were listed in the 1840 trade directories for Manchester and Salford) as well as its markets and street traders, good supplies were available. However, it is worth noting that for the majority over 40% of food expenditure usually went on bread and potatoes. The lowest paid worker's consumption of meat might be confined to Sundays and one weekday.

Even the diet of a cotton spinner's family might be plain and of barely adequate nutritional value. The wife of a Manchester spinner with five children told an official investigating child labour in factories in 1833 of her family's eating habits. Breakfast was usually porridge, bread and milk. Dinners consisted of potatoes, bacon and white bread and suppers of porridge or occasionally potatoes mashed with milk. Eggs were bought when cheap and fried with bacon. Without reference to quantities consumed it is difficult to assess the quality of this diet, but it is probable that it provided adequate intakes of protein and calories, although not of vitamins and minerals. Such studies of diet that do exist support the reliability of this example. The absence of fruit and green vegetables was a typical deficiency in the northern urban working-class diet. The paucity of local supplies of the former and fluctuations in the cost of the latter generally priced these foods beyond the average pocket, until the railway and then refrigerated overseas imports improved matters later on in the century. At any rate this was not a poor family. They occupied a four-room house, and their cooking utensils included two pans, a kettle and a frying pan. They possessed no chest of drawers and used boxes to store clothes. But the parents had cash to spare for a weekly funeral club in case the children should die, and meanwhile sent them to day school at threepence a week. The household possessions included a bible and several books won by the children as prizes at Sunday school. But even in this case any fall in family income could reduce the quality of the diet. Unemployment of the major breadwinner could have a disastrous effect.[2]

Ancoats was the main mill district in Manchester. A survey at the onset of a downturn in trade in June 1837 revealed unemployment and short-time working. Of 359 mill workers questioned, 27.3% were out of work, and approaching two-thirds of those in employment were working only three or four days a week.[3] Those interviewed were depositors in the savings bank run by the District Provident Society and could perhaps be reckoned among the better off. The sufferings of those less well provided for could be much greater. In 1842 at a time of high unemployment and acute distress, charity visitors for the Town Mission reported on some of the appalling cases of poverty which they knew.

Robert O'Brien, Jersey Street, a dyer with four children; has had no work for many months; his wife has been lately confined; they have been whole days without food; they have sold or pledged all that they could for food or rent for the cellar they occupy.

R. Cann, five in family, three children; all out of work, man sick and one sick child. The child was laying down on a few shavings of wood in the corner of a damp cellar without a rag to cover it. Nothing whatever in the cellar.

A widow with two children living in Brook's Court; clothes in pawn, no bed and in want of food; had nothing for three days till I gave her a soup ticket.

Jones, Great Mount Street, is in great poverty; has a very sickly wife. He is a shoemaker by trade but for want of nourishment is unable to work; he has death printed in his countenance.[4]

Manchester's Irish-born residents were consistently among the poorest in the city. Migrants leaving Ireland had ended up in Manchester ever since the early industrial revolution, but the 1840s and especially the period of the Great Famine (1846–51) marked the peak of Irish arrivals. The Irish were by far the city's largest ethnic minority and also the poorest. One third of Manchester's population increase between 1841 and 1851 was due to Irish migration. Manchester was one of the major centres of Irish settlement in England. Its Irish community was only exceeded in size by those in London and Liverpool. By 1851 some 15% of Manchester's population was Irish born, yet the community provided more than one in three of those in receipt of poor relief. Fleeing starvation and rural squalor, migrants from Ireland were ill-equipped to cope with the industrial environment and generally endured the lowest quality housing and were forced to accept the least eligible jobs. On top of this they faced anti-Irish and anti-Catholic prejudices. Understandably, they sought communal solidarity in their own residential districts – some of the poorest quarters of town. Manchester's stock of cheap housing was already overcrowded and the 1840s were marked by industrial recession and unemployment. The local press reported that homeless Irish families, sometimes with 'dreadfully emaciated' children, had become a frequent sight on city streets.[5]

The long-running debate about whether working-class living standards rose or fell during the industrial revolution will not be settled by Manchester evidence alone. Manchester can be used to support the optimistic point of view by reference to its higher than average wage rates. Further local research may support the emerging national picture of rising real wages between 1820 and 1850, anticipating the undoubted gains of the post-1850 period.[6] Equally, however, the evidence abounds of great impoverishment, enough for contemporaries to regard Manchester as a symbol of the poverty and squalor of urban life in the industrial era. Which perspective is correct? Whilst it would not do to over-accentuate the 'horrors', implying that the extreme examples of suffering and deprivation were typical of all classes of worker in all years, nonetheless it is equally unwise to characterise living standards by reference to the skilled worker alone. Regular employment at good wages in an era of falling food prices undoubtedly produced rising living standards before 1850 for an increasing section of the working class, but industrial capitalism generated inequalities within as well as between social classes. The gains for some were balanced by the losses for others. In any case, poverty is not necessarily a permanent state. It affects people most at certain times in their lives, during childhood, the early

DISTRESS IN MANCHESTER.

EVIDENCE

(TABULAR AND OTHERWISE)

OF

THE STATE OF THE

LABOURING CLASSES

IN 1840-42.

BY JOSEPH ADSHEAD.

" The relief of human suffering is a sacred duty, written from the beginning
on the hearts of men, enforced by the positive precepts of the Gospel, and which
no nation can violate or neglect with impunity."
                                                        DR. W. P. ALISON.

LONDON:

HENRY HOOPER, PALL MALL EAST.

1842.

Title page of J. Adshead, *Distress in Manchester* (1842). One of several investigations of
working-class conditions conducted locally.

years of marriage when children are young and during old age. Moreover, any picture of rising industrial incomes during the first half of the nineteenth century needs to be offset against the economic insecurity of casual labour and cyclical unemployment. Finally, the debit side of the balance-sheet must also include the health and housing record of the first industrial city.

Housing and Health

Housing conditions are an important benchmark of the quality of life. Early nineteenth-century Manchester had some of the nation's worst living conditions. The town's population more than doubled in size between 1811 and 1831. A constant flow of migrant and transient workers was squeezed into an increasingly inadequate housing stock. The better-off working-class family lived in a 'through' terraced house, but the speculative builder's answer to the hugely increased demand for workers' accommodation was the 'back-to-back': that is, housing built in double rows, often forming courts, each house having its only door and windows at the front. These were usually 'one up and one down', since there was no way of admitting light to a back room. Although back-to-backs were generally an advance on rural housing, they were poorly ventilated (no back yard), and water pump and privy (drained to a cesspool or ashpit) were shared, commonly between 20 houses. Nonetheless they had minimal amenities such as a cooking range or fireplace in the kitchen. The worst were in closed courts which made the disposal of domestic refuse and 'night soil' a very great problem. Back-to-backs were to be found in most working-class areas of the city which were developed before the 1840s. A local bye-law of 1844 banned the building of new back-to-backs and many were converted to 'through' houses later in the century.

Perhaps the worst category of accommodation to be found was the cellar dwelling. These were often the residue of former grandeur, being higher grade housing which had declined and been converted into several tenancies occupying whole floors and single rooms, of which the meanest part was the cellar. These varied in quality like any other form of housing but were often damp, dark and unhealthy. In the 1830s and 1840s up to 20,000 people existed in these almost subterranean dwellings. The figure for Liverpool was even higher. No other cities in the country had such a concentration of squalid habitations. Census returns and sanitary reports reveal rooms occupied by more than one family or being shared with pigs and donkeys. A report for the Manchester and Salford Sanitary Association in 1853 found a cellar in the Oldham Road area with ten people sleeping in one room, seven on the ground and three others (father, mother and grown up daughter) in a single bed. If the cellars were by the riverside at the Irk near Ducie Bridge or in the curve of the Medlock known as 'Little Ireland' conditions could be dire.

The dwellings of Little Ireland were so low-lying that even though some were three-storeys high only their chimneys could be seen from Oxford Road. As the name suggests this squalid ghetto was occupied by the newest and poorest of Irish migrants. Engels' description of it is justly famous.

> In a rather deep hole, in a curve of the Medlock, and surrounded on all four sides by tall factories and high embankments covered with buildings, stand two groups of about two hundred cottages, built chiefly back-to-back, in which live about four thousand human beings, most of them Irish. The cottages are old, dirty, and of the smallest sort, the streets uneven, fallen into ruts and in part without drains or pavements; masses of refuse, offal and sickening filth lie among standing pools in all directions; the atmosphere is poisoned by the effluvia from these, and laden and darkened by the smoke of a dozen tall factory chimneys. A horde of ragged women and children swarm about here, as filthy as the swine that thrive upon the garbage heaps and in the puddles ... The race that lives in those ruinous cottages or in dark, wet cellars, in measureless filth and stench ... must really have reached the lowest stage of humanity.[7]

An earlier account of Little Ireland had reported damp, flooded cellars, each inhabited by around ten persons struggling to keep warm on beds of straw. In this district a single privy was shared among 250 people.[8] A few years after Engels had written the above passage most of Little Ireland was demolished to make way for Oxford Road Station.

Contemporary observers understandably concentrated on the worst examples of squalid housing, generally to be found on the overcrowded periphery of the central district. Little Ireland and the like were the worst examples that could be found and the cellar dwelling was a particular outrage. Conditions were generally better in the purpose-built terraces of the inner residential ring, in districts like Hulme and Chorlton-on-Medlock. The latter was a working-class suburb south of the River Medlock. A report of 1844 noted that two-thirds of the houses had their own 'necessaries with middens or cess pools attached', the contents of which were removed by cart. Several newly-finished streets had been paved and sewered at the owner's expense. The paved streets were swept by Whitworth's patent street-cleansing machine. However, the quality of housing in Chorlton-on-Medlock varied and some un-paved streets and courts were very dirty. About one-third of inhabitants lived in back-to-backs, although cellar-dwelling was uncommon.[9] These were undoubtedly better conditions than in the back streets and courts

Houses by the Irwell. Some of the worst living conditions were by the riverside. The Cathedral tower in the background enables us to pinpoint this location exactly.

of the central area, but it was the latter which captured the attention of contemporaries and the reason is not hard to find. Manchester's health record was notoriously bad.

Manchester had expanded so quickly and the provision of public services was so poor that conditions inevitably deteriorated in the face of the mass migration of the 1820s to 1840s. Little wonder that overcrowding in decayed or cheaply built housing combined with in-adequate communal sanitation and water supply to pose a major health hazard. Crude death rates were well above the national average at 33 per thousand of the population for 1841–50 compared to the national figure of 22 per thousand. Only Liverpool was worse with a rate of 36 per thousand. Moreover, decennial figures obscure mortality peaks of 34 and 37 per thousand in the late 1830s and mid 1840s respectively. These were years of industrial recession as well as of epidemics of typhus, influenza, diarrhoea and cholera and of a mass influx of poor Irish escaping the Great Famine.

Of the major infectious diseases which afflicted Mancunians in the nineteenth century, the chief killer was pulmonary tuberculosis, accounting for 10% of all deaths. Spread by droplet infection, it was mostly contracted by the poorly fed, living in overcrowded homes and working in inadequately ventilated workshops and factories. Typhus, spread by the body louse, was also rife in congested conditions. The more fatal typhoid was spread through sewage-contaminated water and food and thus could affect all classes. (Prince Albert died of it in Windsor Castle in 1861.) Infant mortality was notoriously high in the city and remained so till the end of the century. Up to 50% of all recorded deaths occurred amongst children under five years of age, the majority being under twelve months. Diarrhoea arising from infected water or food was a major cause of fatalities among the very young. Other childhood diseases – smallpox, scarlet fever, diphtheria, whooping cough and measles – spread by droplet infection, were most common in the under-nourished child, living in cramped conditions.

Cholera is the best documented and most notorious of the epidemic diseases. Outbreaks occurred in 1832, 1849, 1854 and 1866, bringing to light the insanitary conditions of Manchester's poorest quarters. Sufficient was known about the connection between disease and housing conditions to direct attention to the cholera's place of origin and its pattern of diffusion. Cholera did much to arouse government interest in housing and sanitation. In a report to the General Board of Health on the cholera epidemic of 1849, H. K. McKeand, the Poor Law medical officer for the London Road district, described conditions in an area bounded by the River Medlock and the Rochdale Canal and bisected by the Ashton and Stockport Canal. Here lived about 30,000 people. Like Manchester's other rivers, the Medlock was notorious for its pol-luted state. McKeand called it a 'filthy ditch' into which 'Innumerable privies, connected with the back of long terrace ranges ... empty them-selves', mixing with the residues from the dye and chemical works which lined its banks. The Medlock would periodically flood. Stagnant water was plentiful. Piped water was supplied through standpipes operating only for an hour or two a day. McKeand, who lived in his district, noted that 'all who can afford, filter it. I am supplied through the same source at my own dwelling, of course, always filtered for table use'. Polluted drinking water was, however, almost unavoidable since even standpipe supplies were often contaminated by sewage from surrounding cess pits and midden privies. The cholera began in the worst part of McKeand's district, between the Medlock and Granby Row. This was an area of cellar dwellings and back-to-backs in courts without yards. An over-flowing graveyard at one end exhaled 'the most foetid smells'. Cattle and pigs were commonly butchered in open alleys or in ill-run slaughter houses. In September 1849, at the height of the epidemic, well over 600 cholera deaths were registered in central Manchester alone.[10]

It did not escape the attention of the better off that urban living could be damaging to your health. Whilst disease took by far its greatest toll of the lives of the poor it did not ignore the propertied classes. Edwin Chadwick's *Report on the Sanitary Condition of the Labouring Population of Great Britain* in 1842 made famous the fact (originally contained in a report commissioned by the Manchester Statistical Society) that the average age at death of 'professional persons and gentry, and their families' was no better in Manchester at 38 years than the life expectancy of 'mechanics and labourers' in rural Rutland. The health hazards of city life were a further stimulus to suburban growth. Those who could generally chose to live beyond the reach of 'King Cholera' and the other diseases of urban life. They also encouraged the development of a vocal sanitary lobby for public health reform, and pushed the municipal authority into more vigorous measures to combat sanitary and health problems. Although the new borough did not appoint a medical officer of health until 1868, it passed local bye-laws in advance of national legislation. The banning of back-to-backs in 1844 is a case in point. Cellar dwellings were regulated from 1853 and the Corporation took powers to demolish property, although much effective slum clearance actually came with construction of the city's railway lines, warehouses and stations. Demolition, however, was not accompanied by the building of new housing. It often served to increase overcrowding by squeezing the population into existing housing stock.

Manchester's health improved only slowly. Local reforms un-doubtedly helped. Also, the building of isolation hospitals from the 1870s onwards contributed to the reduced virulence of infectious dis-eases. Perhaps more important, however, was a general improvement in the standard of living. The real wages of the majority rose towards the end of the century. A consequent decline in poverty for the bulk of the working class led to improved standards of nutrition and personal hygiene. Inadequate environment was a major cause of ill health but so also was the poverty of low wages, irregular employment and general economic insecurity which was the experience of many in the first industrial city.

Leisure and Recreation

Although living in Manchester could be notoriously unhealthy and the hours of labour long, there always remained some time for leisure, which begs the question: how did working people enjoy themselves in the first industrial city? The growth of the towns of the industrial era marked a break with the traditions of the past. However, old customs and traditional pastimes did not disappear overnight, although there was many a moral reformer who wished they would. Fairs and wakes were the most durable of traditional festivities. In 1792 the *Manchester Herald* reported how thousands thronged to the Easter Monday fair at Knott Mill 'to listen to the discordant jargon … droll concert of whistles, halfpenny trumpets, and threepenny drums'. The greatest jubilee of all was at Whit Week.

> Beside the fair and the races, plays, concerts, assemblies, and that cruel unmanly sport, cock fighting, make out the amusements of the week. Business is nearly at a stand; and Pleasure reigns with almost Parisian despotism.[11]

It was partly the hedonistic and heathen character of the Whitsun festivities that caused the churches to try to reclaim them by the organisation of controlled processions, the Whit Walks. Moreover, by 1834 there remained only eight statutory half-day holidays in England. The old pre-industrial calendar of feast days and celebrations had been considerably pruned at the behest both of employers and the church. Nonetheless, popular culture remained essentially gregarious and public.

When Angus Bethune Reach, an investigator for the *Morning Chronicle*'s national survey of labour and the poor, set out one Saturday night in 1849 to find the Apollo music saloon on London Road, he passed through a thoroughfare made gaudy by gaslight and alive with the bustle of late night shopping and weekend entertainments. 'Cheap shops', pubs and pawnbrokers were busy, and on the street:

> Itinerant bands blow and bang their loudest; organ boys grind monotonously; ballad singers or flying stationers make roaring proclamations of their wares. The street is one swarming mass of people. Boys and girls shout and laugh and disappear into the taverns together. Careful housewives – often attended by their husbands, dutifully carrying the baby – bargain hard with the butcher for a halfpenny off in the pound … From byways and alleys and back streets, fresh crowds every moment emerge. Stalls, shops, cellars are clustered round with critics or purchasers – cabmen drive slowly through the throng, shouting and swearing to the people to get out of the horse's way; and occasionally … the melodious burst of a roaring chorus, surging out of the open

Market Street in the early 1820s. Over the next few years this narrow, steep, winding street was to be widened and most of its half-timbered houses demolished. One of John Ralston's 'Views of the Ancient Buildings of Manchester'.

windows of the Apollo, resounds loudly above the whole con-glomeration of street noises.[12]

The principal everyday focus of working-class leisure was the public house. The traditional attractions of the alehouse were refined by the Beershop Act of 1830 which allowed any ratepayer to obtain a licence to brew and sell beer on his premises. Beershops proliferated, often oper-ating from the front room of a terraced house. In response some publicans began to specialise in spirits. By 1843 the *Manchester Directory* recorded 920 beershops, 624 taverns and pubs and 31 inns and hotels: a total of 1,575 liquor establishments, or one for every 154 inhabitants. For many the quickest way out of Manchester was through the pub doorway. Pubs, however, were not merely places for drinking. The 'free and easy' spontaneous sing-song was a traditional feature of the ale house. In the early nineteenth century these were often formalised into the tavern concert or 'singing saloon', a prototype of the music hall. Singers, dancers and jugglers performed their various acts. Audience participation was active and vocal with the communal singing of everything from traditional melodies to hymn tunes. When Reach finally arrived at the Apollo in 1849, he found it to be a long, narrow, smoke-filled and crowded room, where a small 'orchestra' of three fiddles and a piano accompanied the singers and dancers who performed on the tiny stage.

Many Manchester pubs boasted a music room. Even a small beer-house such as the Lamb, part of a back-to-back row at the end of Tame Street, was advertised in 1866 as having its own room for music or club meetings. Robust entertainments sometimes gave way to the more respectable practice of working-class self-help. Another Ancoats pub, the Nelson Arms (later known as the Star Inn), advertised its 'large club or music room where two extensive benefit societies hold their meetings'.[13] Friendly society lodges met in club rooms such as these. In 1834 there were 66 Manchester lodges of the Odd Fellows and 34 of the Foresters, not to mention the smaller benefit societies. The public house was thus a venue for working-class thrift as well as amusement.

The existence of a large urban population stimulated several ventures in commercialised leisure. Travelling circuses and street entertainments were common. There were permanent sites too. In Mount Street a wooden building was erected in 1842 to house Cooke's Circus which staged equestrian displays. The Kersal Moor Races were exceptionally popular during Whit Week. Most of all Manchester was famous for its pleasure gardens. The first opened by Robert Tinker in 1796 on a 23-acre site in the Irk Valley offered a brief escape from the industrial city; a brass band, roundabouts and swings plus a chance to 'partake of tea and other refreshments at small tables standing under overhanging trees or in alcoves covered with creepers'.[14] Later known as Vauxhall Gardens, this amusement park attracted visitors of varied social backgrounds for over fifty years. The Pomona Gardens in Hulme opened on similar lines in the 1840s.

Mancunians also had the opportunity to visit animal collections, including monkeys, pelicans and polar bears, at the Zoological Gardens in Higher Broughton. An entry fee of one shilling and the necessary omnibus journey may have excluded all but the better-off working family. This establishment closed in 1840 and its stock was acquired by Manchester's most famous zoo, Belle Vue, which its proprietor, John Jennison, had first opened in 1836. Covering 36 acres and including a maze, bowling green, deer paddock, boating lake, flower beds, brass band, licensed dancing saloon and tea room, as well as the animals, it was an exceptional magnet for the crowds.

Literacy and Reading Habits

The industrial revolution did not require a high level of literacy among its factory operatives. In fact, if the ability to sign the marriage register is regarded as reliable evidence, then there was an actual decline in literacy in the cotton district of Lancashire in the late eighteenth and early nineteenth centuries. The factory system required not only long hours of labour but also the fulltime employment of children, at least until the factory acts of 1833 and 1847. Moreover, the corresponding decline in the wages of handloom weavers' families made it less easy to afford schooling for their children. These factors, combined with the rise in population, reduced the proportion of children who could obtain a school education. In 1818 only 8% of Manchester children attended its 'low class day schools'.[15]

It might be thought that the Sunday school movement would have corrected this trend. After all, as early as 1788 there were over 5,000 children attending Manchester's Sunday schools. This was not merely for a few hours in the afternoon. Hours of attendance at the Anglican Sunday schools in the Collegiate Church district were 9 to 12 and 1 to 5. But the religious character of some of these schools inhibited the curriculum. The Anglican and Methodist schools in Manchester only taught the children to read. Writing as well as arithmetic were quickly abandoned in the 1790s as a violation of the Sabbath. Whatever such schools may have contributed to the 'christianisation' of the working class, many did nothing to teach the people to write. It was not that there was no demand for such skills. Edwin Rose, an engineer mill-wright, told the Commissioners on the Employment of Children in Factories in 1833 that he had abandoned the Methodist Sunday School in Lever Street and went instead to the Unitarians on Lower Mosley Street because they taught him to read and write.

Literacy levels were lower in Lancashire towns like Manchester than in the rural districts. It has been estimated that in the 1830s only 36% of Manchester's population was literate. This varied greatly by occupation and by gender. In a survey of Lancashire occupations, whilst around 80% of traditional craftsmen such as watchmakers, carpenters and shoemakers could sign their own names, figures of only 40% are calculated for spinners and 33% for labourers. Women generally fared worse. Whilst 43% of female domestic servants might be able to sign the register at their wedding only 6% of women weavers could do so. Yet there was evidence of a rise in reading ability from the 1820s onwards. Whilst surveys in the late 1830s found very few heads of families in Miles Platting able to understand a book and only 174 out of 436 parents in Irlam O'th'Heights able to read, their children did better: 467 out of 612 Pendleton 15 to 21 year olds were found to be capable readers in 1838.[16]

Given the possibility of rising standards by the 1840s, what did the people enjoy reading? We have a rare and valuable insight into this in the evidence of the Manchester bookseller and publisher and future mayor of the city, Abel Heywood.[17] Heywood was the principal distributor of cheap literature in the cotton district. Most of what he sold came from London, arriving daily via the London and North-Western Railway. At the bottom of his market were the penny weekly novels

produced by the London publisher, Edward Lloyd, the pioneer of
fiction for a working-class public. His popular tales of murder, high-
waymen and 'horrors were profusely adorned with woodcut illustrations.
With such titles as *Gentleman Jack*, *Almira's Curse*, *Gallant Tom*, *The
Hangman's Daughter* and *Ela the Outcast* they averaged a total weekly
sale of 6,000 from Heywood's shop alone. Ela was one of Lloyd's most
popular heroines. A foundling with a hidden aristocratic parentage, she
is seduced by a villain called Rackett and spends much of the story as
a gypsy, imprisoned and pursued by her harridan of a mistress. Stories
such as these appealed to the existing audience for broadside ballads,
the flimsy illustrated single sheets which for generations had sold on
the streets and in the markets of the town. Such popular fiction shared
space on Heywood's shelves with various other lines from comic song
magazines to religious tracts.

By 1850, Lloyd's 'penny dreadfuls' were being ousted by a more
sophisticated style of periodical which appealed to a broader audience.
Heywood sold around 8,000 of *The Family Herald*, a successful weekly
penny paper of family reading started in 1842, and 9,000 copies of
G. M. W. Reynold's first publication, *The London Journal* devoted exclusively to fiction. Reynolds, one of the most important figures in
nineteenth-century popular journalism, left this paper in 1845 and
started his own *Reynold's Miscellany of Romance, General Interest, Science
and Art* which, as the title suggests, mixed fiction with instructive articles
of an 'improving' nature. *Reynold's Miscellany* had a weekly sale of 3,700
from Heywood's. Other 'improving' papers selling at a penny ha'penny
a week included *Eliza Cook's Journal* and *Chamber's Information for the
People* with sales of over a thousand each. By contrast Heywood sold
only small numbers of the cheap editions of Dickens, around 250 copies
a week.

These are only Heywood's figures. There were other sellers and each
copy may have had several readers. Moreover, there were libraries
attached to many tobacco and stationery shops and even public houses
loaning penny fiction and stocking a range of periodicals. Abel Heywood
himself ran a penny reading room open between six in the morning
and ten at night to serve the needs of the working man. Heywood
assured the Commissioners investigating the popular press in 1851 that
the better weeklies like *The Family Herald*, which his own family read,
were improving the morals and the habits of the people. This may have
reassured them, but it could not entirely dispel the impression that
Manchester remained one of the 'dark corners of the land'. This seemed
confirmed by the startling statistics published in the same year implying
that Manchester and the cotton towns were centres of ignorance and
religious indifference.

The 1851 Census found only 32% of Manchester's 5 to 14 year olds
in school. Although an advance on 1818, this compared unfavourably

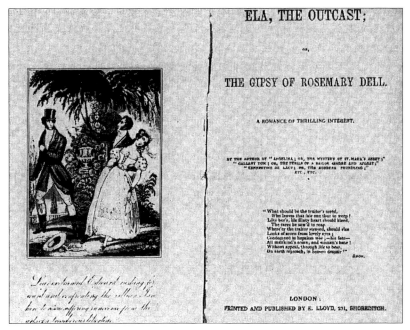

Ela, The Outcast was one of Heywood's most popular titles.

with the average for the 67 English towns surveyed of 52% and was the fourth lowest percentage. The religious census of the same year added to the picture. Manchester, along with the other cotton towns was near the bottom of the table for numbers at religious worship. Fewer than one person in ten attended either church or chapel on the Sunday of the census and this figure included all social classes. If it had not been for Manchester's Irish community these statistics of worship would have been worse. Although Irish migrants accounted for 15% of the population of Manchester in 1851, Roman Catholic church-goers, the vast majority of whom were Irish, provided approaching a quarter of Manchester's total. Add to such figures the common perception that Manchester was a disorderly and criminal place and you had a recipe to disturb even the most complacent among the propertied classes.

Separation of the Classes

What was a question of leisure and custom to the working class could become a matter of popular morality and public order to their employers and to the moral reformers. Perhaps the most common explanation expressed by Victorians for what they saw as a decline in morals and a rise in social unrest in the industrial era was the theory of the 'separation of the classes'. By this was meant that urban living, especially in the industrial towns, had removed the 'civilizing' influence of the rich from the lives of the poor. An oft repeated complaint was that most industrial employers had no relationship with their workers beyond paying their wages. There had been a decline of paternalism. Moreover, the physical pattern of a town like Manchester meant that the middle class, living in their tree-lined suburbs and travelling to work by omnibus or train, had no idea of the conditions in which the working class lived, let alone understood the moral depravity of the 'dark side of the town'. To the moral reformer this was a situation potent of much danger, and Manchester seemed a national symbol of the trend.

Reverend Richard Parkinson, canon of Manchester, claimed in 1841: 'there is no town in the world where the distance between the rich and the poor is so great or the barrier between them so difficult to be crossed'. The French visitor, Leon Faucher, described the effects of the exodus of the rich more graphically:

> ... at the very moment when the engines are stopped, and the counting-houses closed, everything which was the thought – the authority – the impulsive force – the moral order of this immense industrial combination, flies from the town and disappears in an instant. The rich man spreads his couch amidst the beauties of the surrounding country, and abandons the town to the operatives, publicans, mendicants, thieves and prostitutes.[18]

J. P. Kay's *The Moral and Physical Condition of the Working Classes Employed in the Cotton Manufacture in Manchester*, published in 1832, had been extremely influential in encouraging this view. Kay described not only the squalor which had facilitated the spread of the cholera, but also another 'disease' which, he claimed, was equally virulent, that of moral degeneracy. Urban industrial life, he maintained, had produced the conditions in which immorality (defined as careless personal habits, lack of thrift, drunkenness, idleness and sexual promiscuity) could spread like a highly contagious disease. Moreover, the moral and the physical seemed intrinsically linked. Even though contemporaries like Kay recognised that ill-health often arose from people living like pigs, they tended to blame the 'pig' as much as the 'stye' which he occupied, and they were obsessed with his personal habits. They thought it was no good improving the environment without reforming the moral and social behaviour of the people. To do this the gap between the classes had to be bridged by restoring 'civilizing' influences over the lives of working people. Thus in the 1830s and 1840s there were concerted efforts to provide various forms of 'rational recreation' to rival the singing saloons, charitable endeavours to bring the classes closer together and, finally, police action to control the unruly and rebellious.

There was a tradition of paternalism which some employers had inherited from the pre-industrial squirearchy. Some were even patrons of entire communities, which they had often themselves created. A prime example is that of the Gregs of Styal. Such employers assumed a role in providing for the education, social welfare and leisure hours of their workers. In the 1830s the Gregs' employees could exercise in specially provided gardens, use the playground for games, attend music classes and enjoy regular tea parties in the winter months: rational and sober recreations. The Gregs' intention was to shape the behaviour of their workers. Samuel Greg Junior observed that the mill operatives were 'quite capable of being made very worthy, sensible, respectable, and happy ... By gently leading them ... you may ... succeed in making them what you wish them to be'.[19] This appeared easier to do in the isolated rural setting of Styal in Cheshire than in the urban environment of Manchester. But Samuel Greg was also an active member of Manchester's middle-class elite, lectured at the Mechanics' Institute, and delivered papers on education and crime to the Statistical Society. Factory masters like the Gregs joined forces with bankers and merchants to extend employer paternalism to the reform of urban morals and leisure.

The Manchester Mechanics' Institute, the first in the provinces, opened in 1824. An early fruit of the adult education movement it became a self-conscious rival of working-class leisure. Originally it offered mechanics and artisans the chance of self-improvement. For five shillings (25p) a quarter they could attend classes of a scientific and technical character. Financial sponsorship of the original scheme came from local employers like William Fairbairn and Joseph Brotherton and the banker Benjamin Heywood. Heywood was a central figure in the work of the Institute and among the first to realise its over-ambitious character. Clerks, warehousemen and shopkeepers receiving basic lessons in grammar, writing and arithmetic soon outnumbered mechanics attending science classes. Moreover, as attendances declined in the 1830s, it became increasingly necessary to sugar the pill of 'useful knowledge' with entertainments, social evenings, concerts and excursions. Much the largest section in the Institute's library was that entitled 'novels, romances and tales'.

Heywood became convinced that the original scheme of vocational subjects was too demanding for the leisure hours of the exhausted factory operative. Thus in the lyceums set up in working-class districts in the 1830s as auxiliaries to the Institute, the emphasis was upon recreation rather than instruction and the fees were lower. The lyceums were an attempt to reach the broader working class. Heywood made the intention plain when speaking of the first of these new style institutions at Miles Platting.

> We are endeavouring to make our reading-room there very popular, to have in an evening a blazing fire, red curtains, easy chairs, a capital cup of coffee, chess, pictures, now and then a good story read aloud; in short to see if we cannot make it a match for the public house as a place of resort for the working man after his day's work.[20]

At first these lyceums enjoyed popularity, but by 1850 they had had their day. The atmosphere was too earnest and the air of instruction too intrusive. The moral influence of the lyceum could never really compete with the conviviality of the pub.

Public parks and free libraries were other attempts to provide recreational and instructional facilities for the working class. Despite the urban growth of the first half of the nineteenth century, even cities like Manchester were within easy reach of open fields. The novelist Elizabeth Gaskell opens *Mary Barton: A Tale of Manchester Life* (1848) with a working-class family's excursion to Greenheys Fields.[21] There were, however, few open spaces in the inner residential belt. Urban parks were considered vital for the health and leisure of factory workers. In 1840 Parliament voted money to assist local authorities in providing city parks, and in 1846 Manchester's first three public parks were opened: Queen's Park in Harpurhey, Philip's Park in Bradford (in honour of Mark Philips the Manchester MP who campaigned for it and who part financed it) and Peel Park in Salford (supported by £1,000 from Sir Robert Peel and subsequently sold to Salford Corporation). These were meant to be places of respectable recreation. For example, in 1856 the City Council gave in to an orchestrated campaign of protest from the Sabbatarian lobby and banned brass band concerts from the new public parks on a Sunday. Ironically this concession to respectability removed what must have been a powerful attraction in drawing people away from the beershop and gin palace.

The free library was another arm of the rational recreation movement. Manchester Free Library opened in 1852 in the former Owenite Hall of Science at Campfield on Deansgate. It was part financed by rates but depended upon voluntary subscriptions for the purchase of books. This attempt at 'intellectual engineering' greatly increased the range of books and periodicals available to Manchester readers, who previously relied on the Mechanics' Institute and various other smaller collections.[22] The first Chief Librarian, Edward Edwards, reported that in its initial year of operation over 138,000 volumes were issued, with novels and romances the most popular category and Charles Dickens's Christmas story, *The Chimes*, the most frequently borrowed title.

Mechanics institutes, lyceums and free libraries were agencies of self-improvement for a dedicated minority of workers. But most merely selected what they wanted from the rational recreations on offer. Whilst an elite learned from lectures and libraries, the majority felt able to enjoy both park and pub. They were not mutually exclusive.

Crime and the Police

The 'carrot' of rational recreation was accompanied by the 'stick' of police action. The 1840s witnessed drastic reform in the policing of Manchester. The 'New Police' were formed in response to a demand for public order and the more efficient control of the roughest working-class areas. Again, the reform of working-class behaviour was a prime target.[23]

It was widely held that Manchester had an exceptionally high crime rate. In 1840, W. B. Neale, an expert on juvenile delinquency, quoted a 19-year-old just out of Salford Gaol as remarking: 'If you say in any other part of England that you are from Manchester, you are at once supposed to be a thief'. This reputation had much to do with the contemporary debate over the moral effects of industrialism. But it was Manchester's rapid population growth and its attraction to migrants rather than factory labour itself which caused it to appear disorderly and dangerous. It was 'not manufacturing Manchester, but multitudinous Manchester' which gave birth to its reputation for criminality.[24] Some notion of its appeal can be gained from a police estimate in 1841 that 40,000 persons arrived each week by coach and train. It was this transient population which caused most anxiety to contemporaries. The

Manchester's new police on parade in the 1840s.

poorest found their way to the cheap lodging houses of Angel Meadow or the rookeries west of Deansgate. It was areas such as these which were regarded as breeding grounds for crime and disorder. Indeed the growth of crime mirrored the decay of these shabby districts and the rise of the respectable business and retail quarter of Market Street, King Street and St Ann's Square. The coexistence of the two was not peaceful. Many arrests took place in the central market and business areas as well as in the slums.

What sort of crimes were committed? Of offences against the person, street brawls and drunkenness accounted for nearly 75% and common assault another 10%. The overwhelming majority of crimes against property were cases of non-violent theft or contraventions of the vagrancy laws. There was little in the way of organised crime and most offences were minor. What really disturbed the authorities was the threat of a disaffected populace. The fear of public disorder was behind the campaign in the town during the 1830s and early 1840s for an effective police force. Periodic disturbances in the 1830s culminated in the events of August 1842. This month saw simultaneously a major cotton strike (the 'Plug Strikes'), in which Chartist agitators succeeded in closing all the mills, accompanied by riots from the poorest quarters against unemployment and high food prices.

It was in 1842 that Manchester's New Police began their operations. The old day and night watch had been widely criticised for its failure as a police force. It had proved so ineffective against public disorder that the military were routinely called in to suppress disturbances. As elsewhere in the country, the rationale of police reform was the danger to property and the need to patrol the slums. The intention was 'to guard Ardwick by watching Angel Meadow'. It was to be expected that the residents of the poorer districts would resist the new arm of the law. The Irish-born in particular were alienated by their poverty and the hostility of some among the host community. One in three of those arrested for rioting and breach of the peace were Irish.

In the 1840s the reformed Manchester police force adopted an aggressive policy in the 'low' areas of the town. All street gatherings were regularly broken up, people 'moved on', and beershops closely regulated. The number of arrests was initially very high. One consequence of such high profile policing was a large number of assaults on officers which culminated in anti-police disturbances such as those in Ancoats in May 1843. On this occasion a beerhouse arrest for brawling led to an angry crowd breaking into Kirby Street Police Station and beating the officers inside. The ring-leaders, two soldiers, were later arrested in Port Street but local residents turned out to effect a rescue. Rioting spread throughout Ancoats and a crowd of one thousand marched on Piccadilly. Troops had to be called in to quell disturbances which lasted over two days.

Despite such resistance the New Police became well established by 1850. A more 'softly softly' approach to the policing of the poorer districts improved police–public relations. So much so that when Queen Victoria visited Manchester in 1851 she commented very favourably on the quiet and orderly behaviour of the crowds which lined the streets to greet her. Manchester was losing its reputation for disorder. But the 'criminal classes' were not finished. During the later nineteenth century Angel Meadow and the like once more became a focus for anxiety, although by then fear of crime was reduced to concern about a small subgroup rather than the working class as a whole. In the eyes of many the 'dangerous class' of the 1830s had been tamed and civilized. What rational recreation had failed to do, strict policing may have achieved. As we shall see, improved real wages and living conditions also had much to do with the process.

References

1. B. Disraeli, *Coningsby or the New Generation* (1844), Vol. VIII of the Bradenham edition, Peter Davies, London, 1927, p. 161; A. de Tocqueville, *Journeys to England and Ireland*, trans. G. Lawrence and K. P. Mayer, Faber and Faber, London, 1958, pp. 107–8.

2. British Parliamentary Papers (BPP), *Factory Inquiry Commission, First Report, Employment of Children in Factories, XX*, 1833, App. D 1, pp. 39–40; J. C. McKenzie, 'The composition and nutritional value of diets in Manchester and Dukinfield, 1841', *Transactions of the Lancashire and Cheshire Antiquarian Society*, 72 (1962) pp. 123–40; R. Scola, *Feeding the Victorian City: The Food Supply of Manchester 1770–1870*, Manchester University Press, 1992, ch. 5.

3. Manchester Central Reference Library, Archives Dept., MSF 310/6/M5/ 115–16.

4. All from J. Adshead, *Distress in Manchester: Evidence of the State of the Labouring Classes in 1840–2* (1842), reprinted in *Focal Aspects of the Industrial Revolution*, Irish University Press, Shannon, 1971, pp. 151–2.

5. See W. J. Lowe, *The Irish in Mid-Victorian Lancashire*, Peter Lang, New York, 1989, pp. 34–5, 47. See also M. A. Busteed and R. I. Hodgson, 'Irish migrant responses to urban life in early industrial Manchester', *Geographical Journal*, 162 (1996), pp. 139–53.

6. See Scola, *Feeding the Victorian City*, pp. 261–2; although the most detailed local evidence is by no means clear, see R. K. Fleischman, *Conditions of Life among the Cotton Workers of Southeastern Lancashire, 1780–1850*, Garland, New York, 1985, ch. 4 and pp. 348–9.

7. E Engels, *The Condition of the Working Class in England* (1844), Granada, London, 1969, p. 93.

8. J. P. Kay, *The Moral and Physical Condition of the Working Classes Employed in the Cotton Manufacture in Manchester* (2nd edn, 1832), E. J. Morten, Manchester, 1969, p. 35.

9. BPP, *Commissioners for Inquiring into the State of Large and Populous Districts, First Report*, XVII, 1844, Appendix, pp. 58–70.

10. BPP, *The Report of the General Board of Health on the Cholera Epidemic of 1848 and 1849*, 1850, Appendix A, pp. 93–4.

11. J. Aston, *The Manchester Guide*, privately printed, Manchester, 1804, p. 245.

12. J. Ginswick (ed.), *Labour and the Poor in England and Wales 1849–51*, Vol. 1, Frank Cass, London, 1983, pp. 80–2.

13. Quoted in N. Richardson, *The Old Pubs of Ancoats*, Neil Richardson, Swinton, 1987.

14. Quoted in C. Aspin, *Lancashire: The First Industrial Society*, Helmshore Local History Society, 1969, p. 166.

15. BPP, *Digest of Parochial Returns ... Education of the Poor; 1818, i, County of Lancaster*, 1819, IX, A.

16. M. Sanderson, 'Literacy and social mobility in the Industrial Revolution', *Past and Present*, 56 (1972), pp. 84–5.

17. See BPP, *H. C. Select Committee on Newspaper Stamps*, 1851, q. 2474–2617; also Ginswick, *Labour and the Poor*, pp. 61–3.

18. Rev. R. Parkinson, *On the Present Condition of the Labouring Poor in Manchester* (1841), reprinted in *Focal Aspects of the Industrial Revolution*, p. 114; L. Faucher, *Manchester in 1844* (1844), Frank Cass, London, 1969, pp. 26–7.

19. S. Greg, *Two Letters to Leonard Horner on the Capabilities of the Factory System*, 1840, pp. 21–3, cited in P. Bailey, *Leisure and Class in Victorian England*, Routledge, London, 1978, p. 54.

20. Sir B. Heywood, *Addresses Delivered at the Manchester Mechanics' Institute*, Charles Knight, London, 1843, pp. 107–8.

21. Elizabeth Gaskell, *Mary Barton: A Tale of Manchester Life* (1848); Penguin edn, 1994.

22. For the view that this was also 'cultural disempowerment' see M. Hewitt, 'Confronting the modern city: the Manchester Free Library 1850–80', *Urban History*, 27 (2000), 62–88.

23. For what follows see esp. S. Davies, 'Classes and police in Manchester 1829–1880' in A. J. Kidd and K. W. Roberts (eds), *City, Class and Culture: Social Policy and Cultural Production in Victorian Manchester*, Manchester University Press, 1985 and D. Jones, *Crime, Protest, Community and Police in Nineteenth Century Britain*, Routledge & Kegan Paul, London, 1982, ch. 6.

24. W. B. Neale, *Juvenile Delinquency in Manchester*, Gavin Hamilton, Manchester, 1840, p. 58; W. L. Clay, *The Prison Chaplain: A Memoir of the Reverend John Clay*, Macmillan, Cambridge, 1861, p. 518.

CHAPTER 4

Manchester Men:
Power and Prestige in the
First Industrial City

The Manchester of the industrial era was largely the creation of a new order of businessmen, an urban elite of merchants, manufacturers and bankers: the 'Manchester Men' of legend. Industrialisation had enhanced their prestige and power, and the first industrial city was a stage for the display of that power in local politics and in public institutions as well as in the workplace. Moreover, Manchester's business elite came to seek a national role. It must be remembered that we are not talking about a provincial backwater. 'Manchester men' took to the national, even the world's, stage. Out of the growth of a local political identity grew the so-called 'Manchester School' ideology of free trade and the national campaigning of the Anti-Corn Law League. Manchester was the seed-bed of a new philosophy which set fair to become not only the ideology of a class but the policy of the nation. This was the local history which gave birth to the saying: 'What Manchester does today, London does tomorrow'.

What manner of men made Manchester? What do we know about the people who created and governed the first industrial city? Were they a united group or were they divided by politics and religion? How did they bring Manchester from manorial rule to municipal corporation? Was it merely a matter of urban management or was it part of a deep-rooted political struggle? What of their public image? How did the world view them, and how did they see themselves? Do they conform to the stereotype of the northern industrialist, the uncouth, unsophisticated self-made man? First we need to turn to the pattern of local government and politics before considering the manners and tastes of a Manchester 'gentleman'.

Local Government and Politics

During the 1830s Manchester was brought into the national political arena. The Great Reform Act of 1832 gave the town its first MPs, and the Municipal Corporations Act of 1835 led to the incorporation of the borough of Manchester in 1838, and confirmation of its powers by the Borough Charters Incorporation Act of 1842; thus began the municipal management of a town which had hitherto been run by manorial court and police commissioners. Manchester was granted city status in 1853. The story of how Manchester's local government was transformed from Court Leet to Corporation is more than a matter of improved urban management. However, the early administration of the first industrial city needs to be outlined before the political character of the struggle over local government can be explored.

Numerous visitors to early industrial Manchester commented on its remarkable lack of regulation. Until it became a municipal borough in 1838 the town was governed by a curious and confusing array of antique and *ad hoc* agencies of local government. It was partly this lack of uniformity, plus the absence of guild restrictions, which may have encouraged the growth of industry. But equally, the town's unregulated character facilitated its horrendous living conditions. In past centuries many important towns had been granted charters allowing them to be governed by town councils elected by ratepayers. By contrast Manchester was administered almost as the medieval manor it once was. Several different bodies exercised authority. The oldest was the Court Leet, the major organ of the town's government till the late eighteenth century. The chief manorial official was the Boroughreeve assisted by two constables. These posts were voluntary. A permanent paid official, the Deputy Constable, had responsibility for the daytime police force or 'watch'. A second agency of authority was the parish vestry which, through the churchwardens and parish overseers, levied rates and administered poor relief. The vestry also selected surveyors of the highways responsible for the upkeep of roads.

Finally, the most recent and most important arm of local government was the Police and Improvement Commissioners established by Act of Parliament in 1792. The Police Commissioners had wide ranging responsibilities, from street paving, lighting and cleansing to refuse collection and the fire service. They were also charged with providing a night watch, so that Manchester had two police forces, one for the day and another for the hours of darkness. The Police Commissioners were reformed in 1828 and the voting qualification lowered, but it was still a very restricted franchise in which only around 2.5% of the population could vote. The Commissioners, nonetheless, were active agents of improvement. They even launched their own gas company in 1817, the first such municipal venture in the North West and, until the amalgamation of Liverpool's two gas companies in 1848, the largest. Manchester's public gasworks actually made a profit which was spent on street paving and refuse disposal in the town centre. However, the diversion of profits for town improvements at the expense of the gas consumers (chiefly shopkeepers and other small traders) was behind a

Mosley Street in 1824 still retained the quiet residential character it was soon to lose. On the left foreground is the Portico Library and in the distance St Peter's Church.

prolonged dispute in the 1820s over gas prices and the running of the gas venture. The gas consumers had no say in the management of the town but they were expected to pay for its improvement. In fact, the gas dispute was part of a broader struggle for political mastery. Indeed, the local government of industrial Manchester cannot be understood without reference to the structure of local politics.

It might seem on the surface that the demise of the Court Leet of Sir Oswald Mosley, lord of the manor of Manchester, was a mere matter of modernisation. In class terms the advent of a corporation for Manchester could be seen as the middle class replacing the aristocracy and assuming the political power appropriate to its economic position after decades of industrialisation. But this picture is too simple for two reasons. First of all, unusual among nineteenth-century towns, Manchester was almost devoid of aristocratic influence. The county gentry had taken little interest in a town unrepresented in parliament. Moreover, there had been an exodus of landed families from the vicinity of Manchester. By 1795 the only family of antiquity were the Traffords at Trafford Hall. Merchants had even moved into the seats of the Mosleys at Ancoats and at Hulme after the family retired to Staffordshire. Sir Oswald's only interest in the town was the collection of rents and fines. Lord Ducie owned Strangeways Hall but lived in Gloucester. The Earl of Wilton and Lord Francis Egerton survived the exodus, but neither played any part in local society. By 1825 most landed seats in the neighbourhood of Manchester were occupied by merchants and manufacturers or by minor gentry of no political importance. Several were even divided up into separate dwellings.

Secondly, the town's industrial and commercial leaders themselves were divided and the divisions ran deep.[1] The fault lines were political and religious rather than economic in character. All Manchester's leaders owed their wealth to the same economic miracle, but they worshipped in different denominations and gave allegiance to rival political parties. There were two distinct factions in Manchester politics before 1838, the one Tory and Anglican, the other Liberal and Nonconformist. Due to the lack of a resident gentry, Manchester Toryism was middle-class rather than aristocratic. Manchester's leading Tory families were manufacturers and merchants. But they often intermarried with county society or their warehouses employed the younger sons of gentry families. There were also kinship connections with Liverpool's mercantile elite. Great Tory manufacturing dynasties like the Peels and the Birleys looked to the county for traditional paths to status. The three brothers John, Hugh Hornby and Joseph Birley were each Deputy Lieutenants of Lancashire. But access to county society did not prevent others amongst Manchester's Tories from running the town between the 1790s and the 1830s. Among those to be found enjoying the convivial company of 'John Shaw's' punch club, Manchester's traditional Tory meeting place, would be the leading figures in the Court Leet or the town's Police Commissioners as well as the sidesmen and churchwardens from the collegiate church. Their shared memories might stretch back to school days at Manchester Grammar School and their club outings might include riding in the Manchester Yeomanry. It was these men, under the leadership of Hugh Hornby Birley, who played such an infamous part on the day of Peterloo (see below, Chapter 5).

The rival, Liberal, faction in Manchester politics, by contrast, got its identity from the town itself for, by the laws and conventions of the time, the religious nonconformity of most of its members barred them from entry not only to the nation's universities and professions but also from marriage into landed society. This faction was dominated by the great Unitarian families who worshipped at the Cross Street and Mosley Street chapels. These families, linked through business and marriage, formed an influential network. The Heywoods, Percivals, Philipses, Hibberts, Potters, Gregs and others gave Manchester many of its leading commercial, professional, scientific and literary figures; and the nation at large nearly a dozen MPs after 1832. Mark Philips, MP for Manchester, 1832–1847, worshipped at Cross Street Chapel and was related to the Hibberts and the Heywoods. Several of these families were descended from ejected puritan ministers of the seventeenth century. Unitarians were prominent members of most of the town's cultural institutions, notably the Literary and Philosophical Society. They played a part in local social and cultural leadership out of all proportion to the size of their congregations. Out of the 22,255 people recorded as being at worship in Manchester in the Religious Census of 1851, only 1,670 were Unitarians. They were a closely knit group, to whom Manchester's voluntary societies and institutions were important since they were denied access to the traditional avenues of status.

The political and religious divisions within Manchester's middle class generated much bitterness and acrimony. Nonconformists looked to Parliament for the hoped for repeal of the Test and Corporation Acts which denied them civil rights (finally repealed in 1829). The Tories looked to 'church and king' to defend tradition. The French Revolution of 1789 exacerbated the situation. Manchester's middle-class radicals, under the leadership of Thomas Walker, a prominent merchant and former Boroughreeve, stirred by the ideals of the 'rights of man', campaigned for parliamentary reform. They formed the Manchester Constitutional Society in 1790, and when the existing press denied them access created the *Manchester Herald* as their voice. Manchester's Tory loyalists, who had formed the Church and King Club, responded by engineering 'church and king' riots in December 1792. Manchester's Tory controlled authorities (magistrates and constables) stood by as a drunken mob attacked dissenters' chapels, wrecked the *Herald*'s offices and for three successive nights besieged Thomas Walker and other radicals in their homes, breaking windows and threatening bodily harm to the occupants. In the year after war had broken out with revolutionary France, Walker and others were tried for sedition. Such harassment had its effect. Despite further sporadic campaigns the Manchester reform impetus remained subdued for a generation. Many of the middle-class radicals moderated their politics as the war with France continued. Patriotism got the upper hand. The outcome was a Tory stranglehold on the town's political institutions (Court Leet, parish vestry, Police Commissioners and magistracy) which lasted for more than a generation.

Not until Peterloo in 1819, when a huge reform meeting was brutally dispersed, was middle-class politics in Manchester once more set alight. Whigs and Tories were firmly divided over the Massacre and it marked the beginning of a shift of local power away from the Tories. During the 1820s reformers were involved in successive campaigns against church rates and Police Commission powers, including the dispute over the gas supply. It was during these campaigns that the roots were laid of the strategies and policies used so successfully in the battle for incorporation. A 'small but determined band' of middle-class liberal reformers set a course to avoid the treatment meted out to earlier radicals such as Thomas Walker and Joseph Hanson (see page 81).[2] By the late 1830s they were ready to challenge the power of the Tory elite. After a nine-month agitation spearheaded by Richard Cobden, J. E. Taylor, William Neild and Thomas Potter, the Liberal faction finally secured a municipal corporation for the town in 1838.[3] The

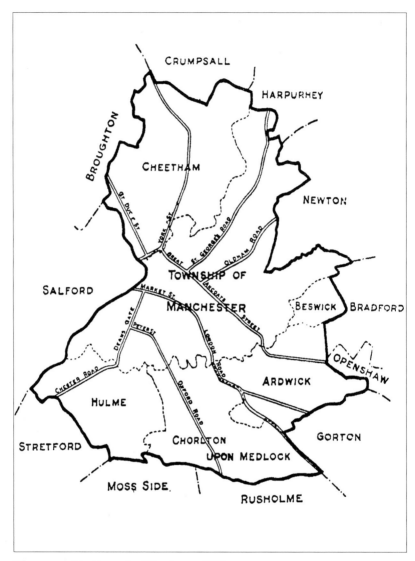

The new municipal borough of Manchester, 1838.

Municipal Corporations Act gave unincorporated towns the opportunity to petition the Privy Council for a charter. Cobden couched his appeal for incorporation on the grounds of liberty and representative government against monopoly and privilege; that the town's 'Chief Municipal Officers should be a body popularly chosen instead of being nominated by the Lord of the Manor's Court Leet'.[4] His appeal was to liberal and democratic principles but also to the self-interest of those excluded from manorial government, especially the town's shopkeepers.

Opposition to the municipal charter came from an alliance of middle-class Tories, and working-class radicals (the latter felt aggrieved at the Whig government of Earl Grey which had not enfranchised the working class in the Parliamentary Reform Act of 1832, had introduced the hated New Poor Law in 1834 and was responsible for the Municipal Corporations Act which offered only middle-class local government to Manchester). The conflict did not end with the granting of the Charter. The new Council was denied access to the Town Hall on King Street by the Police Commissioners and the first meeting of the Council was held in the nearby York Hotel. Legal challenges to the Charter continued until 1841. The Police Commissioners did not relinquish their powers until 1843 and the last meeting of the Court Leet was in 1845. But nonetheless the granting of the Charter was a watershed in local politics. A municipal corporation for Manchester was a chance for the middle-class Liberal nonconformist elite to supplant the older Tory-dominated oligarchy, with whom it had struggled for more than a generation, as the natural governors of the town. The advent of the Manchester Corporation ushered in a Liberal era in Manchester politics which was to last for most of the century.

Anti-Corn Law League

Richard Cobden had been the driving force behind the campaign for local government reform. A calico manufacturer with a Sussex farming background who had only settled in the town as late as 1832, Cobden was one of a long line of Manchester radicals who, from the time of Thomas Walker in the 1790s, had endeavoured to shift middle-class opinion in the direction of political and economic reforms in the industrial interest. Such men were political activists, self-appointed spokesmen for their class, who, whilst not representative of the majority, carried opinion for the duration. For radicals like Cobden, parliamentary and municipal reform were part of a broader policy of 'liberalism', the lynchpin of which was the doctrine of free trade and the political intention of which was 'anti-feudal', i.e. to strike a blow at the privileged landed aristocracy which governed Great Britain. Thus whilst municipal reform was significant for Manchester itself, it was the town's role in the campaign to achieve a government policy in the middle-class interest which secured its national importance. Central to this was the agitation against the Corn Laws and the activities of the Anti-Corn Law League.

The Corn Laws were a symbol of the political dominance of the landowning class and of the agricultural interest. They were introduced in 1815 to maintain farm prices by imposing a duty on imports of corn. Manufacturers objected on the grounds that high food prices forced up wages, ate into the profits of industry and thereby undermined the

wealth of the nation. Living standards and productivity, they maintained, were thus kept artificially low by government policy. Cobden
held that free trade between nations would generate international
understanding and peace.[5] The motives of many manufacturers who
supported the campaign may have been more directly self-interested,
and the implicit anti-statism of Cobden's creed never convinced the
Manchester business class as time was to show.

In the second quarter of the nineteenth century, however important
the provincial business communities might be on their own terms, they
were of marginal significance nationally. Even after the 1832 Reform
Act the landed class retained control of national political patronage.
The Anti-Corn Law League was always in the position of a lobby
outside the charmed circle of the governing class. It was never even in
the position of a modern political party. Nonetheless, under the skilled
chairmanship of George Wilson and with the benefit of the oratory of
Cobden and John Bright, the Quaker manufacturer from Rochdale, the
League proved a remarkably efficient pressure group.

The Manchester Anti-Corn Law Association, formed in 1838, was
the model for the national organisation. Although the League had
offices in London, Manchester was always its first home. Wilson and
Cobden had developed an effective working relationship during the
incorporation campaign. But the League depended upon more than
effective leadership. At its Manchester headquarters in Newall's Buildings on Market Street there was a large staff working in a number of
clearly defined departments. Its organisation combined the best business
efficiency with acute political acumen. For example, its offices contained
a complete set of electoral registers for the whole country, and reports
from the League's local agents were used to update them constantly
with such information as voters' allegiances and qualifications, changes
of address and so on. It was by modern means, such as effective and
accurate leafleting, made possible by the introduction of the Penny
Post in 1840, as well as by a campaign of public meetings, that the
League's propaganda reached the voter. Its impact upon public opinion
was perhaps more instrumental in achieving a change in the law than
any frontal assault on the national government.

Cobden was elected MP for Stockport in 1841 and voiced the
League's arguments within Parliament. But the League's major policy
decisions were still made in Newall's Buildings. Moreover, the significance of the League to Manchester and of Manchester to the League
was symbolised in the building of the Free Trade Hall to house League
gatherings. The first Free Trade Hall was built in six weeks in 1840,
on the site of the Peterloo Massacre. This timber pavilion was replaced
three years later by a brick structure and finally, in 1853, by the
magnificent stone edifice designed by Edward Walters. The Free Trade
Hall became an expression of Manchester's priorities. As A. J. P. Taylor

Richard Cobden at the age of 57.

has remarked: 'Other great halls in England are called after a royal patron, or some figure of traditional religion. Only the Free Trade Hall is dedicated ... to a proposition'.[6]

Cobden once wrote, 'The League is Manchester'. And this view was propagated by the League's first (and most influential) historian, Archibald Prentice,[7] who had chaired the first meeting of the Manchester Association in 1838. Prentice was the radical editor of the *Manchester Times* and the moving spirit of a small group of ultra enthusiasts in the

League. The Manchester business community, on the whole, supported
the League, even if they did not always agree with the Prentice group.
Prominent Manchester men made the transition from local government
agitation to League politics, most notably such impeccable representatives of respectable opinion as the rich merchant Thomas Potter,
the town's first mayor and soon to be knighted, and the celebrated
manufacturer Robert Hyde Greg of Styal Mill.

During the early 1840s League propaganda was moving public opinion towards free trade. But it took a national crisis to secure the
removal of restrictions on imported grain. The food shortages which
resulted from the Great Famine in Ireland enabled the Prime Minister,
Sir Robert Peel, to obtain Commons support for the repeal of the Corn
Laws in 1846. But Manchester was forever to be associated with the
policy of free trade.

To contemporaries what became known as the 'Manchester school
of economics' epitomised the town's contribution to the ideology of
liberalism; its own peculiar version of Victorian values. First coined, in
a derogatory sense, by Benjamin Disraeli this school of thought favoured
unfettered commerce on the assumption that the pursuit of self-interest
and the free exchange of goods and labour would ultimately be to the
benefit of all mankind. This view of free market economics, derived
from Adam Smith's *Wealth of Nations* (1776), gained international
currency through the Anti-Corn Law League as a (sometimes hated)
expression of selfish economic behaviour. It was characterised by
German critics in the abstract noun *das Manchestertum* to symbolise
what they saw as the British ideology of economic individualism. Thus
'Manchester' itself became abstracted as the free trade symbol of
Britain's economic power and of the British middle class.

In reality the picture is more complicated, even with regard to the
Manchester middle class. 'Manchester school' and *das Manchestertum*
were less representative of the economic preferences of the town's
business community than might be thought. Support for the campaign
of radicals like Cobden and Bright was often a matter of political
expediency. Once a national policy of free trade had been secured there
seemed little further use for such an alliance with radical politicians.
Despite the reputation for radicalism acquired through the Anti-Corn
Law agitation, Manchester Liberal politics were inherently conservative
and deferential. Activists like Cobden and Bright were atypical in their
desire to 'take on' the landed class. Manchester's middle-class elite by
contrast were eager to become integrated into a national system in
which rural elites still played a key part, even after the repeal of the
Corn Laws. Thus when the Liberal Party under Lord Palmerston
adopted a more aggressive foreign policy to protect trade, Manchester's
electors took the opportunity, in 1857, to ditch their radical MPs,
including John Bright who had attacked Palmerston's policy and had

also opposed the Crimean War. Economic self-interest not an idealised version of international harmony or a moral crusade against 'feudalism', had always been the driving-force behind the respect of Manchester's business community for what an enthusiast was to call 'the beauty and holiness of free trade'.[8]

Although the town remained represented by Liberal MPs – John Potter topped the poll in 1857 – the demise of 'Manchester school' Liberalism in its home town heralded the national rise of business support for the Conservative Party during the second half of the nineteenth century: Manchester elected its first Conservative MP in 1868. Although incorporation and the League had revealed the radical edge of Manchester Liberalism, the shift to the right after 1857 was more in tune with the politics of the town's middle-class elite, which despite party labels had always been conservative with a small 'c'.

'Manchester Man'

Manchester was thus the symbol of a new order of society and a new economic philosophy. It was important because of the new wealth it created. But was it a place devoted solely to the pursuit of gain? And what of the men who made Manchester? The conventional stereotype, then as well as now, was of a class of austere, vulgar, self-made men with limited leisure. They were greedy of gain and lacking either cultural pretension or artistic sense. The famous contrast between 'Liverpool Gentleman' and 'Manchester Man' opposed the traditional refinement of the older merchant with his aristocratic leanings to the ignorant manners of the new men recently risen from the *hoi polloi*.

Charles Dickens had such men in mind when he created Josiah Bounderby of Coketown and in doing so summed up a new class:

> He was a rich man: banker, merchant, manufacturer, and what not. A big loud man, with a stare and a metallic laugh. A man made out of coarse material, which seemed to have been stretched to make so much of him ... A man with a pervading appearance on him of being inflated like a balloon, and ready to start. A man who could never sufficiently vaunt himself a self-made man. A man who was always proclaiming his old ignorance and his old poverty. A man who was the bully of humility.[9]

Bounderby's *alter ego* was Thomas Gradgrind, the dull unimaginative utilitarian: 'A man of realities. A man of fact and calculations'. Gradgrind instructs the schoolmaster, Mr MacChokumchild, to teach 'nothing but facts. Facts alone are wanted in life'. If there was to be knowledge it had to be 'useful'. Coketown represented all that Dickens hated about the new order of society, and it was partly through such caricatures

that Manchester acquired a reputation as a dull working town, its
business class unmoved by art, music, literature or the wonders of nature
and excited only by the jingle of the cash box. As one contemporary
had earlier observed:

> A thorough Manchester man ... hears more music in the everlasting
> motion of the loom than he would in the songs of the lark or the
> nightingale. For him philosophy has no attraction, poetry no
> enchantment; mountains, rocks, vales and streams excite not his
> delight or admiration; genius shrinks at his approach.[10]

How much of this conventional stereotype is valid? First of all, the
issue of the 'self-made' man. Much depends on what is meant by this
term. If it is synonymous with the 'rags to riches' stories of 'Bounderbys'
risen from the gutter by their efforts alone, then it is largely a myth.
There were a few among the early factory masters who had started out
with nothing but a shilling and a deal of determination, but most already
had some capital either of their own or borrowed from kin. The
humblest of origins appears to have been 'lower middle class': shopkeepers, skilled craftsmen, yeomen farmers. Among Manchester's first
industrialists, James McConnel and John Kennedy were farmers' sons
from south-west Scotland. Similarly, Henry and Thomas Houldsworth,
also fine cotton spinners, were from Nottinghamshire farming stock.
With the help of a legacy they established their first mill. Thomas
made a fortune in Manchester and became MP for Pontefract. There
were a few who rose from the humbler ranks of the wage earner,
generally through promotion. Thus James Halliwell began as a porter
in one of the warehouses belonging to the famous Peel family in Cannon
Street in the 1780s. Recognition by his employers resulted in promotion
to packer, then traveller and finally agent. Through his dedication and
managerial talents Halliwell was eventually offered a partnership in the
Peels' Bolton, Bury and Holcombe concerns.

Much more common, however, was the cotton spinner who began
as a merchant-manufacturer in domestic industry or who was already
an industrialist in another field. For example, Peter Drinkwater, the
pioneer Manchester industrialist who built his steam-powered factory
at Piccadilly in 1789, was already a wholesale fustian manufacturer with
a warehouse in King Street and an extensive export trade. He had
earlier established a water-driven mill at Northwich in Cheshire. Samuel
Oldknow was the largest manufacturer of muslins in England when, in
the early 1790s, he set up two large mills at Stockport and Mellor.
Men with money, manufacturing experience or monied associates
became industrialists.

As we have seen in Chapter 2 it is misleading to regard Manchester's
middle class as merely a millocracy. The 'Manchester Man' could just
as easily be a merchant or a banker or a member of one of the

The Royal Manchester Institution (1823), now the Manchester City Art Gallery.

Below: Also designed by Charles Barry were the Italianate premises of the Athenaeum Club, founded in 1835. 'The institution whch perhaps most clearly revealed the concern of Manchester's middle class with the cultural image of the city.' (*Photographs: Ian Beesley*)

professions as a manufacturer. But how did this new social class see itself? It will not surprise us that many in Manchester rejected the common caricature of the northern businessman. But less obvious that, as a rising class, several within its ranks saw the need for a new urban culture to rival that of the aristocracy.

The middle-class leaders of the industrial towns expressed their collective identity in the public institutions of their town. The voluntary societies, libraries and museums, institutes and clubs which they founded, and the buildings which they commissioned to house them, were emblems of a class identity, expressions of a self-image, in much the same way as the country house estate, with its classical architecture and great paintings, was for the landed aristocracy. This was the face they chose to display to the world. Thus we can understand something of Manchester's elite through their cultural institutions.

To begin with there was the 'Lit. and Phil'.[11] Apart from the Royal Society, the Manchester Literary and Philosophical Society is the oldest enduring English institution devoted to scientific discourse and publication. Founded in 1781 for the study of 'rational pursuits', and excluding discussion of religion or politics, it concentrated on science or 'natural knowledge' as an appropriate subject for a 'Manchester gentleman'. Between 1781 and the opening of Owens College (now Manchester University) in 1851, the 'Lit. and Phil' was the chief Manchester forum for the advancement of knowledge and the exchange of ideas. An impressive sequence of major scientific figures passed through its portals, including Thomas Percival, John Dalton, William Sturgeon and James Prescott Joule. The Society was the haunt of formidable technologists and engineers such as Richard Roberts, James Nasmyth and William Fairbairn. Moreover, merchants and manufacturers from Manchester and the surrounding district were drawn to its sessions and were active in its work. Manufacturing families like the Gregs and the McConnels, merchant and banking dynasties such as the Heywoods and the Philipses, were each represented in its membership. The list of prominent Manchester names is long.

Manchester has contributed much to the advance of science and the 'Lit. and Phil' played its part. The rooting of the Society in the local middle class belies the myth of the ignorant industrialist. The knowledge was intentionally 'useful' and thus characteristic of a class dependent upon the 'practical arts'. But does this perhaps confirm Dickens' charge of 'Gradgrindery' – 'Facts, facts, facts'? Manchester's cultural life, however, was not confined to the 'Lit. and Phil'. 'Manchester Man' could also be a patron of the arts.

The Royal Manchester Institution founded in 1823 and housed in what is now the Art Gallery building on Mosley Street, suggests the importance of Art to at least a section of the Manchester middle class. This neo-classical edifice was designed by Charles Barry, most famous for his later commission, the rebuilding of the Houses of Parliament. This institution devoted to art was funded by voluntary subscriptions to the tune of £32,000. The Royal Manchester Institution represented the belief that middle-class culture could be artistic as well as rational; that these new men could be patrons of art just as much as the traditional aristocracy. The Institution's rooms housed exhibitions and auctions of artwork and provided a space for lectures and painting classes. It was also a meeting place where busy men, otherwise engaged in the pursuit of profit, could come together in a more civilized atmosphere.

The new art institution built upon an existing art market in the town.[12] Growing prosperity and the increased leisure time that came with riches already found an outlet for some in the purchase of paintings, generally 'old masters'. Perhaps Manchester's most exceptional art collector at the end of the eighteenth century was William Hardman, a prosperous drysalter, whose collection of seventy pictures, said to include works by Titian, Canaletto and Rembrandt, had cost around £40,000. This was displayed in his house on Quay Street to which he had also added a spacious music room for 'gentlemen's concerts'. Hardman was clearly a connoisseur. Major collectors in the early and mid-nineteenth century included the cotton manufacturer, Henry McConnel, the banker John Greaves and the merchant Samuel Mendel.

The Royal Manchester Institution stimulated the local art market, bringing art dealers and working artists to the city. By 1861 Manchester boasted 181 professional painters, the largest number in any provincial town. Of these, forty were women. But women were at a disadvantage. Generally absent from the lucrative portrait market, they were also excluded from the city's art clubs and associations. Although they could exhibit at the Royal Institution, they were denied entry to the Manchester Academy of Fine Arts, established in 1857, for almost thirty years. The nineteenth-century art world was a male preserve. Manchester artists were plentiful, and local patrons bought their work. Moreover, famous artists of the day were commissioned by Manchester men. For example, after admiring William Holman Hunt's paintings at the Royal Academy in London, Thomas Fairbairn, of the famous engineering firm founded by his father, contracted Hunt to paint several pictures for him, including his family and personal portraits. The painter G. F. Watts began his career as a protege of Lord Holland in the 1830s, but later enjoyed the patronage of the Manchester merchant C. H. Rickards. Thus some of Manchester's prominent merchants and industrialists became patrons of the leading artists of their day.

Manchester's place as a cultural centre was confirmed in the great success of the Art Treasures Exhibition of 1857. Leading members of the business community were involved in its preparation, including Thomas Fairbairn. Housed in a specially erected building at Old Trafford, it included paintings from numerous aristocratic collectors as well as the royal family. It attracted nearly 1.5m. visitors and made a profit. The Exhibition was an event of international importance. According to *The Times*, Manchester had been the rival of London for a season.

Queen Victoria at the Art Treasures Exhibition, 1857.

And the *Illustrated London News* described Manchester as the equal of any of the major cultural centres of Europe and America. 'Manchester Man' had arrived.[13]

Lest it be thought that Manchester's cultural life was confined to the fine arts, other cultural institutions founded by the city's supposed philistines may be added. Love and Barton's guide to the 'metropolis of manufactures', published in 1839, lists numerous cultural and scientific societies including the Natural History Society (founded in 1821), Botanical Society (1827), Architectural Society (1837) and Geological Society (1838). Most famous of these learned gatherings was the Manchester Statistical Society. Founded in 1833, it was the first in the country and a pioneer of British social science. The bankers William Langton and Benjamin and James Heywood, the cotton manufacturers Samuel and W. R. Greg of Styal, the lawyer James Herford and the physician James Phillips Kay (later Sir James Kay Shuttleworth) were prominent members. Among the first papers read to the Society were W. R. Greg on criminal statistics, Kay on swimming baths for the people and Langton on the 1831 Census. 'Social' knowledge could thus be added to 'Natural' and 'Artistic' knowledge as an appropriate subject for a Manchester gentleman.

Later on those with historical, antiquarian or literary inclinations might also join the Chetham Society (1843), the Manchester Literary Club (1862), the Lancashire and Cheshire Antiquarian Society (1883) or the Manchester Geographical Society (1884). There was no shortage of learned organisations to patronise. However, intellectual pretensions

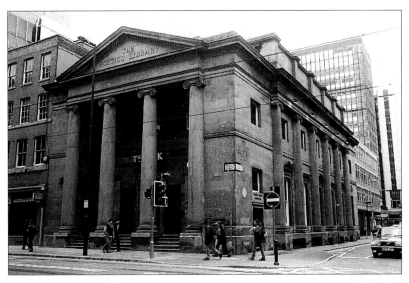

The Portico Library. (*Photograph: Ian Beesley*)

could most readily be satisfied by membership of the Portico or the Athenaeum. The buildings in which both were housed survive today. From the early years of the century the Portico on Mosley Street had provided an elegant and exclusive retreat from the bustle of the town outside. Opened in 1806 as a subscription library and newsroom, it operated as a private club. The Portico was open only to subscribers and was patronised by the town's leading commercial and professional men.

Founded a generation later, the Athenaeum Club on Princess Street, has been described as 'The institution which perhaps most clearly revealed the concern of Manchester's middle class with the cultural image of the city'.[14] Designed by Charles Barry on a site behind the Institution (now the Art Gallery Annexe) it was funded by a public subscription of £10,000 and completed in 1839. With an eye to the education of the town's future leaders, the intention was to provide, what might reasonably be called, 'rational recreations' for the sons of the middle classes. The Club boasted a membership of 2,000 and extensive reading rooms, lecture halls and a library. Its debating and musical societies were popular, but social facilities, such as the restaurant and billiard room, were strong rival attractions. Although its finances were never entirely secure, the Athenaeum was host to literary soirees addressed by the likes of Charles Dickens, Douglas Jerrold and Benjamin Disraeli.

The first industrial city arose from the profits of manufacture and trade. However, its leaders were not a class of money-grubbing philistines but an urban 'aristocracy' with pretensions to grandeur which reached beyond economics and politics to artistic and intellectual pursuits, and which so often found expression in the magnificence of their public buildings. But it would be unwise to transform them into a heroic caste. Their motivation was self-interest, exalted to the status of a creed. The city over which they presided long lacked the most basic amenities of civilised life for the majority of its inhabitants. Their great pride in the town was for its wealth rather than its health. Moreover, an account which only makes reference to the politics of Manchester's rulers gives less than half the picture. Industrial Manchester could be a turbulent place. For much of the early-nineteenth century it was more or less permanently garrisoned with troops. It was a difficult town to control. The manufacturing and commercial middle class was not the only social order created by the industrial revolution. The newly emerging working class did not so readily adjust to the new economic system. The politics of the industrial worker was often the politics of protest.

References

1. The work of V. A. C. Gatrell is central to our understanding of the structure of political and social leadership in Manchester between the 1780s and the 1830s. See especially, Gatrell, 'Incorporation and the pursuit of Liberal hegemony in Manchester 1790–1839' in D. Fraser (ed.), *Municipal Reform and the Industrial City*, Leicester University Press, 1982. See also the references in A. J. Kidd, 'The middle class in nineteenth-century Manchester' in A. J. Kidd and K. W. Roberts (eds), *City, Class and Culture: Studies of Cultural Production and Social Policy in Victorian Manchester*, Manchester University Press, 1985.

2. See M. Turner, *Reform and Respectability: The Making of a Middle-Class Liberalism in Early Nineteenth-century Manchester*, Manchester, 1995.

3. For the struggle for the Charter see A. Redford and I. Russell, *The History of Local Government in Manchester*; Vol. 1, Longmans, London, 1939, pp. 321–56; S. Simon, *A Century of City Government: Manchester 1838–1938*, George Allen & Unwin, London, 1938, pp. 70–116.

4. Cobden speaking at a public meeting in February 1838, quoted in D. Fraser, *Urban Politics in Victorian England*, Leicester University Press, 1976, p. 119. This important book compares Manchester with other provincial centres.

5. See, for example, D. Nicholls, 'The Manchester Peace Conference of 1853', *Manchester Region History Review*, V:i (1991), pp. 11–21.

6. A. J. P. Taylor, 'The World's Great Cities: I, Manchester', *Encounter*, 8 (1957), p. 9. The observation was not original to Taylor; see W. Haslam Mills, *Sir Charles Macara: A Study of Modern Lancashire*, Manchester, 1917, pp. 28–9.

7. A. Prentice, *The History of the Anti-Corn Law League, Vols I & II* (1853), Frank Cass, London, 1968.

8. W. H. Mills (ed.), *The Manchester Reform Club*, privately printed for the Club, Manchester, 1922, p. 33.

9. C. Dickens, *Hard Times* (1854), Penguin edn, Harmondsworth, 1985, p. 58.

10. J. S. Gregson, *Gimcrackiana: or Fugitive Pieces on Manchester Men and Manners*, privately printed, Manchester, 1833, pp. 156–60.

11. For the 'Lit. and Phil' see A. Thackray, 'Natural knowledge in a cultural context: the Manchester model', *American Historical Review*, LXIX (1974), pp. 672–709.

12. See J. Seed '"Commerce and the liberal arts": the political economy of art in Manchester, 1775–1860' in J. Wolff and J. Seed (eds), *The Culture of Capital: Art, Power and the Nineteenth-century Middle Classes*, Manchester University Press, 1988.

13. *The Times*, 30 Oct. 1857; *Illustrated London News*, 9 Oct. 1857, p. 432.

14. M. E. Rose, 'Culture, Philanthropy and the Manchester Middle Class', in Kidd and Roberts, *City, Class and Culture*, p. 111.

CHAPTER 5

The Politics of Protest:
From Food Riots to Chartism

The mechanisation of cotton production and the emergence of industrial society dramatically affected the economic interests and political actions of wage-earners in the new industries and the surviving handicraft workers such as the weavers. As first spinning then weaving became mechanised, trade associations were formed. More traditional forms of economic protest such as the food riot, whilst still a force in the eighteenth century, had virtually dried up as an aspect of urban protest by the early 1800s. Popular politics which could carry a distinct 'church and king' flavour in the 1790s became radicalised during the Napoleonic War. The radical reformers of the post-1815 era pursued the politics of protest through to the climax and disillusionment of the 1832 Reform Act. Ultimately the movement fed into the national programme of Chartism and its doomed campaign for universal suffrage in the 1830s and 1840s. Manchester played an important and often central role in all this. What happened in the cotton district of Lancashire and Cheshire during the early industrial era was often of national significance, and events such as the Peterloo Massacre of 1819 not only caught the headlines of the moment but captured the imagination of succeeding generations.

Food Riots to Trade Unionism

On Thursday 30 July 1795, during a time of national food shortages and high bread prices, a crowd of women and boys gathered in Market Place, Manchester. They quarrelled with stall-holders and, ignoring attempts to quieten them, smashed the windows of flour dealers' warehouses and homes. The rioting crowd had to be dispersed by a charge of cavalry soldiers with drawn swords. Several people were injured. Despite this end to the day's proceedings, the next morning groups of women once more gathered, this time at the New Cross Market near Ancoats. They seized a cart carrying meal, opened the sacks and after distributing some of the contents between them, scattered the rest. More windows were broken before the military were once more called out.

The 1790s were marked by food riots in several North West towns, and Manchester was repeatedly the scene of such unrest. The last food riots in the town occurred in 1812. Such popular disturbances had been a traditional means of protest or even of bargaining between people and magistrates at a time when JPs were supposed to set 'fair' prices by law.

But the Manchester riot of 30 July 1795 was violently suppressed and achieved no sense of agreement over a just price for bread. The food riot only worked where pressure could be brought to bear on all those involved in the pricing of food, including the producers. In industrial urban society this was to prove impossible. As early as the 1790s oatmeal and wheat for Manchester bread came from as far afield as Wales and the South East. With such lengthy supply lines neither crowds nor magistrates could pressurise the producers. In industrial society living standards had to be protected by other means; not by influencing prices but by pressing for higher wages. Thus from the early days of industrialism the workers formed trade unions.

The early textile unions operated at a time of official opposition and employer antagonism. Laws against workers' combinations (trade unions) were frequently strengthened and the infamous Combination Acts of 1799 and 1800 were specifically directed against Lancashire's textile unions. Even after the repeal of these laws in 1824, trade unions carried on their activities in the climate of hostility and suspicion which was to see the Tolpuddle labourers transported in 1834. Workers who organised to protect wages and conditions in the early industrial era often did so at considerable risk to their persons as well as their livelihood. Leaders faced arrest and imprisonment, and the military might be used to suppress strike action. In the face of such co-ordinated hostility it is no surprise that there was little continuity in trade unionism before the mid-nineteenth century. Nonetheless it should not be assumed that that there were no attempts to organise nor that the blanket of oppression suffocated all protest.

The most successful Manchester trade unionists of this era were the mule-spinners. A creation of the industrial revolution, they peopled the spinning factories which began to multiply in Manchester during the 1790s. The manually controlled mule was operated by adult males only. The work of the mule spinner was physically taxing and required constant close attention to the drawn-out threads in the oppressively humid atmosphere of the mill floor. Moreover, the spinner had direct authority over his subordinate workers, the women and children who performed such tasks as the repairing of broken threads and the cleaning of machinery. The mule-spinners soon became regarded as the 'aristocratic' elite of the cotton labour force.

Manchester and Stockport led the way when the first spinners' unions were formed as early as 1792. These unions soon proved militant and effective. In 1795 the Manchester spinners held two successful strikes in support of pay claims, the second sustained for a month. Further strike action in Manchester around the turn of the century aroused the ire of the employers. The Combination Acts strengthened their arm, and several spinners' leaders were arrested and imprisoned. Despite its illegal status the Manchester spinners' union remained effective. So much so that in 1803 a meeting of the Manchester masters at the Bridgewater Arms agreed to raise a 'fighting fund' of £20,000 against the operatives 'dangerous and wicked combination to compel the master spinners to raise their wages'.[1] The purpose was to finance prosecutions of trade unionists and indemnify individual employers who suffered from industrial action. The masters vowed not to employ union members. Despite such tactics the men were successful in securing higher rates of pay for the town's spinning operatives than anywhere else in the cotton district.

Such collective action was the platform for the first county-wide federation of Lancashire's spinning unions in 1810. The level of organisation was remarkable. During the economic boom of 1810 an ingenious 'rolling-strike' took place, whereby the strikers in a single area at a time were supported by the resources of the entire county. The objective was to bring 'country' spinners rates up to those paid in Manchester. The Manchester union itself raised £600 a week for the strike. The whole county became involved in four months of industrial action during which the Lancashire federation, directed by a 'general congress' in Manchester, distributed £17,000 in strike pay. This ambitious action ultimately failed. The employers operated a countywide lock-out and after four months union funds were used up. With the end of the boom in trade the operatives were forced to return at the old rates. The Lancashire federation collapsed. Defeat forced the spinners onto the defensive. Strikes in Manchester during 1811 were against actual wage reductions. More than a decade of success for the Manchester spinners' union had come to a close, and the events of 1810 were a portent for the future.

The depression which followed the end of the Napoleonic War in 1815 further eroded wages. The Manchester spinners were forced to accept reductions of up to one third during 1816. They resorted to massive industrial action once more in June 1818 in an attempt to restore wage levels, bringing out almost 20,000 other operatives whose livelihood depended on the cotton industry. When the masters, who had enforced a lock-out, opened the mills again on 24 August, what had been a peaceful dispute turned violent as frustrated strikers vented their anger both on returning workers and on the 'knobsticks' ('black-legs') brought in by some masters. The military fired on protesting spinners, killing one and wounding several. Under government pressure the local authorities used the charge of riot to justify the arrest of

Emblem of the Associated Cotton Spinners of Manchester, c. 1829.

pickets. Union leaders were imprisoned and known activists 'blacklisted'. Three local leaders were sentenced to two years at Lancaster Assizes. Others were pressured to sign a written declaration against combinations. Eleven years later, Daniel Brough, 'the captain of the pickets', was still victimised, eking a living as a rag and bone man.[2] Striking operatives were once again driven back when union funds were exhausted. These were the years of repression in which trade unionists suffered alike with radicals and reformers. Home Office spies sent alarmist reports back to London, and troop movements in Lancashire intimidated workers. Union action was extremely difficult, even hazardous. But the spinners' union was not yet broken.

The repeal of the Combination Laws in 1824 was greeted with such an outburst of militancy that a parliamentary enquiry in 1825 led to legislation which hedged-round the new freedoms with restrictions so as to render much trade union activity illegal once more. For the Manchester spinners the 1820s was a decade of shop-floor consolidation. By 1828 the Manchester mills were all but a closed-shop and this despite a growing disparity between the wage-rates of the fine and coarse spinners. The election of John Doherty as secretary of the Manchester Spinners' Union in 1828 marked the renewal of militancy. But a

Manchester Masters' Association was also formed, resolved to reduce fine spinners' wages. Despite the threat of wage cuts if they supported the fine spinners, the coarse spinners joined their fellow workers in a bitter strike which lasted nearly six months. But the employers never lost the initiative and used the dispute to push the spinners' union to breaking-point. Again as strike funds ran low, the strike crumbled, and the spinners returned to work at the new rates.

The defeat of 1829 led to a revival of union federalism. Links were forged with other areas, and under John Doherty's leadership a Grand General Union of Cotton Operatives of the United Kingdom was formed. Doherty's ambitions for a more general unionism was also the stimulus for his work to create the National Association for the Protection of Labour (NAPL), formed in 1830 as a general union of all trades. Such attempts at federal and general unions were over-ambitious. The Grand General Union's call for a general strike in 1830 in support of the Ashton spinners was unsuccessful and the Union collapsed. Doherty's NAPL was also finished by 1832. The membership of the Manchester Spinners' Union was severely hit by these defeats. Formerly the largest in the country, it had lost half of its 2,000 members by 1835. It is not hard to see why. Repeated strike defeats followed by wage cuts were compounded by unemployment. Despite the slow development of a self-acting mule, other technological developments were undermining the hand-mule spinners. Longer, more productive, mules reduced the number of operatives required per mill. Unemployment amongst the spinners was hardly comparable to the redundancy of the handloom weavers, but this set the seal on the employers' victory. The spinners were subdued for a generation and took little part in the Chartist agitation of the 1830s and 1840s.

Compared to the spinners, the obstacles to trade-union organisation amongst the cotton handloom weavers must have seemed insurmountable. They lacked a specific skill with which to bargain. Weaving was a grossly overstocked trade flooded by newcomers during the Napoleonic War. Manchester and the other cotton towns in the region became a magnet for thousands of displaced and impoverished migrants from England and Ireland keen to become settled in a manufacturing town. In these circumstances it is remarkable that weavers were able to organise petitions and strikes across Lancashire between 1799 and 1818. The essential difference between their unionism and that of the spinners was its defensive character. Whilst the spinners used 'boom' years to press for wage increases the weavers mostly protested against declining living standards. The rapid spread of the power looms from the 1820s onwards marked the final phase of the handloom weavers' long decline to eventual extinction.

By 1808 a decade of petitioning and the existence of at least informal committees in towns like Manchester had given the weavers enough

Joseph Hanson, the
Weavers' Friend.

experience of organisation to attempt a strike, sparked off by news of
the defeat of a minimum wage bill in Parliament. The turn-out was
supported by mass meetings, the scale of which the authorities would
not accept. A meeting of 5,000 at St George's Field, Manchester, on
25 May 1808 was refused leave to allow delegates to meet with magistrates to discuss the starting of negotiations with employers. The cavalry
was summoned and, near nightfall, the Riot Act was read. But the
weavers held their ground, encouraged by the appearance at the scene
of their most prominent supporter, the radical manufacturer, Joseph
Hanson. Hanson had departed before several cavalry charges dispersed
the crowd, during which one man was killed. The other casualty of the
day was Hanson, whose radicalism had earned him many enemies in
Manchester. Popularly known as 'the weavers' friend', Hanson was
found guilty at the next Lancaster Assizes of having encouraged riot,
fined £100 and imprisoned for six months. After his trial nearly 40,000

donated a penny each to present him with a gold cup. Despite the
violence which opened the dispute the weavers' strike was remarkably
solid and after only one week the masters met and offered a 20% pay
increase. But this was the high point of the weavers' success.

Ten years later a Lancashire-wide strike in 1818 was the weavers'
last attempt to take industrial action, before the threat of the power
loom intervened. It achieved only a temporary respite. As mechanised
weaving was introduced in the 1820s the weavers' frustration resulted
in machine-breaking. The summer of 1826 was a period of intense
violence. Such Luddism, although widespread, was largely confined to
the outlying towns of the cotton district. The only incident of note in
Manchester occurred on the evening of 27 April 1826 when a crowd
broke the windows of several mills containing power looms and attempted to set fire to Beaver's Mill in Jersey Street, Ancoats. This was
among the last gasps of the expiring weavers movement in Manchester.
An occupational survey in the 1830s of 170,000 inhabitants of Manchester and Salford discovered only 3,192 hand weavers of all fabrics.[3]
In Manchester this decaying craft was concentrated to the north and
east of the city, especially in New Cross and Miles Platting. By now
handloom weaving had become a highly marginalised occupation, the
resort of the most desperate or impoverished.

Outside textiles, industrial action was even more fragmentary and
ill-coordinated. This was especially so in the metal trades where union
organisation remained craft based and localised. For example, the Manchester Society of Tinplate Workers (founded in 1802) and the United
Journeymen Brassfounders and Finishers Society of Manchester (1825)
retained an independent identity within their national unions well into
the second half of the nineteenth century. Newer craft unions, such as
the boilermakers society, later the major craft union of the iron ship-
yards and founded in Manchester in 1834, were equally sectional.

There was limited industrial action outside the manufacturing sector.
A strike of Manchester lamp-lighters in 1830 was 'snuffed out' by the
employment of a new set of men. There was some unionisation in the
warehouse sector, especially amongst calenderers, who pressed and gave
the final finish to the cloth, and amongst the packers, who operated
the hydraulic presses. The Hydraulic Packers Society took strike action
in 1834 and 1835. Other warehouse workers were a mixture of labourers,
clerks and salesmen.

The mid-1830s were a period of industrial unrest in Manchester.
The shoemakers and tailors each took strike action to no avail. The
most militant activities at this time were to be found in the building
trade. There was a building boom in the mid-1830s. Masons, painters,
plumbers, glaziers, plasterers and slaters were involved in overlapping
disputes. They experienced varying rates of success, but the Manchester
brickmakers provide an illustration of the lengths to which some artisans

would go to defend craft traditions. Manchester was a major centre of brickmaking. There was a long local history of opposition to innovation. In 1843 resistance to the introduction of larger brick-moulds involved a strike and an assault on Pauling's brickyard by 300 men. The yard was defended by an armed guard. Despite this the manager's house was ransacked and the works pillaged. Two kilns and 100,000 bricks were destroyed by fire. Further disputes followed, and more outbreaks of violence occurred in the 1860s.

Political Radicalism

The imbalance of social forces in a very unequal society, and the limited success of trade unionism, impelled many to seek changes in the political constitution. They came to believe that economic improvement would only come through political reform. Popular radical societies and associations formed from the 1790s onwards most commonly comprised a membership of handloom weavers, artisans and small traders with a leavening of labourers and factory workers. Although the evidence for actual revolutionary intent is sparse, the climate of opinion created by the French Revolution made the aristocratic-dominated governments of the era paranoid about all forms of popular political protest. This is a national story, but one in which the Manchester region played a prominent role.

Thomas Paine's *Rights of Man* was the national focus for radical agitation in the 1790s. Sales of the cheap sixpenny edition were phenomenal, reaching a total of 200,000 by 1793 and this in a population of only ten million. It is no surprise that Paine was driven into exile by the authorities and his book banned as seditious libel. It was Paine's vision of a democratic society with complete manhood suffrage, equality before the law and freedom of speech which caught the popular imagination.

Paine was avidly read and discussed in Manchester's radical circles. Popular societies were formed with democratic programmes. The Patriotic Society and the Reformation Society were both founded in 1792, with workingmen as members. Manchester was already a centre of middle-class radicalism, and members of the two popular societies frequented joint meetings with the middle-class radicals of the Constitutional Society. The Patriotic Society held its own gatherings in premises owned by Thomas Walker. However, the atmosphere in Manchester at this time was hostile to reformers of any social class. In 1792, 186 Manchester publicans met at the Bull's Head to sign a declaration refusing the use of their rooms to radical societies. Manchester taverns commonly displayed the slogan 'No Jacobins Admitted Here'. The 'church and king' sentiments of the mob were used by those opposed to reform in the Manchester riots of December 1792 (see Chapter 4). Moreover, the course of the French Revolution (the execution of the king, the Terror and the outbreak of war), added to the persecution of 'respectable' reformers like Walker, encouraged a middle-class withdrawal from radical politics in the mid-1790s.

The reforming spirit among Manchester's artisan radicals was kept alive by the political line of the *Manchester Gazette* (anti-war and anti-taxes) founded by William Cowdroy in 1795 and the Manchester Corresponding Society formed solely by workingmen in 1796. But as the war continued reform societies were made illegal and reform politics became more extreme. Many were forced underground into secret republican organisations such as the Society of United Englishmen which boasted several hundred members in Manchester before being proscribed in 1798.

Despite wartime repression of political dissent, the era of 'church and king' populism was coming to an end, killed off by a combination of industrial unrest (especially of the weavers), food shortages during wartime and political alienation. If slogans scrawled on walls are any guide, the privations of the war had seen a dramatic turn in popular sentiments. 'Church and king' slogans had been replaced by radical rhetoric. In 1800 the Manchester magistrate Thomas Butterworth noted how 'The public eye is daily saluted with sedition in chalk characters on our walls. And whether the subject regards Bread or Peace – "NO KING" introduces it'.[4]

Manchester had become a centre of radical protest. In 1810 a public address sent from the town in support of the Radical MP Sir Francis Burdett carried nearly 18,000 signatures. Moreover, the cause of reform was accompanied by an increase in public disorder which peaked in the Luddite year of 1812. Manchester was not a centre of Luddism but was considered sufficiently difficult to govern to justify the permanent quartering of troops there. Political and economic unrest were by now common bedfellows. That the days when 'church and king' mobs could be turned out by the dispensing of free ale were long gone was symbolically demonstrated by the Exchange Hall Riot of 8 April 1812. A meeting called to congratulate the Prince Regent on the retention of the Tory ministry was cancelled at the last moment due to fears that it might become a protest meeting against a government which held out no prospect of reform. But it was too late. Thousands gathered in the building and the event turned into a riot. An eyewitness who rushed to the scene on the news that the Exchange was on fire 'found the windows of the newsroom broken and much of the furniture … destroyed or damaged, and soldiers engaged in driving the crowds from the neighbourhood of the Exchange'.[5] An intended affirmation of loyalty had turned into a day of violent protest. The symbolism was not lost on Manchester's business community. The new Exchange building, opened in 1809, was the centrepiece of Manchester's business and cotton's commercial palace. The Exchange Riot alarmed the Manchester gentleman and made him fear for his family and his property. In its aftermath some felt obliged to seek armed escorts in the streets, as there were reports of popular hostility to the finely dressed. The presence of soldiers in the town was a consolation and, in fear of Luddism, detachments were ordered to protect some mills. There existed an atmosphere of class hostility, exacerbated by the food riots which followed a few days later. These lacked any political element and followed a similar pattern to those of the 1790s. The magistrates, however, linked the food riots with Luddism and political protests like the Exchange Riot. Repression was harsh and convicted rioters were hanged. Vengeance fell on the hungry at a time when all protest was regarded as insurrection.

The advent of peace in 1815 after 23 years of almost continuous conflict was marked not by a return to 'church and king' deference but by what has been called 'the heroic age of popular Radicalism'.[6] The end of the war brought even greater economic hardship. The depressed post-war economy could offer little immediate relief for the thousands of demobilised soldiers and sailors who returned home to unemployment. Radicals on all sides linked the reform of government with the demand for economic justice. During the four years which culminated in the Peterloo Massacre of 1819, a nationwide campaign for universal suffrage and annual elections gripped the public imagination and alarmed the government of the day into a policy of severe legal repression. The industrial districts were at the centre of political protest. This was the age of the provinces. The pace of political change was being set by the regions rather than by the capital. The new social forces conjured up by industrialism generated a regional radicalism possessed of an independent and working-class character. The mass reform campaign of the post-war years was strongest in the North West, and Manchester was its chief platform.

Radical consciousness was raised during 1816 and 1817 by the work of the Hampden Clubs. Inspired by Major Cartwright, these radical societies were formed throughout the provinces. By March 1817 there were about forty in the Manchester region with a claimed membership of 8,000. The authorities in London feared revolution, and in February 1817 the Habeas Corpus Act was suspended and Acts passed to prevent public meetings and extend the law against sedition. In Manchester the local authorities reflected government anxiety. More special constables were enrolled and other preventive measures taken. Such concern seemed justified as the organisational base provided by the local Hampden Clubs allowed the planning of a march on London in a mass petition of the Prince Regent. On 10 March 1817, 12,000 gathered on St Peter's Field, Manchester, to support the march of the 'Blanketeers' as the petitioners were called, each man carrying a blanket, rug or coat to sleep in *en route*. Most of the marchers were handloom weavers and the connection between economic hardship and political reform is reflected in the petitioners' claim that the burden of heavy taxes and high prices would have been less 'If the House of Commons had emanated from and been wholly and annually appointed by the People at large'. The Manchester magistrates acted swiftly and effectively. The crowd was cleared by troops, and soldiers accompanied magistrates in pursuit of 300 marchers who had already embarked on their journey. Most were stopped at Stockport, although a few got further afield.

Whether or not the government was correct to see revolution in the 'Blanketeer' protest, there is evidence to suggest that London 'revolutionaries' had made contact with Manchester militants through the Hampden network. It is certain that some radicals were planning a national revolt which would consist of simultaneous uprisings in the towns of the Midlands and the North followed by a march on London. It had been hoped the 'Blanketeers' might stir up something of the sort. Samuel Bamford, the Middleton radical, had boycotted the march for this reason. Anger or frustration at the dismal failure of the 'Blanketeers' may have determined a quick response from some of the more militant radicals. Certainly the authorities believed they had uncovered the plot for the Manchester uprising when they raided a secret meeting held at Ardwick Bridge on 28 March 1817. The so-called 'Ardwick Plot' was to make 'a Moscow of Manchester', i.e. set it in flames as a signal for the local revolt. Bamford and seven other leaders were arrested and charged with high treason. But insufficient evidence could be amassed and only four of the charged were imprisoned. Was there a conspiracy? Bamford, who was released, gives an account of what some had proposed, proposals from which he carefully distanced himself. Samuel Priestly, a Manchester dyer, had carried the news of the uprising to Bamford, informing him that the sight of Manchester ablaze would be the signal for the country people to come in.

> The whole force would be divided into parties, one of which was to engage the attention of the military and draw them from their barracks; another was to take possession of the barracks and secure the arms and magazine; another was to plunder and then set fire to the houses of individuals who were marked out; and a fourth was to storm the New Bailey and liberate the prisoners, particularly the Blanketeers confined there.[7]

That such a rising was planned seems indisputable. That the support the conspirators were likely to receive was small is equally probable. Most northern radicals doubted the value of violence and correctly assessed that the odds against success were too great. Moreover, the planning of insurrection played into government hands, allowing the reform campaign to be discredited. The discovery of the Ardwick Plot had called a temporary halt to the radical campaign which, however, was to be reignited in the most dramatic fashion by the momentous events of 1819.

The Hampden Clubs did not survive 1817, but the radical campaign was kept alive through similarly organised Union Societies. The first was founded at Stockport with the ambitious title of the Stockport Union for the Promotion of Human Happiness. By August 1819 most towns surrounding Manchester had at least one Union Society and these were instrumental in sending contingents to Peterloo. Parallel women's societies were formed, and many Union Societies founded radical Sunday schools to attract scholars away from the existing loyalist schools. Supporting the Union Societies was the radical press. Perhaps the best conducted working-class radical newspaper of the period was the *Manchester Observer*. Started in 1818, it publicised the radical campaign in the months leading up to Peterloo. At the height of its fame in the aftermath of the Massacre, the *Manchester Observer* claimed a weekly sale of 4,000, the highest circulation of any provincial newspaper. The political clubs and the radical press were not, however, the chief vehicles of the reform campaign. The radical politics of the Peterloo era were the politics of the mass meeting.

The Peterloo Massacre

The reform meeting held at St Peter's Field, Manchester, on 16 August 1819, which ended so tragically, was the culmination of a campaign of mass meetings in the Manchester region, held in the hope that a show of popular support would bring pressure to bear for reform. Oldham, Stockport, Ashton and Rochdale as well as Manchester were the venues. On 8 January, 8,000 had assembled on St Peter's Field to hear the reformers' national leader, Henry Hunt, urge them to approve a Declaration to be sent to the Prince Regent affirming 'That the only source of all legitimate power is in the People' and 'That all Governments, not immediately derived from and strictly accountable to the People, are usurpations and ought to be resisted and destroyed'. Such assertions were derived from the view that 'all men are born free, equal and independent of each other'.[8] Thus the philosophy of the 'Rights of Man' had descended intact from the era of the French and American Revolutions and, for radicals at least, had now entered the mind as 'common sense' demands for justice. In constitutional terms this meant annual elections and universal suffrage.

Henry Hunt and other leaders were addressing mass meetings across the country during 1819. He was invited back to Manchester for the meeting on 16 August which was intended to be the greatest display

of radical strength in the provinces. Hunt's intentions were purely
peaceful. When he heard that preparations for the Manchester meeting
had involved 'secret' military drilling on the moors with pikes and even
firearms, he demanded that the Lancashire radicals 'cease playing at
soldiers' and issued instructions that they must come to the meeting
'armed with no other weapon but that of a self-approving conscience'.[9]
The magistrates were alarmed by the reports of drilling, but even more
so by the sheer size of the demonstration. On the morning of the
meeting, bands of men, women and children arrived from surrounding
towns, marching behind specially made banners and flags. The absence
of pikes and firearms was evidence that Hunt's exhortations had not
gone unheeded. Estimates of the size of the crowd vary widely from
30,000 to 150,000. In fact it was impossible for eye-witnesses to count
those present with any degree of accuracy. The highest and lowest
figures represent the arithmetic of propaganda rather than reliable
assessments of numbers, but even the lower estimate would suggest a
gathering of unprecedented proportions.

The assembling thousands had been closely watched as they marched
into town. The Manchester magistrates registered their concern by
calling the military to stand by. In the early morning Lieutenant-
Colonel Guy L'Estrange, officer in command of the Manchester district,
had summoned a force of 1,500 consisting of the 15th Hussars and
troops of the volunteer Manchester and Cheshire Yeoman Cavalry. The
Manchester Yeomanry, comprised of local manufacturers, merchants,
shopkeepers and publicans, was led by the Tory cotton master Hugh
Hornby Birley. They formed-up in the streets near St Peter's Field.

The magistrates decided to have Hunt and the other speakers arrested
and the meeting dispersed as a danger to the town. Almost as soon as
Hunt had reached the hustings and before he could address the crowd,
Manchester's Deputy Constable Joseph Nadin attempted to effect the
arrest. Nadin, however, reported that his special constables were unable
to secure Hunt without military support. Thus the fateful events un-
folded. The first troops to respond to the request for support were not
regular soldiers but the Manchester Yeomanry positioned just off Portland Street. They made their way via Cooper Street to the scene of
the meeting knocking over a mother and infant *en route* and killing the
child. The magistrates decided not to wait for the Hussars but to send
in the Yeomanry to accompany Nadin as he executed the arrests. They
advanced into the crowd sabres drawn, to cut a path to the hustings.
The arrests were made, but the Yeomanry then began to panic as they
found themselves separated from each other. They struck out with their
swords. But it was not blind panic since the evidence suggests they
took the reformers' flags and banners as targets. At first those posted
at the hustings were dashed at, then, more dangerously, those amongst
the people, the Yeomanry sometimes cutting indiscriminately to the

INHABITANTS

OF

Manchester

And Neighbourhood.

FELLOW COUNTRYMEN:

Our enemies are exulting at the victory they profess to have obtained over us, in consequence of the postponement, *for a week*, of the PUBLIC MEETING intended to have been held on Monday last.

The Editor of the London Courier, (although he admits that we are only *checked* not *subdued*) appears to be as much rejoiced as he, and his *coadjutors*, had for a time escaped unhurt from the effects of an Earthquake or some other great National Calamity; his *blood-thirsty imitators* of the local press of Manchester, cannot disguise the fears of their employers, although I am informed that they attempt to do it, by resorting to the most vulgar and impotent abuse. To reply to any of their malignant and contemptible efforts, would only tend to drag them forth, for a moment, from their natural insignificance and obscurity; therefore you will bestow on their petty exertions the most perfect indifference; for as they are beneath your anger, so you will not even suffer them to attract your notice.

You will meet on Monday next my friends, and by your *steady, firm, and temperate* deportment, you will convince all your enemies, you feel that you have an *important* and an *imperious public duty* to perform, and that you will not suffer any private consideration on earth, to deter you from exerting every nerve, to carry your praiseworthy and patriotic intentions into effect.

The eyes of all England, nay, of all Europe, are fixed upon you: and every friend of real Reform and of rational Liberty, is tremblingly alive to the result of your Meeting on Monday next.

OUR ENEMIES will seek every opportunity by the means of their sanguinary agents to excite a RIOT, that they may have a pretence for SPILLING OUR BLOOD, reckless of the awful and certain retaliation that would ultimately fall on their heads.

EVERY FRIEND OF REAL AND EFFECTUAL REFORM is offering up to Heaven a devout prayer, that you may follow the example of your brethren of the Metropolis; and by your *steady, patient, persevering*, and *peaceable* conduct on that day, frustrate their HELLISH AND BLOODY PURPOSE.

Come, then, my friends, to the Meeting on Monday, *armed* with NO OTHER WEAPON but that of a self-approving conscience; determined not to suffer yourselves to be irritated or excited, by any means whatsoever, to commit any breach of the Public Peace.

Our opponents have not attempted to show that our reasoning is fallacious, or that our conclusions are incorrect, by any other argument but the *threat of Violence*, and to put us down by the force of the *Sword*, *Bayonet*, and the *Cannon*. They assert that your leaders do nothing but mislead and deceive you, although they well know, that the eternal principles of *truth* and *justice* are too deeply engraven on your hearts; and that you are at length become (fortunately for them) too well acquainted with your own rights, ever again to suffer any man, or any faction, to mislead you.

We hereby invite the Boroughreeve, or any of the Nine wise Magistrates, who signed the Proclamation declaring the meeting to have been held on Monday last, *Illegal*, and threatening at the *same time* all those who abstained from going to the said Meeting; we invite them to come amongst us on Monday next. If we are wrong it is their duty as Men, as Magistrates, and as Christians, to endeavour to set us right by argument, by reason, and by the mild and irresistible precepts of persuasive truth; we promise them an attentive hearing, and to abide by the result of conviction alone. But once for all we repeat, that we despise their THREATS, and abhor and detest those, who would direct or controul the mind of man by VIOLENCE or FORCE.

I am, my Fellow Countrymen,

Your sincere and faithful Friend,

Henry Hunt.

Smedley Cottage, Wednesday, August 11, 1819.

Hunt's Address, which exhorted those who attended the St Peter's Field Meeting on 16 August 1819 to come 'armed with no other weapon but that of a self-approving conscience'.

left and the right among the demonstrators. By this time the 15th Hussars had arrived. Colonel L'Estrange immediately ordered them to disperse the meeting. The field was cleared in a mere ten minutes. At least eleven people died and over six hundred were injured as a result of the day's proceedings.[10] Although the Hussars reportedly used only the flat of their swords it was their rapid clearance of the crowd which caused most of the injuries, many of the wounded being trampled on or crushed in the panic of the dispersal. Samuel Bamford's description of the aftermath is unforgettable.

In ten minutes from the commencement of the havoc, the field was an open and almost deserted place. The sun looked down through a sultry and motionless air ... The hustings remained, with a few broken and hewed flag-staves erect, and a torn and gashed banner or two dropping; whilst over the whole field were strewed caps, bonnets, hats, shawls and shoes, and other parts of male and female dress; trampled, torn, and bloody. The Yeomanry had dismounted – some were easing their horses' girths, others adjusting their accoutrements; and some were wiping their sabres.[11]

Almost immediately the events on St Peter's Field of 16 August 1819 became the 'Peterloo Massacre'. The 15th Hussars had seen service at Waterloo in 1815, as had some of the victims. As such Peterloo has become a major event in British history and arguably the single most important day in Manchester's history. Historical interpretations vary; to some it was the unfortunate consequence of a lack of foresight on the part of the Manchester magistrates; in one view it was a panic response to some stone-throwing at the Yeomanry; others suspect it may have been planned as a show-down with the radicals, certainly in the case of the magistrates and possibly even involving the Tory government in London.[12] Whatever the correct interpretation, Peterloo proved the prelude to severe government repression.

In the days that followed the atmosphere in Manchester was uneasy to say the least. On the very evening of the 16th a mob attacked a shop in New Cross on the grounds that the proprietor was a special constable at St Peter's Field and had paraded one of the radical flags as a trophy of the battle. The military killed one of the rioters with gunshot as they cleared the crowd. The next day Manchester was in a state of panic. The Exchange was closed, as frightening but unfounded reports spread that up to 50,000 armed men were marching on the town from Middleton and Oldham: 'All seemed in a state of confusion; the streets were patrolled by military, police and special constables: the shops were closed and silent; the warehouses were shut up and pad-locked; the Exchange was deserted; the artillery was ready'.[13]

The invaders never came. The panic tells us more about the alarmist tenor of middle-class opinion than of radical readiness for an uprising. There was sporadic violence in Manchester over the next few days particularly in the New Cross district, a stronghold of Irish handloom weavers. On the 17th a special constable was fatally injured there and on the 20th locals fought a pitched battle with the cavalry. 'Manchester', *The Times* of 23 August declared 'now wears the appearance of a garrison, or of a town conquered in war.'[14] Soldiers were strategically posted at all commanding positions and troops were quartered in temporary barracks in New Cross.

Meanwhile, Hunt and the others arrested were released on bail from

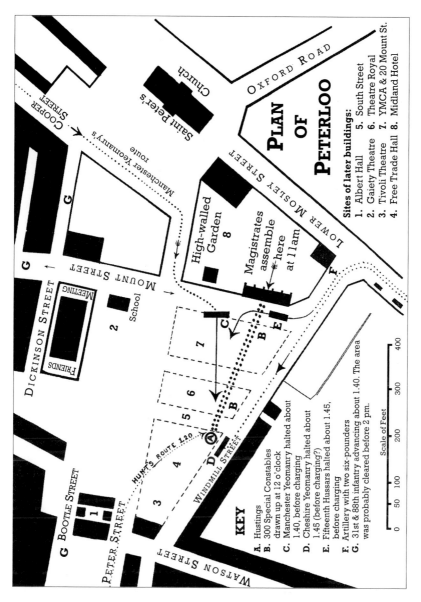

PLAN
OF
PETERLOO

Sites of later buildings:

1. Albert Hall
2. Gaiety Theatre
3. Tivoli Theatre
4. Free Trade Hall

5. South Street
6. Theatre Royal
7. YMCA & 20 Mount St.
8. Midland Hotel

High-walled
Garden
8

Magistrates
assemble
here
at 11am

OXFORD ROAD

Saint Peter's Church

Manchester Yeomanry's route

COOPER STREET

MOUNT STREET

DICKINSON STREET

FRIENDS

MEETING

School

2

7

6

5

4

3

1

LOWER MOSLEY STREET

WINDMILL STREET

HUNT'S ROUTE 1.20

BOOTLE STREET

PETER STREET

WATSON STREET

G
G
G

A
B
C
D
E
F

Scale of Feet

0 50 100 200 300 400

KEY

A. Hustings
B. 300 Special Constables
   drawn up at 12 o'clock
C. Manchester Yeomanry halted about
   1.40, before charging
D. Cheshire Yeomanry halted about
   1.45 (before charging?)
E. Fifteenth Hussars halted about 1.45,
   before charging
F. Artillery with two six-pounders
G. 31st & 88th infantry advancing about 1.40. The area
   was probably cleared before 2 pm.

Lancaster Castle. Tens of thousands lined the route for his triumphal return to Manchester. Despite the urgings of those who advocated an armed uprising, Hunt's popularity ensured that the majority adhered to his peaceful and carefully legal methods. Although tension remained high in the town throughout the winter of 1819–20 the radical campaign was losing its impetus. Economic recovery during 1820 did not lessen the desire for reform but reduced its urgency. Moreover, Peterloo was the high-water mark of Manchester's involvement in the reform

The Peterloo Massacre. (*Courtesy of Manchester Central Library*)

campaign. Even within the cotton district attention shifted elsewhere to the smaller textile communities, like Oldham, Stockport and Blackburn, which had been radicalised by the events of 1819. Popular radicalism in Manchester was not set alight again until the parliamentary reform agitation of 1830–2.

Chartism

The Whig government which came to power in 1830 was pledged to a moderate measure of parliamentary reform. The middle class had most to gain from a limited reform, but working-class radicals hoped for a more ambitious measure. When finally passed by parliament, the 1832 Reform Act greatly disappointed working-class radical hopes. Manchester was enfranchised for the first time, but the £10 householder qualification for the vote brought only a minority of workingmen into the political fold. During the mid-Victorian period up to the Reform Act of 1867, around one quarter of Manchester's electorate was drawn from the better-off working class; a fairly typical proportion for a large town.[15] Whilst this was an advance on the pre-1832 situation it was insufficient to satisfy working-class aspirations. The new popular movements of the 1830s, for factory reform and against the New Poor Law, both looked to parliament for redress, and Chartism itself was predicated on the necessity of universal suffrage, annual elections and the secret ballot, the radical menu of old. The reformed parliament turned a deaf ear to all this. The Great Reform Act of 1832 was regarded as a final settlement of the matter, and it took over thirty years for this view to be undermined and further parliamentary reform contemplated. Manchester was not central to the factory reform agitation of the 1830s and 1840s, and the New Poor Law was introduced relatively smoothly into the town. But as Chartism gained strength in the cotton district, Manchester inevitably became a forum for its activities.

The Chartist movement began when the London Working Men's Association issued a six point Charter in 1837 calling for universal manhood suffrage, secret ballots, annual elections, equally populated constituencies, payment of MPs and the abolition of the minimum property requirement for MPs. Chartism dominated popular politics until the late 1840s. The campaign centred on mass meetings and the petitioning of parliament. Agitation for the Charter in Manchester began with the formation of the Manchester Political Union (MPU) in 1838. The MPU organised the huge Chartist meeting on Kersal Moor on 24 September 1838. This was the greatest of a national series of Chartist demonstrations during that summer. A crowd of at least 50,000 gathered to hear speeches in favour of the Charter and to elect delegates to attend the Chartist National Convention. The sense of historical continuity was clear in the prominent display of banners retrieved from the field of Peterloo. The Kersal Moor meeting also provides evidence of the strength of working-class feeling about the Charter. It is often suggested that Chartism was chiefly the movement of the most economically depressed outworkers and that organised labour remained aloof. Although handloom weavers remained a mainstay of the reform campaign, the attendance at Kersal Moor of formal contingents of unionists from eighteen trades, including textiles, engineering, building and clothing, suggests that Chartism, at least in its early stages (up to 1842), represented the general mood of the working class and not just of the most economically desperate.[16]

Manchester Chartism found formal expression through the Manchester Political Union. In reality this was a loose, decentralised federation. The following branches are recorded as having been founded in 1838: Pollard Street, Pendleton, Salford, Hulme and Chorlton, Whittle Street, Ashley Lane, Bank Top, Deansgate and Brown Street. They mostly acted in their own right and were rooted in their own neighbourhood culture of mutual support and drew on pre-Chartist radicalism. No event stirred memories or instilled support for radical action more than the Peterloo Massacre. It was an icon of popular protest throughout the Chartist era and beyond – from the Chartist Monument erected in commemoration of Henry Hunt to the scores of ballads and poems that perpetuated its memory. The Chartist ranks in Manchester included several Peterloo 'veterans' and added to the radicalism of Manchester Chartism.[17]

The Chartist National Convention sat in London during most of 1839. In July a national petition with over 1.25m. signatures was rejected by the House of Commons. There were plans for a general strike or 'Sacred Month' to force acceptance of the Charter. Tension was already high in the Manchester district. The winter of 1838–9 had been marked by numerous night-time Chartist meetings, which, lit as they were by torchlight, raised fears of incendiarism. It appeared a short step from torchlit processions to factory burning. Even before the National Petition was rejected, Manchester had become a centre of 'physical force' Chartism. Rank and file Chartists in the Manchester region were arming themselves with pikes, and to a lesser extent with firearms.

The calling of a second Kersal Moor meeting for the Whit-weekend in May 1839 thus raised the spectre of a march on London. Such was the alarm of the authorities that General Sir Charles Napier, the officer commanding the Northern Districts, worked out a plan for defending the streets of Manchester against a force of 100,000. Troops brought in from Ireland strengthened the Manchester garrison. But force was combined with a politic reserve. Napier restrained the Manchester magistrates from a repeat of Peterloo and planned to arrest seditious speakers only after the meeting had dispersed. In the event the turn-out was down on the previous September and no violence ensued. 'Physical force' Chartists were being picked-off by the authorities and charged with conspiracy, incitement to riot and the promotion of rebellion. There was a danger of insurrection during 1838–9, but government containment and divisions among the Chartists themselves meant it came to naught. The 'moral force' of petitioning and passive resistance was the alternative to the uncertainties of an uprising.

Chartism was strongest in the spinning towns around Manchester, and the importance of the cotton district to the development of Chartism was clear in the next phase of the movement. The defeat of the National Petition forced the Chartists to look to their tactics. At a conference held in the Griffin Inn, Great Ancoats Street, on 20 July 1840 the decision was taken to establish a permanent organisation, the National Charter Association (NCA). By the end of 1841 Lancashire provided one in six of the NCAs branches. When the National Petition was once more presented in 1842, Manchester contributed nearly 100,000 signatures. James Leach, South Lancashire's delegate to the National Convention of that year, claimed that over 300,000 people had signed the petition in his region. This represented over one quarter of the total population of the area. The North dominated the NCA and Manchester was its metropolis.

Members of the NCA agreed to support the Charter, paid a weekly membership fee of one penny and held a personal membership card.

Officials were elected annually and towns divided into wards with classes of ten each under a class leader. These leaders formed the district or town council of the Association. The elaborate hierarchy of classes, wards and councils was derived from the class system of the Methodists. At this stage Chartist organisation in Manchester was based on four districts: Chorlton-on-Medlock, New Cross, Miles Platting and Strangeways. In addition there were industrial branches of tailors, shoemakers and building trades workers plus a youth section.

Chartism was now a political party, the first devoted solely to the interests of working people. Links with the trade union movement were strong enough to find 64 union delegates at a Chartist meeting at Manchester in March 1842. The second National Convention met in London in April of the same year. Despite its national organisation and widespread support the second national petition was summarily dismissed by the Commons, and the Chartists were left contemplating their own ineffectiveness. Inevitably this led to a resurgence of direct action. Moreover, economic distress was at a peak in the early 1840s. Unemployment and wage reductions were the context of the Plug Plot strikes of August 1842. This was the decisive moment for Chartism.

The Plug Strikes, so called because the strikers immobilised mills by pulling the plugs from the factory boilers, were a spontaneous protest against wage reductions, but they linked up with Chartist demands and incited some to revive the idea of using the general strike weapon to force acceptance of the Charter. The events of August 1842 revealed the futility of such hopes. The strike began in Ashton and soon spread throughout the cotton district. Meetings across the region demanded a return to the old wage rates. Although heavily garrisoned by troops, Manchester was a focus of disorder and unrest. On 9 August a peaceful procession of several thousand weavers and miners marched on Manchester. Met by magistrates and military, they were escorted on a prescribed route round the town. They were refused entry to Irish districts out of fear that they would incite disorder. In the event a party of 500 or so broke away and headed for Little Ireland and the mills of Oxford Road, pursued by dragoons. Meanwhile, others had started a meeting in Granby Row Fields. Manchester's mills began to turn out. Troop presence was heavy but restrained. The memory of Peterloo lingered.

The next day, Wednesday 10 August, at around 6 a.m., a large crowd gathered outside Kennedy's Ancoats mill, which was defended by about 50 police. As the morning wore on the crowd increased to some 10,000. Cavalry were called to disperse them and police made 15 arrests. Once broken up the crowd coalesced into smaller, turbulent groups. Sporadic outbreaks of disorder followed. Mills were closed as workers left their machines to join the demonstrators. Shops were looted, buildings attacked and a police station practically destroyed. By the end of the day the town was unsettled and the propertied uneasy. The only mills at work were those guarded by police and soldiers. The disturbances continued the next day. Up to 15,000 gathered in Granby Row Fields. Local Chartists exhorted them to stay out until their demands were met. The magistrates, disturbed at the size of the meeting and the political content of some of the speeches, had the Riot Act read. Immediately a detachment of officers and dragoons, a company of the 60th Rifles and 50 artillerymen with two six-pounder field pieces, appeared on the scene, supported by over 400 special constables sworn in on the previous day. Not surprisingly, at this display of force the crowd rapidly disappeared into surrounding streets. Throughout the day the streets of Manchester remained congested and unsettled as all gatherings were broken up by police and soldiers. In all, 122 arrests were made and 23 cases treated at the Infirmary. After this the disorder died down, but the factories remained closed and some 50,000 workers were idle.

The Plug Strikes, in Manchester and elsewhere, proved short-lived and unsuccessful. Within a month it was all over. The squeeze on working-class living standards continued. Chartist support for the action gave the authorities the opportunity to arrest 1,500 of the national and local Chartist leaders in an attempt to wind up the movement. Many ended up in prison. The events of 1842 had certainly alarmed the government. Manchester had once more resembled a garrison town. Two thousand troops were transported by rail, the first such use of the railway for troop movements, to strengthen the local garrison.

Chartism went into a decline after 1842. It was never again to be such a powerful force, although the third National Petition of 1848 was a final attempt to use the politics of mass protest. Again a period of acute economic distress provided the backdrop to further agitation and unrest. The last major Chartist gathering in the capital was the assembly on Kennington Common prior to the presentation of the Petition to parliament. The planned march on the Commons was curtailed by police action. The authorities similarly suppressed parallel Chartist gatherings up and down the country. In Manchester the military were out in force and 11,000 special constables were mobilised. Cannons were prominently placed in the streets and the cavalry paraded with drawn swords. In the face of such a show of strength, meetings in support of the Petition, like that attended by up to 20,000 at Smithfield Market on 9 April 1848, ended peacefully. The authorities once more exploited Chartist weakness to arrest 15 local leaders. Chartist trials were held in Liverpool in December and most were sent to gaol. To all intents and purposes the Chartist campaigns were at an end.

Why did Chartism decline? An upturn in the trade cycle may be an important explanation, but repeated failure is not a recipe for ripening political allegiance. More fundamentally, the evidence suggests that popular politics was adapting to the industrial system. In the years following Chartism the working-class movement became more reformist in character.[18] The authorities had less reason to fear violence and insurrection. The spectre of revolution disappeared, only to return in the 1880s, but then in London rather than the industrial north. The Manchester region had been the focus of industrial unrest in the early industrial era, but in the later nineteenth century the district was quiet. Its political respectability was symbolised by the restrained response of the Lancashire mill workers during the Cotton Famine of the 1860s. Although unrest and violence would return to the streets of Manchester, the town was to lose its earlier national image as a turbulent and unruly place.

References

1. *Cowdroy's Manchester Gazette*, 15 Oct. 1803, quoted in A. Redford, *Manchester Merchants and Foreign Trade 1794–1858*, Manchester University Press, 1934, pp. 66–7.

2. See A. Fowler and T. Wyke (eds), *The Barefoot Aristocrats: A History of the Amalgamated Association of Operative Cotton Spinners*, George Kelsall, Littleborough, 1987, p. 21.

3. Manchester Statistical Society, *On the Condition of the Working Classes in an Extensive Manufacturing District in 1834, 1835 and 1836*, Manchester, 1838, Table 5.

4. Quoted in A. Booth, 'Popular loyalism and public violence in the northwest of England 1790–1800', *Social History*, 8 (1983), p. 311.

5. A. Prentice, *Historical Sketches and Personal Recollections of Manchester* (1851), Frank Cass, London, 1970, p. 51, citing an eyewitness whom he had interviewed.

6. E. P. Thompson, *The Making of the English Working Class*, Pelican edn, Harmondsworth, 1968, p. 660.

7. S. Bamford, *Antobiography, Vol. II, Passages in the Life of a Radical* (1841), Frank Cass, London, 1967, pp. 37–8.

8. For the Declaration and Remonstrance see *Manchester Observer*, 23 Jan. 1819. The full text is reprinted in D. Read, *Peterloo: The 'Massacre' and its Background*, Manchester University Press, 1958, Appendix A, pp. 210–16.

9. Quoted in J. Belchem, *'Orator' Hunt*, Oxford University Press, 1985, p. 106.

10. For an assessment of the casualties see M. and W. Bee, 'The casualties of Peterloo', *Manchester Region History Review*, III:i (1989), pp. 43–50.

11. Bamford, *Passages*, p. 208.

12. For a review of the various interpretations see N. Kirk, 'Commonsense, commitment and objectivity: themes in the recent historiography of Peterloo', *Manchester Region History Review*, III:i (1989), pp. 61–6.

13. Bamford, *Passages*, p. 214.

14. Quoted in Read, *Peterloo*, p. 143.

15. D. Fraser, *Urban Politics in Victorian England*, Leicester University Press, 1976, pp. 22–3.

16. See R. Sykes, 'Early Chartism and trade unionism in south-east Lancashire', in J. Epstein and D. Thompson (eds), *The Chartist Experience*, Macmillan, London, 1982.

17. P. Pickering, *Chartism and the Chartists in Manchester and Salford*, London, 1995. This detailed and imaginative study does much to recreate the world of the rank and file Chartist.

18. For Hewitt this was a question of changed tactics rather than of altered norms or values and he argues that working-class consciousness remained fundamentally unaffected by the demise of Chartism; see M. Hewitt, *The Emergence of Stability in the Industrial City: Manchester, 1832–67*, Scolar, 1996.

Part II
Commercial Metropolis: 1850–1914

CHAPTER 6

The Capital of Cotton

The industrial revolution had made Manchester one of the world's great cities. Apart from London, it was the foremost commercial, banking and transport centre in what was the most economically advanced country in the world. If Manchester's comparative importance was to decline during the second half of the nineteenth century, as other cities and other industries caught up, it nonetheless remained one of the great trading cities of the world. It certainly dominated the commercial life of the cotton district of Lancashire and Cheshire. Some contemporaries referred to Manchester as a 'metropolis of manufactures', but it would have been more accurately described as a citadel of commerce.

As the world's largest market for cotton goods Manchester remained a centre of wealth creation. The weekly turnover in trade rose from £1m. in the 1850s to £10m. by the 1880s. The Royal Exchange was the economic heart of Manchester, and the central business district was dominated by warehouses, banks, hotels, railway stations, shops and markets. Manchester's increasing wealth was reflected in an 85% rise in the rental value of city centre properties between 1861 and 1891; and this despite periodic slumps in the cotton trade (the Cotton Famine of the early 1860s and the cyclical pattern of the 'Great Depression' of the 1870s–1890s) plus the growing challenge of foreign competition.

Manchester was also a major industrial city with an increasingly diverse manufacturing base. Whilst the Lancashire cotton industry as a whole continued to expand, within Manchester's industrial sector cotton faced several rivals. Chief amongst these were metals and engineering, but the production and sale of food and drink, road and rail transport and the clothing industry were also significant employers of labour. In fact, the clothing workshops of Strangeways were to become a more characteristic feature of the local economy than the mills of Ancoats. Finally, the city's trade and industry were boosted by a most extraordinary venture. The opening of the Manchester Ship Canal in 1894 soon made the inland city of Manchester the fourth most important port in Britain in the value of its trade. Among its spin-offs was the construction of the world's first industrial estate, at Trafford Park.

'Manchester Goods'

The Manchester market for cottons united and mobilised Lancashire's chief industry. The city had long controlled the export trade. Between 1830 and 1880 Manchester merchants also established supremacy over London in the expanding home market. Merchant houses specialising in the home trade exploited growing domestic demand after 1850. Rising real wages and the statutory establishment of the Saturday half-day holiday all stimulated the popular demand for goods. Ready-made clothing and the rising influence of the fashion cycle were changing the dress habits of the lower middle classes and of young working women. Manchester's home trade firms, with the aid of rail transport, sent an army of commercial travellers to the linen drapers of the land. Fitting their trade to suit the market, they extended their range beyond cotton to include all cloths, making 'Manchester goods' a synonym for textiles in general.

The export of textile goods to the self-governing colonies (Australia, New Zealand, Canada, South Africa) passed gradually into the hands of the home trade houses. Foreign trade firms sold across the globe, but exports became increasingly concentrated in a few far-flung markets. India came to dominate, taking nearly 40% of piece-goods and 27% of manufactured goods exported by the British cotton industry in 1896. From the 1870s to 1913, Manchester despatched, every year, well over one thousand million yards of cloth to India. Other large markets included Latin America and China. Improved communications enabled Manchester to remain the controlling influence in this global market. The completion of a world-wide network of telegraph cables in 1872, under the guidance of the Manchester merchant John Pender, further reinforced Manchester's control by greatly improving contact with distant customers and agents.

Cotton was not without crisis. Periodic booms and slumps characterised the cotton trade throughout the century. The Cotton Famine itself began as a cyclical slump made worse by the Northern blockade of exports of raw cotton from the Southern United States during the American Civil War. This event destroyed the myth that the British economy would collapse without cotton. Apart from the Cotton Famine, the most severe dips in cotton's trade cycle during the second half of the nineteenth century were those of 1877–9, 1884–5 and 1891–3. In general, there was a crisis in the cotton trade from the late 1870s through the 1880s. These were years of depression in the Manchester economy. In common with other staple industries of the industrial revolution it was feeling the bite of foreign competition, which was to sink ever more deeply after the First World War. Under the impetus of low wages (Japan) or of technological adaptation (USA), the overseas challenge was developing. By the end of the century cotton no longer dominated Britain's export trade as it had done for about a generation between the 1830s and the 1870s. But despite periodic crises and a declining share of the nation's exports, cotton remained an attractive investment down to 1914 and even enjoyed something of a boom in the years preceding the First World War.[1]

Cotton was not the sole item of Manchester commerce. The city was a major centre for the distribution of imported food and industrial raw materials. At first it depended upon imports via Liverpool but later through the Ship Canal and the Manchester docks. Moreover, Manchester was the region's distribution centre for food and other supplies, with specialised markets and exchanges. The Corn and Produce Exchange attracted a thousand dealers each week. The Coal Exchange's 227 members in 1879 had risen to over a thousand by 1914. The wholesale butter market was the largest in the UK, and specialised meat, fish, poultry, fruit, vegetable and flower markets supplied Manchester and its region. Manchester's chief wholesale food market took place under the great iron and glass roof of the Smithfield Market off Shudehill. Purchased by the city in 1846, it was constantly expanded until by 1897 it covered four and a half acres. For those who rose early enough, Smithfield provided one of the sights of Manchester as, around 6 a.m. each market day, the surrounding streets were congested with hundreds of horse-drawn 'lurries' and carts, heavy-laden with vegetables, coming to market.

The commercial core of the city expanded rapidly in the decades after 1850 as warehouses, shops, offices and banks lined former residential streets. Railway building and municipal street improvements added to the restructuring of the city centre as a business and market zone. This is reflected in the population statistics. Although 'greater' Manchester with its suburbs continued to grow throughout the century, central Manchester's population actually fell. Thus began a vital feature of the city's history over the ensuing 100 years, an absolute decline in the population of the central area. The population of the Manchester region as a whole, which had risen from an estimated 322,000 in 1801 to a shade over 1m. by 1851, more than doubled to 2.1m. by 1901. The opposite trend was represented in the figures for the economic heart of the region. The central Manchester subdistricts of Market Street, Deansgate and London Road housed 92,176 people in 1851 but only one third of this figure fifty years later. Offices and shops replaced dwelling houses, and commercial occupations escalated, reflecting the greater complexity of business life. Between 1871 and 1914, the number of firms occupying office space increased by 41%. A comparison made of the Manchester Directory for 1881 with that of twenty years earlier revealed a threefold increase in the number of accountants and commission agents and a 60% rise in the number of attorneys and solicitors.[2] More business meant more legal advice and a corresponding rise in

Watt's Warehouse (1858), now the Britannia Hotel. *(Photograph: Ian Beesley)*

costly litigation. Others to benefit from the increased business of the city centre were the host of dining rooms and cafes which sprang up to feed Manchester's growing army of office workers.

Warehouses Like Palaces

The cotton trade gave central Manchester a distinctive physical appearance. At the mid-century its architecture was regarded as the most advanced and innovative in the country. What so impressed contemporaries were the great warehouses which gave a new look to the city centre. The architectural style adopted from 1839 onwards was that of the *palazzi* of Renaissance Italy but exploiting the latest construction methods and materials. Manchester's 'merchant princes' thus likened themselves to real Italian princes of the past, and the architect Thomas Worthington felt justified in dubbing the city the Florence of the nineteenth century. Manchester's mid-Victorian warehouses are one of the glories of its architectural heritage. Surviving examples are little more than glanced at by the passer-by but their often grand proportions repay a longer look. The principal features of the Manchester warehouse are rows of regular windows to four storeys or more, with a central doorway at first floor level reached by a flight of steps, and the top of the building marked by a prominent cornice. These often palatial edifices were 'structures fit for kings ... which many a monarch might well envy'.[3]

The greatest of these palaces of commerce were to be found flanking the principal thoroughfares of the commercial district. By 1850 this meant Portland, Princess and Mosley Streets. The most spectacular and showy of the Portland Street warehouses was that of S. & J. Watts (now the Britannia Hotel). Beginning in a Deansgate shopping bazaar which they sold to Kendal, Milne and Faulkner in 1836, the Watts brothers built up the largest wholesale drapery business in the city. They operated from warehouses in New Brown Street and Fountain Street before opening their imposing Portland Street premises in 1858. Sir James Watts, twice Mayor of Manchester, was knighted on the occasion of the Queen's visit to the Art Treasures Exhibition of 1857. A classic merchant prince, Watts entertained the rich and the famous including aristocrats and royalty at his country house, Abney Hall in Cheadle.

The warehouse was such an important element in the everyday business of Victorian Manchester that it is worth a brief description of what went on inside. Customers would reach the sample rooms on the upper floors via the central staircase. Here goods could be inspected in the light of the tall front windows. The ground floor and basement below housed, respectively, the offices and the packing room. This latter was the hub of the warehouse. It let out at the side to a loading bay. In the packing room could be found:

> men ... working the hydraulic press; porters ... groaning under heavy bales; clerks ... perambulating with note-books in their hands; waggons ... standing at the door, each in its turn receiving pack after pack, till the whole is made up and rolls away like a moving mountain.[4]

If Manchester's warehouses were the arteries of the Lancashire cotton trade, the Royal Exchange was its heart. Attempts to build rival cotton exchanges at Blackburn and Rochdale came to nothing, and the railway strengthened Manchester's grip on the region's commerce. The 'Change was rebuilt and enlarged several times during the nineteenth and early twentieth centuries. A visitor who entered the third building (completed 1874) at High 'Change, 2 p.m. each Tuesday and Friday, encountered a dense mass of around six thousand men engaged in a myriad number of discussions and deals. The Cotton Exchange was for foreign trade only. Here buyers and sellers from far and wide could meet a large number of business contacts in quick succession, as well as gather the 'intelligence' on the state of the various markets so important to their trade. The building was in essence a huge internal space for meeting and dealing. The last extension was commissioned in 1913, to house the more than 10,000 subscribers. It finally closed

Manchester Royal Exchange. Members are singing the National Anthem in April 1911 to mark the coronation of King George V and Queen Mary – hence the bare heads. Note the day's trading prices on the board at the St Ann's Square end of the building.

for business in 1968, by which time the number of members had dwindled to 660. The last day's prices can still be seen on the display board in what now houses the Royal Exchange Theatre.

Manchester's commercial importance can be measured by the annual settlements at the Manchester Clearing House, established in 1872 and embracing twelve local banks. Between 1872 and 1896 the annual turnover of these banks rose from £69m. to £191m. This was the greatest of all the provincial clearing houses. In 1902 Manchester clearings amounted to eight times those of Bristol, four times those of Birmingham and were 48% larger than those of Liverpool. Manchester was the North's financial centre. Its long-standing private banks were gradually being absorbed by the newer joint-stock ventures. Thus Heywood's, the most prominent name in Manchester banking for almost a century, was absorbed in 1874 by the Manchester and Salford Bank. This merger was succeeded by another which marked the transformation of a local concern into a national business. In 1890 the Manchester and Salford Bank took over their London agents to form what became William Deacon's Bank. Thus Sir Benjamin Heywood's bank at the corner of St Ann's Square (and the original Heywood home adjacent to it) became, what it remains today, a branch of a national bank, at present the Royal Bank of Scotland.

Victorian Manchester could justifiably claim to be a major centre of insurance as well as banking. By the late nineteenth century most industrial and personal risks could be insured against, and the major life and fire insurance companies had offices in the city. In addition, specialist companies had grown up to deal with particular kinds of risk. Given the importance of Manchester to Britain's engineering industry it is not surprising that the city was the foremost centre for engineering insurance and home to the three leading specialist engineering insurance companies, Vulcan Boiler (originally founded in 1859), National Boiler (1864) and British Engine (1878). In the field of life assurance, 'The Refuge Friend in Deed Life Assurance and Sick Friendly Society' was transformed into the Refuge Assurance Company in 1881, assuming its massive Oxford Street premises in 1895 (designed by Alfred Water-house, architect of the Town Hall). The various elements in cooperative insurance eventually gathered together in Manchester under the umbrella of the Cooperative Insurance Society.

Finally, Manchester's retail sector was assuming something approaching its modern importance to the city's economy. The key to this was Manchester's part in the retailing revolution which saw the advent of the department store and multiple-shop trading. Large-scale retailing came to Manchester with the opening of Lewis's Market Street store in 1880.[5] Its success was immediate, and as new departments were added several building extensions were required, culminating in the seven-storey structure completed in 1885. The age of mass shopping

Lewis's Department Store.

had begun. Thousands came by train and omnibus to Lewis's to purchase goods and services not available in surrounding towns. David Lewis's retail empire was built on low profit margins and a large turnover of goods. Aggressive advertising and bargain sales based on bulk-buying were designed to capture the rising wages of the working and lower middle classes.

Kendal Milne's, by contrast, was the antidote to cheapness. Unlike Lewis's, which originated from Liverpool, this was a local firm. The title 'Kendal Milne' was assumed upon the death of Adam Faulkner in 1862. This furniture and drapery business was carried on in separate stores facing each other across Deansgate, each catering for 'the elite of society in town and country'. Both Lewis's and Kendal Milne differed from modern department stores in several respects, most notably in their combination of production with retail. In the 1880s Lewis's building included workshops employing 300 tailors and almost as many others making boots and shoes to be sold to customers. Kendal Milne were listed in trade directories of the time as 'cabinet makers, uphol-sterers, general house furnishers and drapery warehousemen'. Their cabinet factory occupied a separate seven-storey building at the rear of the Deansgate furniture store. Although there was understandable initial opposition to Lewis's from specialist retailers, ultimately the greater attractiveness of Manchester as a shopping centre benefited the entire city. The strength of Manchester's retail sector contributed to the rise in city centre land values.

The other element in the retailing revolution was the retail chain or multiple store. Wholesale distribution and the branch system revolutionised retailing techniques: both were pioneered by the Co-operative Movement. The Cooperative Wholesale Society supplied local cooperative stores which, in effect, acted as multiple branches of the same company. The grocery trade was first affected and the Coop. provided good quality, cheap food for the better-off wage-earner who could wait six months for the 'divi'. Cooperative stores never generated the same degree of customer loyalty in commercial cities like Manches-ter as they did in the smaller towns of the North West, although the Manchester and Salford Equitable Cooperative Society had 19 branches in the area in the 1880s as well as an impressive headquarters in Ardwick, with drapery, tailoring, boot and shoe, butchers and grocery depart-ments. Commercial retailers soon adopted the same multiple-store strategy, and from the 1870s the grocery trade entered a transformation, exploiting new opportunities for the cheap import of bacon, butter, cheese and eggs which then ceased to be special luxuries on the working-class table. Grocery chain-stores multiplied, and national chains like Liptons, Home and Colonial and Maypole Dairy had branches throughout the area. In addition, local chains developed like Burgons Supply Stores and Williams Grocers. The latter began in

Didsbury and catered for the middle-class suburbs to the south of the city centre.

A Broader Industrial Base

Lancashire cotton became a highly specialised industry during the second half of the nineteenth century. Towns concentrated on either spinning or weaving or even specific kinds of cotton goods. Most weaving towns were to the north like Blackburn, Burnley and Preston, whilst spinning dominated in south-east Lancashire towns such as Bolton, Oldham and Rochdale. Manchester itself spun the finest of all cotton yarns. Most of this production found its way into the city's own weaving sheds, although its share of Lancashire's looms was steadily declining. Whilst the number of cotton operatives in Lancashire as a whole almost doubled between 1850 and 1914, Manchester's cotton workforce was shrinking. This was already clear by the 1860s. For example, although Manchester was the regional centre for organising charitable relief during the Cotton Famine, there were actually fewer operatives laid off in the city than in much smaller places like Ashton-under-Lyne and Stockport.[6] By 1911, out of a total occupied labour force of nearly 350,000, the official Census listed a shade over 20,000 men and women working in textiles in Manchester. This was lower than the textile figures for each of the much smaller towns of Bolton, Oldham, Burnley and Blackburn. Moreover Manchester's textile workers were preponderantly female. Mill girls outnumbered male operatives by roughly three to one. The industry as a whole was noted for its high proportion of women workers, but this was more marked in Manchester than almost anywhere else. Despite this, although for many the mill lass remained the typical image of the Manchester working woman, by the later nineteenth century domestic service in the city had actually become a more important source of female employment than mill work.

Cotton, however, remained an indirect employer in Manchester through the textile engineering industry. The major British textile machine makers were in Lancashire, including such engineering giants as Platt Brothers of Oldham, Dobson and Barlow of Bolton, and Mather and Platt of Salford. Manchester firms included Curtis and Madeley, Hetherington and Sons, and Samuel Brooks. But Manchester engineering was not solely dependent upon textiles. The local machine-tool industry maintained the pre-eminence established before 1850. Joseph Whitworth's exhibits dominated the machine-tool section of the Great Exhibition at the Crystal Palace in 1851. Manchester's reputation in this field was maintained by new firms such as those of Muir, Hulse, and Craven's. It was not until the 1890s that American competition undermined the Manchester producers. Manchester engineering was also important in

A shop floor at British Westinghouse, Trafford Park.

other sectors. For example, the enormous Beyer-Peacock locomotive works in Gorton employed over one thousand men by 1875, and railway carriage and wagon construction companies, such as Ashbury's, were of national significance. By the 1900s munitions, electrical plant, structural steel, chains and wire were all manufactured on an extensive scale. Manchester and district had become one of the world's foremost engineering centres with famous local firms such as Armstrong-Whitworth, Crossleys, Mather and Platt and British Westinghouse. By 1911, Manchester's workforce in metals and engineering was more than twice that employed in textiles. In terms of industrial production Manchester engineering had far outstripped Manchester cotton.

In Manchester's manufacturing sector engineering and metals were rivalled only by the importance of the city's clothing industry. The growth of a working-class market for ready-made clothes had, by the mid-nineteenth century, stimulated the expansion of a clothing industry in most of the major urban centres. Diverse and decentralised, generally carried on in small workshops, it was easily overlooked and its import-ance unrecognised. Yet, according to the Census of 1911, over 40,000 were engaged in various branches of clothing manufacture by this date. This was easily the largest concentration of clothing workers in Lanca-shire, and Manchester was second only to Leeds among northern clothing centres. Tailoring, the most important branch of the industry, flourished in the ill-regulated 'sweatshops' of Strangeways and Chee-tham. Underclothes, shirts and collars were often made up by poorly paid home-workers, mostly women. The making of blouses and dresses was chiefly in the hands of large firms who also manufactured the cloth, such as Tootal Broadhurst Lee. The 'sweatshop' end of the trade was finally regulated by the Trade Boards Act of 1907. Manchester's clothing sector included rubberised rainwear. By the early twentieth century two-thirds of the waterproof garments made in the UK came from Manchester and Salford, while the entire British production supplied 90% of the world market. It had all begun in 1824 when Charles Macintosh had opened his works in Chorlton-on-Medlock. Considering its reputation for inclement weather, it might seem appropriate that Manchester was the indisputable home of that essential item of wet-weather wear, the 'macintosh'. Other industries important to Manchester's economy included food, drink and tobacco; wood and furniture; the building industry; paper and printing and vehicle manufacture. The chemical industry was well represented especially in the field of textile dyes. Although aniline dyes were a British invention, German firms led the field. The largest home producer of aniline oil and aniline salt was the Clayton Aniline Company, founded in 1876 by the young chemist, Charles Dreyfus. The owner of a rival firm, Ivan Levinstein, had begun by making magenta from aniline in a converted cottage in Blackley. Levinstein's soon expanded into larger premises in the adjacent Crumpsall Vale, thus forming the basis of the future ICI Dyestuffs complex at Blackley. Far from being merely a cotton town, Manchester had become an industrial centre of the first rank with a diverse manufacturing base. It was also a major centre of transportation and communications. In 1911 over 27,000 worked on Manchester's railways, roads and docks.

At the Centre of the Railway Web

Transport and communications were central to Manchester's economic success. The development of Lancashire's railway network strengthened Manchester's hold over the region's commerce and industry and added to the national standing of the region's economy. A French observer (Leon Faucher) used the analogy of a spider at the centre of its web to describe the way in which Manchester presided over the intricate pattern of rail routes which linked it to the surrounding mill towns. These routes acted almost as production lines in which materials and men could rapidly reach the citadel of commerce. The railways quickly became an integral element in the economy of the cotton district. Their blockage by heavy snowfalls in January 1854 made Manchester a 'beseiged city ... deprived of all postal communication with the metropolis', and the victim of a 'very serious interruption of mercantile transactions'.[7]

The commercial potential of the railway in the Manchester region produced sharp competition between the railway companies. As many

A scene at Central Station in the 1890s.

as nine were rivals for access to Manchester, a figure only exceeded in London. Rivalry between them was vigorous and could be violent, such as at the so-called 'battle' of Clifton Junction in 1849 when, in a dispute over the payment of tolls, Lancashire and Yorkshire Railway workmen constructed a barrier of timber and empty carriages to obstruct illegally the passage of an East Lancashire Railway train to Manchester. By 1860 amalgamations had reduced the number of companies operating to three; the London and North Western; the Manchester, Sheffield and Lincolnshire; and the Lancashire and Yorkshire. These were later joined by the Midland. Rivalry over new routes, especially to the south of the city, continued for decades. Most of the new lines to the south were completed by 1885 and the essentials of the regional rail network were by then in place.

Whilst such competition benefited Manchester's business community and facilitated suburban growth, it did not produce a rational plan for the traveller across the city. Victorian Manchester came to have four railway terminals, all on the edge of the central district. In 1842 Hunts Bank Station (later Victoria) and Store Street Station (later London Road, now Piccadilly) were opened. These two terminals, a mile apart, were joined after nearly forty years of wrangling, by Central Station on Lower Mosley Street, completed in 1880. However, the weary trudge between the stations was never done away with. Much talk of an east–west linking line or of a tunnel system came to naught. Manchester's fourth terminal, Exchange Station, was effectively an adjunct to

The GNR Goods Warehouse (1898). *(Photograph: Ian Beesley)*

Victoria. In addition, the rail traveller to Manchester was ill-served by the absence of a good railway hotel, a facility common in most other northern cities. Plans to build on the front of Central Station were abandoned in the 1880s and when, at last, the Midland Hotel opened in 1898 it was on a separate site.[8]

The construction of railway lines, stations, goods warehouses and depots, not to mention hotels, was costly (in terms of land purchase), socially intrusive (in terms of the clearance of existing property) and took up a lot of urban space. For example, between 1861 and 1871, 600 houses were demolished to clear a site for a goods station at London Road, and another adjacent to Central Station in 1898 cost £700,000 for the nine-acre site alone. The railway companies also constructed huge warehouse complexes for the storage and handling of goods. Although some could be physically imposing, like the Great Northern Railway Company's Goods Warehouse between Watson Street and Deansgate, they were generally plain, utilitarian buildings which lacked the architectural flourish of their city centre counterparts

The Manchester Ship Canal

Canals gave way to the railway in the middle of the century, but in the 1890s one of the greatest engineering projects of the era was to reinstate

Navvies at work on the Ship Canal pause for the photographer.

water transport as a vital feature of Manchester's economy. Manchester's role as a centre of international trade and of regional distribution was maintained by the city's imaginative sponsorship of a ship canal linking it with the sea. It is fitting that Manchester's engineering know-how and commercial endeavour should combine in such a project. The original impetus was the burden of port charges at Liverpool and the punitive rates charged by the railway companies for the carriage of freight between Liverpool and Manchester. After the depression years of the late 1870s and mid-1880s, the building of the Ship Canal heralded a distinct economic revival, but one which was to benefit engineering more than cotton.[9]

The Manchester Ship Canal and the Ship Canal Company which administered it were corporate endeavours of great magnitude. The Company was based on the financial sponsorship of the Manchester Corporation in the shape of a loan of £5m. (32.5% of the Company's total capital of £15.4m.) plus the investment of 39,000 shareholders, the largest number of investors in any private company at that date. In 1904 arrears on the loan were partly written off, in return for a new and permanent financial arrangement which gave the Manchester Corporation a dominant role in the Canal Company. Support for the Canal was an enterprising move for the city. The Canal linked Manchester to the sea. As well as dramatically reducing transport costs, it transformed Manchester into a port of international standing and gave

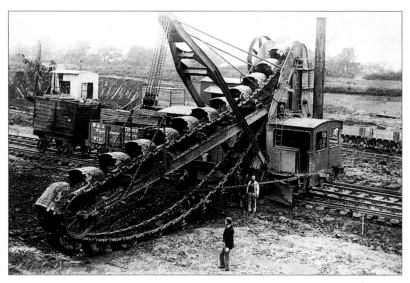

A steam-powered 'Navvy' or excavator used in the construction of the Ship Canal.

Manchester and Salford their own docks. By 1914 the Canal had captured nearly 5% of UK imports by value and 4.4% of domestic exports. It liberated the twin cities from their long-standing dependence on the port of Liverpool.

In engineering terms the Ship Canal was remarkable. Built between 1887 and 1894 it was 35 miles in length and included notable technological feats such as the triple entrance locks and the unique Barton Aqueduct which carried the Bridgewater Canal over the new navigation. Contemporaries were fascinated by the construction plant used, which included 75 steam excavators, 124 steam cranes and seven earth dredgers working from the banks. It was dug to the same depth as the Suez Canal. When completed, the Manchester Docks, mostly located in Salford, consisted of three main units. The main docks lay west of Trafford Road; on the opposite side of the Canal was Trafford Wharf; and the shallower Pomona Docks (on the site of the Pomona pleasure gardens) lay upstream to the south of the River Irwell.

Originally intended to revive the cotton trade, its chief economic impact was on the local engineering industry. Easier export opportunities stimulated a boom in textile machine-making, although this proved to be a mixed blessing considering the build-up of foreign textile competition which resulted. The Trafford Park Industrial Estate, adjacent to the Canal and designed to exploit its trading opportunities, effectively shifted the industrial focus of the city towards its south-western fringes. The Estate, the first of its kind in the world, was intended to attract a cross section of firms in textiles, engineering, food production and brewing. In the event, medium to heavy engineering, the oil industry and chemicals preponderated. The British Westinghouse Electric Company, a subsidiary of the American parent firm, bought up 11% of the Estate and erected the largest engineering works in the UK. Westinghouse soon became the biggest employer in Trafford Park, with 12,000 workers by 1903. The firm introduced US production methods, employed American foremen and retrained English engineers at Pittsburgh. Westinghouse were the advance guard. Many more American firms established themselves in the Park before and after the First World War. George Westinghouse founded Trafford City, fourteen miles from Pittsburgh, to commemorate his UK endeavour.

The Ship Canal further secured Manchester's regional role in the distributive trades. Imported grain, meat, oil and fruit each necessitated specialist warehousing and distribution. Specialist trades were stimulated, such as that for imported fruit. American apples joined those from the Mediterranean in the flourishing fruit markets of the city. Profiting from this blossoming trade, Manchester's fruit merchants formed their own trade association. The Canal also benefited the chief arm of the distributive trades, the Cooperative Wholesale Society (CWS). The Society remained a staunch supporter of the Canal. It pioneered the industrial development of the Canal banks by the establishment in 1894 of its Irlam soap works. It had expanded into margarine manufacture by 1914 and by then also had a bacon factory and flour mill at Trafford Wharf. The Canal also created a regional boom in the haulage industry and once again the CWS played a central part. The number of carriers in Manchester rose from 61 to 151 between 1894 and 1914. Thanks to the Ship Canal, the centre of gravity in the North's distributive trade drifted away from Liverpool and Preston and towards Manchester. Thus communications joined commerce and industry as the lynchpins of Manchester's economy.

Despite some periods of slump and sluggish trade, between 1850 and 1914 there had been no lasting check to Manchester's economic vitality. Although cotton remained essential to Manchester's success the city's industrial base had diversified and its significance as a commercial centre had continued to grow. There had been numerous economic problems, but each had been regarded as a challenge to be overcome. It was characteristic that the planning for the Ship Canal had begun in the depths of the depression of the 1880s. Yet future stresses were to be more profound and long-lasting. During the 1920s and 1930s the textile base was to slide into irretrievable decline. Manchester's greatest days were already over.

References

1. The work of Douglas Farnie is essential for an understanding of the commercial development of cotton in the nineteenth century, esp. D. A. Farnie, *The English Cotton Industry and the World Market, 1815–1896*, Oxford University Press, 1979; see also A. Redford, *Manchester Merchants and Foreign Trade, Vol. II, 1850–1939*, Manchester University Press, 1956.

2. T. W. Freeman, *The Conurbations of Great Britain*, Manchester University Press, 1966, pp. 136–41; H. Baker, 'On the growth of the Manchester population, extension of the commercial centre of the city, and provision for habitation', *Transactions of the Manchester Statistical Society* (1881–82), pp. 1–27.

3. *Bradshaw's Guide to Manchester*, 1857, as cited in C. Stewart, *The Stones of Manchester*, Edward Arnold, London, 1956, p. 36.

4. R. Lamb, 'Manchester by a Manchester Man', *Fraser's Magazine*, 47 (1853), p. 616.

5. For Lewis's see A. Briggs, *Friends of the People: The Centenary History of Lewis's*, Batsford, London, 1956.

6. See, for example, J. Watts, *The Facts of the Cotton Famine*, Simpkin Marshall, London, 1866, p. 229, who gives figures of 25,198, 11,510 and 4,242 for factory operatives in receipt of poor relief on 20 June 1863 in Ashton, Stockport and Manchester respectively.

7. *Manchester Guardian*, 7 January 1854.

8. See J. R. Kellett, *Railways and Victorian Cities*, Routledge & Kegan Paul, London, 1969, ch. 6; J. Simmons, *The Railway in Town and Country, 1830–1914*, David and Charles, Newton Abbot, 1986, ch. 4.

9. For the Ship Canal see, D. A. Farnie, *The Manchester Ship Canal and the Rise of the Port of Manchester, 1894–1975*, Manchester University Press, 1980; D. Owen, *The Manchester Ship Canal*, Manchester University Press, 1983; I. Harford, *Manchester and its Ship Canal Movement*, Keele University Press, 1994.

CHAPTER 7

Living in Victorian Manchester

In spite of Manchester's continued economic importance, interest in the 'shock city' of the industrial revolution waned after the mid-century. Manchester almost slipped from the national consciousness. Although it had been a centre of attention in the 1830s and 1840s, during the second half of the nineteenth century, apart from at particular 'moments' like the Cotton Famine and the opening of the Ship Canal, the nation's gaze was elsewhere. Although Free Trade had ensured the city's enduring symbolic importance, Manchester was no longer the mouthpiece of the provincial middle class. Moreover, in plain terms, the novelty had worn off. Manchester was no longer so remarkable as the model of the new society polarised along class lines. Attention had shifted to other cities and other regions, and the image of the industrial North was being transformed.

Progress and Poverty

When the 'problem of the city' was discussed in the later nineteenth century it was customary to focus on the slums of London's East End. This was reputedly the lair of the 'residuum', the semi-criminal under-class of disreputables which stalked the urban nightmare of the Victorian imagination. Investigations of London poverty, from Henry Mayhew in the 1850s to Charles Booth in the 1880s, caught the public eye. The East End symbolised the apparent failure of self-help and moral improvement to reach a submerged section of the working class which, untouched by the 'civilising' influence of their 'betters', was seen as degenerating both physically and morally in a brutalising urban environment. By contrast the industrial North, especially the textile towns of Lancashire and the West Riding, had come to symbolise the growing respectability of a very different section of the working class which seemed to be civilising itself through a combination of adult education, cooperative society, savings bank and chapel.

Nevertheless, a closer examination of Manchester would have revealed enough similarities with London to distinguish it from the supposed 'respectability' of the textile towns. The poverty exposed by Booth's survey, *Life and Labour of the People of London*, was caused in large part by the operation of a casual labour market, that is irregular employment by the day or by the job. Insecurity of income could be worse than low wages since food had to be bought and rent paid whether or not work was available. The classic case of a casual trade was the work pattern of the dockworker, but several other occupations were similarly blighted, such as building industry workers, those in the handicraft trades, employees in shops and pubs, a range of commercial employments and street traders. Every Victorian city had a pool of casual and seasonal workers, but in Manchester this pool may have been wider and deeper than in most, more akin to the situation in ports like Liverpool and Hull than in other inland cities such as Birmingham or Leeds.

Among casualised employments in Manchester were jobs in transport and storage such as carman, porter, messenger, warehouseman and also in the building trade, especially painter and labourer. The casual worker would not stick to one trade but turned to anything that came along. A factor in Manchester's casual labour market may have been the possibility of temporary work in the mills, especially for the young. At any rate, the necessity of living near to the chance of employment concentrated the casual worker in the most run-down districts in the inner city. Their lot would be poverty, their goal the avoidance of the workhouse. In years of high unemployment it was they rather than the archetypal 'honest workingman' who sought charity or applied for poor

Boy Navvies. There was a plentiful supply of unskilled, often casual, work in Manchester and a large market for juvenile labour. These youths were employed on the construction of the Ship Canal.

relief. When the Manchester and Salford District Provident Society raised £26,000 in a special distress fund during the bad winter of 1878–9, the vast majority of applicants were casual and seasonal workers, mostly from the building trade; only 7% were factory hands. Casual work was concentrated in the city's central area rather than in manufacturing districts like Gorton and Openshaw. Around 70% of all out-relief applications to the Poor Law guardians of the Township of Manchester (the city centre plus Ancoats) between 1894 and 1897 came from the casually and seasonally employed. Workers in the building trade made up the largest group applying in 1905. At this time, approaching half of central Manchester residents were in either part-time or casual jobs. Around 75% of the adult males registered as unemployed with Manchester Corporation between 1903 and 1905 were casual labourers, a high proportion of whom were dependent upon the earnings of other members of their families.[1]

Manchester was never subjected to a detailed social survey of the sort conducted by Booth in London or Seebohm Rowntree in York, but in spite of the city's economic achievements it still had a reputation for poverty: the pauperism figures for the Township of Manchester were among the worst in the country at 55.7 per thousand of the population in 1911. Those surveys that were conducted locally tend to confirm this picture. Among the more reliable of these was that of Fred Scott, whose findings were presented to the Manchester Statistical Society in May 1889. Scott's survey revealed the problem of casual employment. He found 21% of respondents in a section of Ancoats and 40% of those questioned in Salford to be 'irregularly employed'. This was in a good year for employment, when only 3.5% of the Ancoats and 2.5% of the Salford samples were unemployed. Even during the 'good times', however, the degree of impoverishment made a chilling recital. Using Charles Booth's terminology, Scott classified 50% of his Ancoats sample and 61% in Salford as 'very poor' with a weekly income of less than four shillings (20p) per adult.[2]

Yet if levels of poverty in the city were a cause for alarm, there was other evidence of advancing standards of living for the majority of the working class. On average the wages of factory workers rose during the second half of the nineteenth century. Whereas earnings had declined during the 1840s, from the 1850s there was an overall improvement in money wages which was most marked in the post-1865 period. Cotton spinners in the Manchester district had experienced a decline of 6.5% in average weekly earnings in the 1840s but recovered with rises of 11% in the 1850s and 36% between 1860 and 1874. Spinners' average earnings increased from 21s. 10d. (£1.09) in 1850 (lower than their 1840 equivalent) to 33s. 1d. (£1.65) by 1874. Such material advance was not confined to the 'labour aristocrats'. Even the less well paid Manchester piecers experienced rises of 17% and 36%

for the 1850s and 1860–74 respectively, and the wages of cardroom workers (mostly female) doubled during the latter period. Wages in the cotton district were generally high by national standards, and this extended beyond the textile factory. Building wages, for example, were up to 15% in excess of the national average, only exceeded by those in London and the Midlands. The average hourly rate in Manchester for building trade craftsmen in 1886 was 8*d*. (3p); the London equivalent was just a penny more.[3]

We cannot estimate family income on the basis of adult male wages only. The earnings of women, children and young persons should be taken into account. This is especially true of the cotton district. Census data suggests that in Lancashire the proportion of females in employment aged 15 and over was well above the national average at 47% in 1851 and 43% in 1911. The averages for England and Wales as a whole were 39% and 36% respectively. The proportion for Manchester itself may have been even higher considering the numbers of part-time workers and domestic servants in the city. These were occupational categories which consistently confused and occasionally eluded the census enumerator.

Judged by the best indicators,[4] 'real wages' (which relate money wages to changes in the cost of living) rose during the second half of the nineteenth century. Average retail prices actually fell between 1885 and 1900. However, it is clear that income differentials grew and standards of living became more varied. Whilst the casual worker might often languish in poverty, the purchasing power of the factory worker was greater than ever and, as described below, whole industries of leisure and consumerism arose to exploit the commercial possibilities of a working class with money in its pockets.

Migrants

Living in some of Manchester's poorest quarters were its various ethnic communities. The largest was the Irish, who comprised 15% of the city's population in 1851. Nearly half of Britain's Irish population at this time lived in four major cities, London, Manchester, Liverpool and Glasgow. Many had come to escape the Great Famine of the 1840s. As first generation migrants became native Mancunians, the numbers of Irish-born dwindled until by the time of the 1901 Census only 3.6% of Manchester residents gave an Irish place of birth. But the Manchester 'Irish' remained an identifiable community, however difficult it might have been to quantify them.

Irishness was a contested identity in the nineteenth century. The Irish were often conceived as an 'Other' in contrast to an English 'Us', and anti-Catholic and anti-Irish sentiments were never hard to inflame.

Consequently, Irish migrant groups in British cities lived in an environment of cultural as well as economic insecurity. Although the situation in Manchester never achieved the bitter sectarian rivalry found in Liverpool or Glasgow, there was still an undercurrent of hostility to the Irish. Consequently, the descendants of Irish migrants remained in close-knit communities and nurtured an identity that was defiantly Irish and Catholic.[5] A reasonable estimate of the community's size is the Catholic population of the city which was around 14% in 1901. Manchester's Catholic population was concentrated in particular areas. The northern part of Ancoats was 40% Catholic according to a religious census of 1900, and the figure for its poorest quarter, Angel Meadow, was even higher at 50%. Since most of the city's Catholics were of Irish descent, Ancoats could be regarded as a major Irish district.

The Ancoats Irish often found work as day labourers in the building trade (men) or as domestic servants (women), but the biggest single employer was Smithfield Market. One-quarter of stallholders were Catholic and so were large numbers of the porters and labourers employed in the market and the hordes of street sellers and hawkers trading on its margins. Most of these occupations were precarious, and it is no surprise to discover that between 1881 and 1914 on average one half of the paupers in the New Bridge Street Workhouse were registered as Catholic. This was no advance on the 1840s (see Chapter 3), and the Irish community remained poor throughout the century. They were also more likely to end up in gaol. Irish-born offenders comprised around 25% of the total in Manchester between 1841 and 1871, and it was estimated that one third of Strangeways prisoners in 1900 were Catholic.[6]

By far the largest foreign settlement of the later nineteenth century was of Jews from Eastern Europe. They came from Russia, Austria and Romania, escaping popular anti-semitism and an official persecution that was most marked in the Russian pogroms of the 1880s. Manchester's Jewish population rose from under 10,000 in 1875 to over 35,000 by 1914. This was England's largest Jewish community outside London. The East European Jews most readily found work in the workshops of the cheap clothing and household furniture trades in Red Bank, Strangeways and Lower Broughton. These were poor areas of low cost accommodation, numerous lodging houses and a reputation for crime and disorder. Shortage of cash rather than anything else attracted the first immigrants to these quarters, but as Jewish institutions (especially synagogues) grew up they became ethnic centres. Soon upwardly mobile families migrated the short distance north to Hightown (by Cheetham Hill Road and Elizabeth Street) or farther flung outposts of suburbia such as Higher Broughton.

Like the Catholic Irish, Manchester Jewry found its identity contested by elements in the host community. A key adhesive holding the Jewish

Smithfield Market. Many of the traders, porters and labourers were Irish.

community together was its welfare system for the care of the Jewish poor. Whilst unemployed or elderly Irish joined their English counterparts in the workhouses of the Poor Law, the Jews had their own Manchester Jewish Board of Guardians to dispense poor relief. This was one of a network of Jewish secular institutions. No other religious or ethnic group had such a comprehensive welfare system. This distinct 'Jewish culture of welfare' has been seen as a product of the tension between the need for integration and the need for preservation. The rationale was that if Manchester Jewry could demonstrate its ability to care for its own, this would assist integration. Ironically, it may have been precisely the existence of this exclusively Jewish sphere that reinforced separateness. Either way, the mass immigration of East European Jews in the later nineteenth century intensified the apparent need for a Jewish welfare system.[7]

This mass immigration of largely poor, non-English speaking and culturally alien Jews was seen as a problem by Manchester's existing Jewish community, themselves an accepted part of the local business and professional class. They feared this alien influx might destroy the image of Manchester's Jews and threaten their own economic position and status. The hostility expressed by some among Manchester's non-Jewish majority must have fuelled such fears. In contrast to the traditional picture of tolerant acceptance by the host community, there is evidence of an anti-alien revulsion shading off into outright antisemitism. This surfaced in even the most respectable of local

Manchester bricklayers at work. Jobs in the building trade were casual and notorious for fluctuating with the seasons. Bricklaying was one of the better paid and more secure employments.

newspapers, the *Manchester City News*, which complained in 1890 of 'an invading force, foreign in race, speech, dress, ideas and religion'. Other periodicals, like the short-lived *Spy*, used the reductive language of the racist, referring to 'Yids' and 'sheeneymen' and complaining of the 'cancer' of foreign Jewry 'eating away all that is noble in our national character ... We do not want them at any price. We want England for the English'.[8] The response of Manchester's existing Jewish elite was to set about a programme of 'anglicisation' to imbue the immigrant with English culture and traditions. This was ruthlessly followed through – the Jews' School even banned the speaking of Yiddish – and was largely successful. The traditional culture of the East European Jew was gradually abandoned as the price of acceptance in English society.

The People's Health

Manchester remained an unhealthy place in which to live well into the second half of the nineteenth century. Crude annual mortality rates gave no hint of improvement, with figures per thousand population of 31.5, 32.8, 30.5, for the 1850s, 1860s and 1870s respectively. This was

particularly depressing for members of the Manchester and Salford
Sanitary Association, formed in 1852 to promote public health education
and sanitary reform. This influential and active voluntary body had set
about a vigorous programme of health education (selling or distributing
100,000 tracts and delivering 435 free lectures 'in the worst parts of
the town') and campaigning for local health reforms, from improved
sewage disposal to the creation of isolation hospitals. Yet their struggle
seemed in vain. The city's poor health would not respond to treatment.
As an Association report of 1867 remarked:

> Strenuous exertions have been made both to make Manchester a
> more healthy place to dwell in, and to improve the condition of
> the inhabitants. What then has been the result? ... we do not gain
> any sign of progress. When the last ten years are taken together,
> the average annual death-rates for Manchester and Salford are 33
> and 26 in the thousand – almost exactly the same as in the ten
> years from 1841 to 1851. It will be seen at once, then, that the
> death-tax levied upon the inhabitants of our town is as heavy as
> ever.[9]

But improvement eventually came. From the 1880s the overall trend
in mortality was downwards, with crude death-rates of 27.4 and 25.5
recorded for the 1880s and 1890s respectively.

This was the beginning of a long-term trend towards better health.
What had caused this improvement? Did the Sanitary Association's
campaign finally bear fruit? Was this the product of the 'Sanitary Idea',
born of mid-century alarm at the appalling conditions of urban life?
In practice formal public health reforms had less impact than might be
thought.

Almost 88% of Manchester's total reduction in mortality between
1850 and 1900 came from a decline in infectious diseases.[10] The greater
understanding about the spread of infection that came with the 'germ
theory of disease' lay behind the move to establish isolation hospitals
for infectious diseases (like that in Monsall, to the north of the city,
opened in 1871 with a capacity of 128 beds), which contributed to the
declining incidence of smallpox, scarlet fever and some other communicable diseases by the end of the century. However, contemporary
reformers laid most emphasis on pure water supplies and adequate
sanitation as a preventive to water-borne infections such as typhoid,
cholera and gastro-intestinal disorders.

Inadequate sewage disposal continued to threaten the people's health
well after 1850. With ashpits and cesspools in the poorer districts
infrequently emptied, faecal contamination of food and water was
common. In the 1870s the Council began to replace midden privies
with 'Dolly Varden' pail closets (nicknamed after a popular scent of
the time), but it was not until the 1890s that a water-borne system of

sewage disposal was introduced. As late as 1902 only 37% of the city's privies were water closets. Thereafter Manchester's position improved greatly, and research into the problem of sewage disposal in the city led to the invention of the activated sludge process after 1914. If Manchester was slow to improve its sewage disposal, it had led the way in the provision of pure water. Water supply came under municipal control with the completion of the Longendale Reservoir in the 1850s. Thirlmere Reservoir was added in 1894, despite opposition from those who feared for the natural beauty of the Lake District from the construction of such man-made lakes. By 1900, the consumption of water in the city had risen to nearly 32m. gallons a day. Nevertheless, standpipes remained in use in many of the poorest streets. It took twenty years and the construction of a further reservoir, at Haweswater, to meet adequately the city's demands for fresh water.

Sanitary reform certainly saved lives; cholera and typhoid ceased to be significant causes of death during the second half of the nineteenth century. But improved water supply was not enough. Evidence of this is the survival, and actual intensification in the 1890s, of Manchester's notoriously high infant mortality rate. Infant diarrhoea was a major killer, and it has been claimed that its persistence in the city, despite better water supplies, points to the significance of unhygienic food-handling, storage and feeding practices as impediments to good health. However valid the connection between personal habits and health, it is nevertheless probable that the city's slow conversion to water closets contributed much to Manchester's extraordinarily high infant death figures. Young children remained in danger of contracting summer diarrhoea by infection from the large number of midden-privies and pail closets still in use in the early 1900s.[11]

Sanitary reform, however, may only be a sub-plot in the story of the people's health. Reduced mortality from water-borne and food-borne infections had accounted for less than one third of all lives saved in Manchester during the half-century following 1850. Much more sub-stantial had been the reduction in air-carried diseases such as pulmonary tuberculosis, the major single cause of death in Victorian England. Tuberculosis, although a communicable disease, depended less for its spread on exposure to infection than on the general health of exposed individuals. In other words, the most effective preventive against con-tracting tuberculosis in the nineteenth century was the improved diet and general standard of health normally associated with rising real wages. Poverty and ill-health go hand in hand. A mortality map of Victorian Manchester would reveal a variety of experience according to district.[12] The most unhealthy areas formed a ring round the de-populating city centre whilst death rates remained lower in the outer-ring of suburbs. In the 1870s the inner zone of working-class districts consisting of Hulme, Chorlton-on-Medlock and Ardwick provided the highest mortality figures; by the end of the century Ancoats was a death black spot. These were the areas of highest housing density and overcrowding. Congested court and tenement dwellings lurked behind main road shopping façades and street upon street of closely-packed terraces sprawled across the newer districts. Poor housing and a substandard environment made illness more likely, although at the level of the individual family or the single life it was other factors, including regularity of income, quality of diet, genetic endowment and personal habits which determined comparative life chances. The poverty of those on low wages or in casual employment encouraged the mal-nutrition that arises from an inadequate diet and caused the exposure to disease that comes from the necessity of living in the cheapest accommodation in the most unhealthy districts.

There were, however, some improvements in Manchester's housing during the later nineteenth century. For example, within four years of the appointment of Manchester's first Medical Officer of Health in 1868 virtually all the city's cellar dwellings had been closed. But the Corporation proved reluctant to incur the costs of rehousing which was allowed under government legislation passed in 1875. Instead a new set of bye-laws (similar to those passed elsewhere) laid down regulations over the construction of new private houses. Hence there arose the era of the 'bye-law' streets with their small walled backyard and distinctive alleyways. Thus the 'Coronation Street' image of the North was born. Instead of rebuilding, the Corporation pursued a policy of 'recondi-tioning' existing stock, converting back-to-backs into through houses and supplying water-closets and inside water taps. The Unhealthy Dwellings Committee of the Council reconditioned around 500 houses a year between 1885 and 1906, a figure subsequently increased to 2,000 a year. There were also voluntary housing initiatives in Manchester as part of the garden suburb movement of the 1890s and 1900s. Local advocates of housing reform like T. R. Marr and T. C. Horsfall stimu-lated a climate of opinion which looked favourably on private ventures such as Burnage Garden Village and Chorltonville and the municipal estate at Blackley in the 1890s.

Leisure and Recreation

The later nineteenth century saw the advent of the modern entertain-ment and leisure industries. The profit potential of the increased spending power of a growing proportion of the working class did not long escape the attention of the pioneers of commercialised entertain-ment and sport. The music hall, professional football and the cinema each emerged as substantial commercial enterprises before 1914. The music hall developed out of the traditional 'concerts' of the pub music room. Gaining in commercial organisation what it lost in spontaneity, the music hall became the prototype of the modern entertainment industry. Numerous halls were opened in Manchester from the 1850s onwards. One of the earliest was the People's Music Hall (later known as the Casino) run by Tom Burton and opened in 1853 on Lower Mosley Street. In 1897 it was demolished to make way for the Midland Hotel. Other early Manchester halls included the Folly on Peter Street, originally a Methodist chapel and renamed the Tivoli in 1897; the London in Bridge Street, purpose-built in 1862 and later renamed the Queen's; and the Star in Pollard Street, Ancoats.

What kind of audience attended the music hall? They were pre-dominantly working and lower middle class. A correspondent of the Manchester satirical magazine *Free Lance* visited the Wolverhampton, one of the larger Manchester halls in 1867, and witnessed 'smart looking mechanics', numerous commercial travellers, clerks, warehousemen and shopworkers. 'Steady, sober-looking men' had come with their wives and in some cases their children. The hall was spacious and refreshment tables occupied the stalls area to which waiters brought drinks from the bar. As always the cheapest seats were in the balcony. The audience enjoyed a varied programme which included a comic quartet of singers, some child gymnasts and a tenor singing arias from a Verdi opera.[13] This appears an upmarket venue. Prices ranged from 6*d*. (less than 3p) in the balconies to 6*s*. 0*d*. (30p) for a private box. Elsewhere entrance fees were cheaper, often 3*d*. or less for the overcrowded and distant balcony. The cheaper halls crammed people in, and audiences were generally young. A year after the *Free Lance* report, 23 were killed in a fire panic at the Victoria, one of the cheapest halls in Manchester with admission charges of 2*d*. and 3*d*. Most victims occupied low price balcony seats and were killed in the crush on the stairs. Of those who died few were more than twenty years old.

Most Manchester music halls remained small concerns, essentially pubs with music licences catering for an average audience of around fifty drawn from neighbouring streets. By 1891 licences were held by some 400 of these smaller halls. But variety entertainment could be a lucrative business for some proprietors. Music hall entrepreneurs like Edward Moss built 'empires' both literally and commercially. By the turn of the century music hall was big business. In 1899 Moss Empires Ltd was formed with share capital of around £1m. This was the era of the giant hall which combined variety with circus acts. Audiences could be huge. In 1904 two new halls opened in Manchester, the Hippodrome on Oxford Street and the Ardwick Empire at Ardwick Green. The latter could house 3,000 and offered two houses nightly plus a Saturday matinée. It opened in July 1904 with Fred Karno's 'Speechless Comedians' topping the bill.

The Manchester Hippodrome was a feat of theatrical engineering.

More than a third of its area lay behind the proscenium arch, which was adjustable to be used either as a conventional music hall or to accommodate a circus ring. The stage area incorporated 24 concealed water jets for aquatic displays. 'A foot of water to a fathom at the touch of a lever' was the proud boast of a theatre which enabled boats to sail into the arena tank from back stage. At the back of the auditorium lay stables for the circus animals. For entrance fees of 6*d.* to 2*s.* 0*d.* the audience were offered horses, elephants, performing dogs, a trapeze artist plus numerous variety acts. These circus/variety performances left traditional music hall far behind. Such extravaganzas attracted an audience from all parts of the city and beyond and mark the complete commercialisation of what had begun as a spontaneous popular entertainment.

By the turn of the century the larger Manchester music halls occasionally included a film show put on by travelling showmen or local entrepreneurs. Many people saw their first film in a theatre or a fairground tent. The age of the moving picture had begun. The first recorded public film shows in Manchester were held in 1896 at the St James's Theatre, Oxford Street, and at the old YMCA building and the Lesser Free Trade Hall, both on Peter Street. Of these the Lumière brothers Cinematographe shows at the latter venue were the most sophisticated, showing French scenes of card players, factory girls, bicyclists and the arrival of a train at a country station. The admission charge of one shilling (5p) for a half hour performance suggests a select audience. Prices fell as shows multiplied. A year later the ever-enterprising Lewis's department store presented the Cinematographe at one of their 'penny concerts', showing every half hour from noon till 7 p.m. The programme included the death scene from *Trilby*, rough sea at Blackpool and Buffalo Bill's Circus. The Tivoli Music Hall became a regular venue and showed films of the Boer War, an event which demonstrated the appeal of the new medium. A cinematograph licence was issued in 1910, and in the 1920s the Tivoli became the Winter Garden Cinema. The pattern of future entertainment was set.

The city centre's first true cinemas opened after the Cinematograph Act of 1909 which required licences and strict fire regulations. Of these the most prestigious was the Picture House, Oxford Street, formally opened by the Lord Mayor on 15 December 1911 and in use as a cinema until 1980. Another of Manchester's earliest cinemas still shows films, despite a long period as a furniture store: what is now the Cornerhouse Cinema was opened in 1910 as the Kinemacolor Palace, showing colour (hand tinted, frame by frame) as well as black and white films. 'Comfortable tip-up seats' were offered for 3*d.* and 6*d.* and performances were continuous from 2 p.m. till 10.30 p.m. The 1920s and 1930s were the great age of popular picture-going, but prior to 1914 Mancunians had a choice of cinema viewing to complement (or rival)

Street scene, Rochdale Road. This scene of a main road through a working-class district is one of Samuel Coulthurst's fine series of Manchester photographs taken in the 1890s.

the attractions of the variety stage. The importance of this pioneer period is illustrated by the fact that of the 140 venues ever used as a cinema in Manchester, almost 100 had shown films before the First World War.

Thus the cinema, the dominant popular entertainment of the first half of the twentieth century, drew its first audiences in the nineteenth. The same is also true of the country's national sport. In the 1880s it cost around 3*d.* or 4*d.* to see a professional football match, although admission prices rose in the 1890s. It cost nothing to play on the street, and in that pre-car age there might be little to disturb the back-street game. It could be an obsession.

> So far as the boys are concerned ... in the North the game par excellence is football. From the days when they begin to go to school this is the one game which absorbs their attention ... In courts and alleys, on vacant plots of land, on brickfields, indeed where any open space at all may be found, attempts are made to play the game, even though the football be but a bundle of tightly rolled up, string-bound papers.[14]

When Charles Russell wrote those words, English professional football was almost thirty years old and Manchester United had twice been Division One champions (1908 and 1911) and F.A. Cup winners in 1909. The industrial North was a stronghold of the game. Six of the twelve clubs which founded the Football League in 1888 were from the North West (although not from Manchester).

United had begun in 1878, rather humbly, as the Newton Heath Lancashire and Yorkshire Railway F. C. (try shouting that from the terraces!). When financial problems threatened bankruptcy in 1902, a consortium of businessmen, led by the Manchester brewer John H. Davies, saved the club and had it renamed. For the 1906/7 season the re-formed club joined Manchester City (which began life as Ardwick F. C.) to give the town two First Division sides. Professional football was a major commercial enterprise. United's new ground, at Old Trafford, was opened in 1910, and 50,000 attended the inaugural match against Liverpool (which United lost 4–3). Football had become the workingman's sport whether as spectator or as player in the numerous amateur leagues. Club cricket was its only rival. Lancashire County C. C. played at its Old Trafford ground from 1864, and Manchester Cricket Club from even earlier. But the largest single crowd for any sporting event in the area gathered for the annual Whitsun Week Manchester Races.

Although there was never a Manchester wakes week, Whitsun served as the town's annual holiday. On the Thursday, Friday and Saturday of each Whitweek Manchester centre was deserted as the crowds moved to the Castle Irwell raceground in a loop of the river two miles north of the city. This was the week of the Manchester Races. It was not only the horse racing or even the betting which brought them but the sheer exuberance of the event. Manchester's publicans moved with their customers, erecting numerous white canvas drinking booths so that 'for three days in Whitweek the raceground at Castle Irwell becomes a complete canvas city of public houses'. The Manchester Races were the occasion for all kinds of disreputable pursuits from illegal gambling rings to prostitution. But they were very popular.

> You could not collect so many people together in favour of reform
> to save your life – nor even to see a man hanged, which shows
> that folk have their tastes in matters of amusement and that racing,
> whether for good or bad, is the most popular sport we have.[15]

Little wonder that Manchester's churches were so keen to absorb the leisure hours of Whitweek in the famous Whit walks. Alcohol was an essential ingredient of Manchester Races. And Whitweek may merely have occasioned an intensive bout of a distinctive Manchester pastime.

National levels of alcohol consumption were declining from the 1870s, but as late as 1892 Manchester had 3,031 licensed victuallers and beerhouse keepers, or one for every 167 inhabitants. This was little different from the situation in the 1840s and easily the highest ratio in Lancashire. Although Liverpool's population was larger it had over 800 fewer liquor licences than Manchester. The Mancunian's taste for beers and ales was well served by the several local breweries including Boddington's Strangeways Brewery, Joseph Holt's Derby Brewery at nearby Cheetham, Wilson's of Newton Heath, Chester's at Openshaw and the Salford brewers, Groves and Whitnall of Regent Road. Fittingly, Manchester housed the national headquarters of the U.K. Alliance, the body which campaigned for the prohibition of alcohol. However, all temperance reformers were up against it. Licensing laws were permissive until Lloyd George's wartime measure of 1916 severely restricted pub opening times. The desire to regulate the habits of the drinking classes was further complicated by the advent of portable bottled beers in the 1890s. Temperance beverages generally offered no real competition although there were exceptions. Vimto was Manchester's chief contribution to the soft drinks industry. John Noel Nichols, manufacturer of essences and cordials, first mixed his 'Vimtonic' concentrate in a backyard shed in Granby Row in 1908. At first he sold it to temperance bars and herbalist shops who added water and served it hot or cold. By 1911 Vimto was available ready mixed in bottles as a sparkling drink or as a cordial. It proved so popular that by the 1930s production at Nichol's Britannic Works in Stretford was on a scale large enough to supply Vimto to 27 countries.

Alongside the rise of spectator sports there emerged organised amateur recreations such as cycling and rambling. The earliest clubs in the area were formed by the YMCA in the 1880s. Such pursuits were considered 'manly' or 'healthy' for the young clerks and shopworkers who were typical YMCA members. The cycling craze took off after the invention of the safety bike in the mid-1880s and the growth of mass production. Cycling ceased to be the preserve of gentlefolk and came within the reach of working men and women. Cycling clubs proliferated. Best known locally was the Manchester Athletic Bicycle Club (founded in 1883) which changed its name to the Manchester Wheelers in 1889. This was a serious racing club but also had its recreational side, and members made regular excursions into the surrounding countryside. The Wheelers' annual subscription was two shillings (10p) plus one shilling for the National Cyclists Union. Additional costs, apart from the bicycle, involved a uniform for the men of grey jacket and knee breeches with black stockings (women were expected to tackle the bike ride in the long skirts of the period). This was in the reach of the better-off working and lower middle class. Cycling could be healthy and sociable. It offered a means of transport that was relatively cheap (no stables were required!) and very portable. Cycling clubs were a product of the greater leisure time and increased spending power of the skilled working class and the rising army of white-collar workers in office and shop. But the picture of advancing consumerism must not be overdrawn. Whilst rising real wages benefited some young workers many others, especially the unskilled or the casually employed, had to turn to simpler pleasures.

Manchester's city centre was a magnet for the young on a Saturday night even more than it is today. Many working people received their wages on a Saturday morning, and the afternoon football match, the long pub opening hours, the music hall and later the cinema were key attractions. But for those who had little or no wages to spend the city streets themselves provided free entertainment. Nowhere was this more evident than at the Saturday night markets which traditionally sold off food which would not keep till Monday and which were accompanied by a range of free or cheap amusements. Shudehill Market traded till ten o'clock on a Saturday. Alongside those looking for a cheap dinner for Sunday were others out to see the 'sights'; whole families, children in tow, courting couples and others alone or in small groups, but preponderantly young. On a Saturday night Shudehill was 'alive with animation, and amid a blaze of gas all [was] life and bustle'. It had all the fun of the fair with sideshows and street entertainers galore. Walking round the market was an entertainment in itself. Its historian has described it as a 'town within a town' for those 'who lived by economy rather than high fashion'. A contemporary who visited Shudehill at eight o'clock on a Saturday in April 1870 regarded Manchester's 'big market' as a 'great institution'.

> As we look upon the sea of faces, the owners of which swarm in thousands crushing, pushing, elbowing and swaying to and fro, whilst the general din proclaims that something is going on which is engrossing the minds of fifteen to twenty thousand men and women, we cannot help thinking how great is the subject of study before us. Life is here as it really.[16]

Education and Literacy

Mass education was a product of the nineteenth century. Before 1800 there were only a few, voluntarily-organised, schools for the children of labouring families; by 1900 elementary schooling was compulsory and enforced by the state. The key point in the evolution of the state system was the Education Act of 1870 which created a national network of elementary schools by adding locally financed 'Board Schools' to the existing pattern of voluntary provision. By 1899 free and compulsory attendance until the age of twelve was enforced by truant officers. Finally the Education Act of 1902 introduced state secondary schools and created Local Education Authorities to administer both levels of public provision. Manchester's poor record on school attendance and literacy in the first half of the nineteenth century has already been referred to,

A corner of Market Street. This was Manchester's main shopping thoroughfare. This photograph is notable for the newsboy at the bottom displaying a copy of the scurrilous Manchester periodical, the *Spy*.

and may go some way towards explaining the major role played by Manchester reformers in the campaigns for a rate-supported system of public elementary education which culminated in the 1870 Act.

Manchester was the birth-place of the state education lobby. The Lancashire (later National) Public Schools Association (LPSA), founded in 1847, was a product of the same Manchester tradition of radicalism which had given rise to the Anti-Corn Law League. Among its early members were Richard Cobden, Jacob Bright and Samuel Lucas (John Bright's younger brother and brother-in-law respectively). The LPSA campaigned for a rate-aided, locally controlled, non-sectarian education system. Whilst Leeds was the home of voluntaryist resistance to compulsory education, Manchester gave birth to a further movement for state provision. The secular approach of the LPSA was opposed by the Manchester and Salford Committee on Education formed in 1851 by Anglican and Methodist ministers and philanthropic-minded laymen of the Established Church like Oliver Heywood and W. R. Callender. Enjoying the influential patronage of Sir James Kay Shuttleworth (formerly James Phillips Kay), the new Committee got as far as promoting a local Education Bill within a few months. Both Manchester bodies favoured state-aided education but differed over the place of denominational schools in a state system. The debate continued within and beyond Manchester throughout the 1850s and 1860s until W. E. Forster steered his Education Bill through the Commons in 1870.

By this time both Manchester associations had fallen into abeyance and the National Education League, founded in Birmingham in 1869, was heir to the Manchester tradition of education reform. Meanwhile practical efforts within Manchester had further contributed to the public debate.

In response to a series of articles in the *Manchester Guardian* by local businessman Edward Brotherton, the Manchester Education Aid Society was formed in 1864. Brotherton, who had set out to describe at first hand the impoverished lives of the children of the poor, was to die two years later from an infection contracted on one of his slum visits. The Education Aid Society he inspired was a charity, the chief work of which was to pay the school fees of poor children. Its impact on the education debate arose from its self-acknowledged failure to bring more than two-fifths of 'neglected' children to school and the difficulties of keeping them there. The Society believed its work proclaimed 'the inefficiency of even the best constituted voluntary associations to secure the primary instruction of the people'.[17] There were few effective arguments left against a state system. Manchester's first Board School under the 1870 Act was opened in Vine Street, Hulme, in 1874.

Given the increasing literacy arising from the advent of mass education, what of the people's reading habits? The mass market for cheap fiction which grew up in the later nineteenth century affected Manchester no differently from any other provincial area. Apart from a few local publications, region gave way to metropolis in the furnishing of 'penny' fiction for the working class. What was distinctive about Manchester was its range of free library provision and the strength of its locally published newspapers.

The Free Library was founded at Campfield in 1852, but by 1877 had moved to the old Town Hall building on King Street. A central feature of the library system in Manchester was the early development of branch libraries in residential districts. Branch libraries in Hulme, Ancoats, Rochdale Road, Chorlton and Ardwick were all founded prior to the Education Act of 1870. By 1895, the city had eleven branch libraries and 49,516 card-holding borrowers. It was estimated that during 1894/5 the number of library visits totalled over 6.3m. or 18,844 a day. This suggested that use of the city's free library system had trebled since 1870, an increase in usage which far outstripped the city's population growth rate of under 50% for the same period.[18] Such had been the popularity of the system that Sunday opening was adopted in 1878. This controversial decision had generated considerable debate in the Council. A popular feature of Sunday opening was the reading rooms. These were often large halls with comprehensive stocks of periodicals. In addition boys' reading rooms (but none for girls) were provided to prevent their interference with adult readers and to cater for an age group which greatly worried contemporaries. The Hyde

Road Reading Room for Boys was open between 6 p.m. and 9 p.m. each evening and on Sundays. Papers stocked combined the exciting with the wholesome. Weeklies included the *Boys Own Paper, Chatterbox, Chums, Children's Own* as well as adult picture papers such as the *Graphic* and the *Illustrated London News*. Monthlies included the *Children's Friend, Little Folks, British Workman* and the *Band of Hope Review*, a temperance publication. During 1894/5 over 500,000 visits were recorded to the city's reading rooms for boys. That these rooms proved popular may have been due in no small part to the lack of alternative warm places outside the home during winter evenings.

Manchester's free reading rooms stocked local as well as national newspapers. The second half of the nineteenth century saw the origins of the modern popular press and it is likely that it was declining newspaper prices as much as rising literacy which explains the advent of a working-class readership. The repeal of Stamp Duties (the Taxes on Knowledge) made practicable the penny daily. But even at this price the *Manchester Guardian* and the *Manchester Courier* were still too expensive for many. Sixpence (under 3p) a week on newspapers was difficult to justify out of a labourer's wage of around £1. The falling price of newsprint plus increased advertising revenue, improvements in the speed of printing and the spread of the telegraph all cheapened newspaper production. They led to the key element in the emergence of a mass readership, the halfpenny evening paper.

The Manchester reader at the turn of the century could choose between three halfpenny evening papers, the *Manchester Evening News*, the *Manchester Evening Chronicle* and the *Manchester Evening Mail*. The *News* was founded in 1868 as virtually the first of the provincial evening papers. By 1891 it claimed a circulation of 152,000, probably the largest of any evening paper in the country. In 1897 it increased in size from four to six pages and carried extensive advertising and correspondence columns. It was referred to by the *Daily Mail* as 'beyond question the best and most popular provincial evening paper'.[19] The *News* was a stable-mate of the *Manchester Guardian*, broadly Liberal in politics and regarded as a comparatively 'serious' read. The political potential of reaching a mass audience in an increasingly democratic electorate did not escape the attention of the political parties. When the Tory *Manchester Evening Mail* folded in 1902 after 28 years of publication, local Conservatives tried desperately, although unsuccessfully, to come up with a 'really smart sheet' to replace it.[20]

The *Chronicle*, first published in 1897, was reckoned to be the 'lightest' of the three evening dailies but even this paper, as was the fashion of the time, covered its front page with classified advertisements. In fact these halfpenny newspapers were sober and serious by twenty-first-century standards. Although illustrated (with photographs by the early twentieth century) their journalism made few concessions to the

Piccadilly by Wellington's statue at the end of the nineteenth century. Note the broad and busy open space in front of the Infirmary and the roadway congested with horse-drawn trams, carts and hansom cabs.

semi-literate. Political news was the stock in trade, although sports coverage, especially football reporting, and weekend serials were undoubted draws. The less literate end of the market was catered for by a new brand of weekly epitomised by George Newnes's *Titbits*, started in Manchester in 1881. Newnes's distinctive blend of popular psychology and humour, culled from the press of the world (especially the USA), opened up a market for sub-news publications.

Manchester in 1914

By the early twentieth century Manchester covered a much larger area than it had in 1850. The municipal imperialism that had swallowed up the surrounding townships was merely a recognition of the existence of the Manchester conurbation, the arrival of urban sprawl.[21] The green spaces were gone which once had separated the old town from surrounding townships and hamlets such as Ardwick, Rusholme, Harpurhey and Broughton. As for the city centre itself, the street pattern had taken

Manchester's first electric trams. The introduction of this service was an occasion of note (and the excuse for a block-purchase of potted plants!).

on most of its modern shape. Corporation Street had cut a swathe through the rambling byways of the old town in 1845. Portland Street was extended to meet Oxford Street in the 1850s. Albert Square was created in the 1860s as a prelude to the building of the Town Hall in the 1870s. Whitworth Street was laid out and lined with its distinctive terracotta warehouses in the 1890s. By now the central business district incorporated several discrete zones. The warehouse mansions of the cotton merchants around Portland Street contrasted with the more workmanlike premises of the wholesale provision traders at the Withy Grove/Fennell Street end of town where the impressive headquarters of the Cooperative Wholesale Society dominated the northern stretch of Corporation Street. The upper reaches of King Street and Spring Gardens had taken on a sober and serious character appropriate to the city's banking and insurance quarter. By 1914 the Royal Infirmary had been removed from the Piccadilly site it had occupied since 1752, and thus had been created Manchester's most notable open space, although it was to take some time before the decision was finally taken to leave it undeveloped, as a public garden.

What kind of place was it to visit? The day tripper from the suburbs or nearby mill town might well have come for the shopping. The town's importance as a centre of the retail trade has already been referred to. Late Victorian and Edwardian Manchester had no shopping attraction to rival Lewis's department store. Lewis's used the most up-to-date American techniques to pull in the customers. Rather than advertising brand name goods, as is the case in the modern shop, the intention was to advertise the store itself, to make it an exciting place to visit. The use of moving picture shows as a draw had been preceded by stereoscopic machines, distorting mirrors and penny-in-the-slot Edison phonographs. Lewis's boasted the biggest soda fountain in the Empire and once, to proclaim the delights of Venice, flooded the sub-basement and invited customers to sail on gondolas. This was for the mass audience of consumers. The more discerning, because wealthy, shoppers could be found frequenting the most fashionable retailers around St Ann's Square and Exchange Street or along lower King Street. These were places of elegant promenade and exclusive shops selling jewellery, fine dresses and millinery, books and pictures. Laden with purchases the weary shopper might seek refreshment in one of the city's numerous cafes, tea shops and restaurants. Some might come to rest at Parker's in St Ann's Square or Meng and Ecker in St Ann's Passage. Whilst many more would search out the nearest Lyons.

Although the noise and air pollution of the automobile was largely a thing of the future, the streets of the late Victorian city were not without their offensive smells. In an age when the nation had over one million horses in its towns, shoppers knew enough to watch where they walked! Whilst many may have come by train, the horse-drawn omnibus or tram remained the commonest form of public transport for the shorter journey. Manchester's trams were not electrified till after 1900, and in 1893 the 385 tramcars of the Manchester Carriage Company had required 3,583 horses to pull them. City centre streets were regularly congested with horse-drawn traffic of every description. Bearing in mind that a single horse might produce four tons of manure each year, and that horses were not the only large beasts resident in the city (there were 57 registered cow-keepers with 664 cows in Manchester in 1890), then animal droppings seem a potential hazard of literally enormous proportions! Animals require feed, and fortunately this was the occasion of a profitable exchange between farmer and town-dweller. Local farmers provided the hay to feed the horses and cattle and in return purchased the manure for their land. Usually the larger carriage companies dealt directly with farmers. The electrification of the tramways and the advent of the motor bus were to reduce the number of horses on the streets, but it was a slow process and horse-drawn traffic remained a feature of urban life well in to the age of the motorised vehicle.

Manchester in 1914 was a healthier place than it had been in 1850 and there had been some improvement in the housing stock, but much greater advances were to be achieved by the 'housing' and 'health' revolutions of the next seventy-five years. There had been a general advance in real wages, especially after 1885, and the quality of life for many had undoubtedly improved, but stark inequalities remained. Increased leisure and the advent of consumerism for some of the working class was paralleled by the pockets of sometimes desperate poverty that existed in the Edwardian period, and were still there to be discovered by the social investigator in the 1930s. The pattern of working-class housing has changed dramatically since the nineteenth century, and a Victorian visitor to the present would be lost in modern Hulme or Ancoats. However, she would be less surprised by the spectacle of beggars on city centre streets. Despite overall improvements in the quality of life since 1914, which would stagger the time-travelling Victorian, British cities can still offer a display of sometimes startling inequalities.

References

1. For references in this paragraph see A. J. Kidd and K. W. Roberts (eds), *City, Class and Culture*, Manchester University Press, 1985, pp. 50–1, 69.
2. F. Scott, 'The condition and occupations of the people of Manchester and Salford', *Transactions of the Manchester Statistical Society* (1888–9), pp. 93–116.
3. E. H. Hunt, *Regional Wage Variations in Britain 1850–1914*, Oxford University Press, 1973, pp. 68–9.
4. B. R. Mitchell, *British Historical Statistics*, Cambridge University Press, 1988, pp. 149–50.
5. M. Busteed, 'Little islands of Erin: Irish settlement and identity in mid-nineteenth-century Manchester', *Immigrants and Minorities*, 18 (1999), pp. 94–127; *idem*, 'Songs in a strange land: ambiguities of identity among Irish migrants in mid-Victorian Manchester', *Political Geography*, 17 (1998), pp. 627–65.
6. Figures in this and the preceding paragraph from S. Fielding, 'Irish politics in Manchester 1890–1914', *International Review of Social History*, XXXIII (1988), pp. 261–84.
7. R. Leidtke, *Jewish Welfare in Hamburg and Manchester, c. 1850–1914*, Oxford, 1998.
8. Quoted in B. Williams, 'The anti-semitism of tolerance: middle-class Manchester and the Jews 1870–1900', in Kidd and Roberts, *City, Class and Culture*. Henry Yeo, the *Spy*'s disreputable owner and author of its anti-semitic propaganda, was twice imprisoned for criminal libel in the 1890s. Compared with the Jews and the Irish, Manchester's other migrant groups have been neglected, though see P. DiFelice, 'Italians in Manchester 1891–1939: settlement and occupations', *Local Historian*, 30 (2000), pp. 88–104.
9. A. Ransome and W. Rayston, *Report Upon the Health of Manchester and Salford During the Last Fifteen Years*, Manchester and Salford Sanitary Association, 1867, pp. 11, 13.
10. This statistic and most others in this section are from the work of Marilyn Pooley, see M. Pooley, 'Geographical and demographic approaches to

medical history' in J. V Pickstone (ed.), *Health, Disease and Medicine in Lancashire 1750–1950*, Department of History of Science and Technology, UMIST, Manchester, 1980, pp. 60–1; M. Pooley and C. Pooley, 'Health, society and environment in Victorian Manchester' in R. Woods and J. Woodward (eds), *Urban Disease and Mortality in Nineteenth Century England*, Batsford, London, 1984. Together these constitute an important contribution to the history of the nation's health in the nineteenth century.

11. See T. R. Marr, *Housing Conditions in Manchester and Salford*, Sherratt and Hughes, Manchester, 1904, pp. 30–1, 45; also A. Sharratt and K. R. Farrar, 'Sanitation and public health in nineteenth-century Manchester', *Memoirs and Proceedings of the Manchester Literary and Philosophical Society*, 114 (1971–2), p. 67. The claim about the role of personal hygiene is in Pooley and Pooley (1984).

12. For such maps see Pooley and Pooley (1984).

13. *Free Lance*, 1 (1867), pp. 5–6. From a series of articles, 'How Manchester is Amused'.

14. C. E. B. Russell, *Social Problems of the North* (1913), Garland, New York, 1980, pp. 99–100. Other parts of town were host to a different, more menacing type of street gathering as sporadic violence broke out between so-called 'scuttling' gangs of youths between 14 and 19 years of age. There were hundreds of gang-related incidents in the later part of the century involving male youths often armed with knives; see A. Davies, 'Youth gangs, masculinity and violence in late Victorian Manchester and Salford', *Journal of Social History*, 32 (1998), pp. 349–69.

15. *Free Lance*, 1 (1867), p. 202. The Races had moved from Kersal Moor to Castle Irwell in that year.

16. The figures may be an imaginative overestimate. Quotations in this paragraph from the *Shadow* and *Free Lance* cited in A. Davies, 'Saturday night markets in Manchester and Salford 1840–1939', *Manchester Region History Review*, I:ii (1987), pp. 3–12.

17. Quoted in S. E. Maltby, *Manchester and the Movement for National Elementary Education 1800–1870*, Manchester University Press, 1918, p. 97.

18. Library statistics in this section from, W. R. Credland, *The Free Library Movement in Manchester*, Manchester Public Free Libraries, Manchester, 1895; *idem.*, *The Manchester Public Free Libraries*, Public Free Libraries Committee, Manchester, 1899.

19. Cited in J. Nicholson, 'Popular imperialism and the provincial press: Manchester evening and weekly papers, 1895–1902', *Victorian Periodicals Review*, XII (1980), p. 87.

20. See C. Buckley, 'The search for a "really smart sheet": the Conservative evening newspaper project in Edwardian Manchester', *Manchester Region History Review*, I:i (1987), pp. 21–8.

21. For a vivid contemporary portrait of this urban sprawl, see W. Haslam Mills, 'Manchester of Today' in H. M. McKechnie (ed.), *Manchester in 1915: Handbook for the 85th Meeting of the British Association for the Advancement of Science*, Manchester, 1915.

CHAPTER 8

City and Suburb:
Leadership and Authority
in Victorian Manchester

It is a curious fact that, as a rule, the family firms of the industrial revolution did not form durable dynasties. Whereas the aristocratic tradition had been to preserve the family estate from generation to generation a business established by an industrialist or a merchant rarely remained in the family beyond the second generation. The sons and grandsons of successful entrepreneurs often had little taste for business. Sent by their fathers to public school, they acquired the manners and expectations of 'gentlemen'. The next logical step, for those who could afford it, was the purchase of a country estate, preferably in the South, and assimilation into the higher social circles of the county set and the London 'Season'. The industrial and provincial character of their origins would be left far behind.

Many existing country houses were refurbished and new ones built to the specifications of self-exiled northern businessmen. From Manchester the diaspora could be far and wide. Thus the multitudinous branches of the mercantile Philips family set down their roots in four counties; building Heath House in Staffordshire in the 1830s, remodelling Lee Priory in Kent and Abbey Cwmhir in Radnorshire in the 1860s and establishing a country estate at Welcombe in Warwickshire in 1867. An early and exceptional example of how new status could be acquired is that of Samuel Jones Loyd, born in 1796 into an immensely successful Manchester banking family and educated at Eton and Cambridge. In 1848 he assumed control of the London branch of the family business. He and his father, Lewis Loyd, spent almost sixty years between them building up an estate of over 30,000 acres called Overstone Park in Northamptonshire at a cost approaching £2m. The Loyds were multi-millionaires, and Samuel was much respected in the City of London. Reputed to be worth over £5m. and one of the richest men in England, he was popularly known as 'Lord Overgold'. In 1850 he was elevated to the official aristocracy, taking the more respectful title of Lord Overstone. This was one of the few 'industrial' peerages created before 1890. However, only a minority of Manchester's businessmen had the opportunity and resources to gain entry to the

The gates to Victoria Park, Rusholme.

landed aristocracy, and several that could nevertheless chose not to sever all links with the city. But the opportunity seized by an elite few was the tip of an iceberg of ambition of the many.

Middle-Class Havens

The process whereby Manchester's early nineteenth century social elite withdrew from the public life of the city is often remarked upon although not fully researched. In fact it operated on several levels within the Manchester middle class, according to status and aspirations. Many sought to escape from the city's environs as the industrial grime spread outwards and the working class encroached on former suburbs like Ardwick Green in Manchester and the Crescent in Salford. Those who did not depart the world of business entirely sometimes sought refuge along the rail routes into Cheshire or Lancashire, establishing small estates and grand mansions. Still greater numbers bought fine villas in tree-lined suburbs beyond the city smoke or escaped to the exclusiveness of a residential estate like Victoria Park. Some settled for the remoter but more bracing climes of the Lancashire coast, especially Southport and Lytham. Others eventually made use of the good rail link to the Lake District.

The railway greatly facilitated the businessman's escape. Those who moved out to the coast or the Lakes used the train to reach their places of work. By the 1890s the daily ebb and flow of business commuters was so well established that it paid the Lancashire and Yorkshire Railway to offer a 'Blackpool Club Train' whereby first-class season ticket holders paid extra for saloon accommodation with light refreshments

Marylands, Lower Park Road, Rusholme (1860s). (*Photograph: Ian Beesley*)

on the morning and evening expresses. These were the days before corridor trains and the exclusive club cars gave the wealthy a clear mark of distinction. Commuting in this manner was comfortable and feasible, with a journey time to and from fashionable Lytham of only sixty minutes. Later the London and North Western Railway offered a similar service on the longer journey to and from Windermere in the Lakes. By 1910 this took a shade over two hours. Oliver Westall has imaginatively reconstructed the scene as the 'Windermere Club Train' prepared to leave Manchester.

> Imagine the bustle ... of ... Exchange Station at about five o'clock on a Friday afternoon in summer in the early years of this century. Amid the confusion there lies waiting the Windermere Express and attached to this a coach which formed a very private sanctuary from the heat, crowds and muddle, for admission was only for the members of a select club. Within ... sat its members discussing ... the movements on the 'Change during the week ... in a relaxed atmosphere that indicated ... serious work was behind them and ... they were beginning to adjust to the temper of a country weekend.[1]

Regular passengers on this route included Sir William Crossley, the engineer, director of the Ship Canal Company and notable philanthropist, and Sir James Scott, chairman of Haslam's cotton manufacturers and a director of the Manchester and County Bank.

A solution to the problem of exclusiveness which did not require a lengthy rail journey was to surround residential estates with fences and toll-bars to keep out intruders. Victoria Park, Rusholme, established in 1837, set a fashion for such enclosures. Ellesmere Park at Eccles and Fielden Park in Didsbury were the closest imitators. The owner of a 'gentleman's residence' in Victoria Park could combine the advantages of town life with the privacy of a 'country seat'. Once inside the massive iron perimeter gates the resident's carriage curved along crescent and drive to arrive at the pillars and portico of his own private mansion. Victoria Park remained an attractive option until 1914, although its encirclement by the growth of Rusholme 'without the gates' meant that new building became progressively more modest.

The railway, however, was an essential ingredient in this migration to the suburbs. An early illustration was the colonisation of Alderley Edge, also an instance of the contribution made by tourism to the growth of the commuter belt. The Manchester and Birmingham Railway, opened in 1842, stopped at Alderley and soon attracted sightseers to the wooded Edge. The placing of a station barely two miles down the line from the more important stop at Wilmslow was undoubtedly intended to exploit the day-excursion market from Manchester. The day-trippers soon arrived. The resident gentry, the Stanleys at Park House, found these tourists a great nuisance, though Lady Stanley complained that Manchester's 'cottentot grandees' were more annoying than the operatives 'as one can neither hand cuff nor great dog them if they are intrusive'.[2] The Stanleys must have been alarmed when the 'cottentots' began building their villas on the hill approaching the Edge. A further line of advance was created when the Manchester South Junction and Altrincham Railway was opened in 1849. Although there had been a few merchants and manufacturers resident along the Chester Road at Timperley, Altrincham and Bowden prior to 1849, without the railway these places would have remained rural backwaters until the advent of the motor car.

Alderley and Altrincham marked the limits of the suburban invasion of Cheshire. By the end of the century they were among a string of dormitory suburbs along the rail routes to the south. Suburban clusters surrounded the stations of the London line at Wilmslow, Cheadle Hulme, Bramhall and Heaton Moor. Sale and Stretford grew up on the Altrincham line. Closer to Manchester, Withington and Didsbury had developed on the Wilmslow Road horse omnibus route since the 1830s, but the Midland line from Central Station ensured their future in the 1880s. In the 1890s Withington and Didsbury stations together were booking around 1,250 passengers each working day. With season ticket holders this rose to 2,500. The opening of an electric tram route in 1904 cut into this traffic but did nothing to decrease population growth in these suburbs. By this time the social mix of the inner suburbs

included better-off artisans and clerks. The suburban ideal was beginning its inexorable progress down the social scale. By 1900 the railway
had given the Manchester conurbation its modern shape and Manchester had spread itself across northern Cheshire. The escape routes north
were less attractive as one quickly ran into independent-minded Lancashire towns such as Oldham and Rochdale. The 'unspoilt' pleasantness
of the south was more conducive to the creation of a rural idyll. Minor
exceptions were the suburban developments along the Bury line at
Prestwich and Crumpsall and astride the Warrington line at Urmston
and Flixton.

Before leaving Manchester's 'cottentots' in their mansions and villas,
it is worth a brief diversion to consider the character of the dormitory
villages they created. Katherine Chorley has left us a vivid portrait of
life at Alderley Edge around the turn of the century.[3] Her autobiography
describes the 'man-made and man-lorded' society they gave birth to.
Each morning the businessmen caught the 8.25, 8.50 or 9.18 trains into
Manchester. They travelled first class in a male preserve. For any woman
to join them 'would have been unthinkable ... a sort of indelicacy'.
Wives and daughters who had to travel on the 'rush hour' trains went
third class. After the 9.18 had pulled out of the station, the Edge became
exclusively female. The only males to be found on the roads were the
gardener, the plumber or perhaps the doctor. The Alderley Edge ladies
lived a life of polite gentility. Paying calls took up a couple of afternoons.
The younger ladies played golf and tennis whilst the older ones indulged
in more sedentary games at the card table. Some gave time to philanthropic pursuits such as 'sewing for charity' or even visiting Ancoats
housewives, carefully selected from the lists of an accredited charity.
All the ladies produced embroideries; needlecraft was still the hallmark
of a 'useful' upbringing. But each afternoon and by midday on Saturday
the women of Alderley prepared themselves once more 'to bask in the
sunshine of masculine society' as the men came home from business.
They were the dependent sex in a man's world. Trained to be passive,
the Alderley ladies offered little support to the suffrage movement.
Suburbs like these were enclaves of middle-class respectability in which
snobbery was endemic and suburban rivalry almost tribal. Whilst Edge
society assumed that 'no good thing would come out of Wilmslow', the
settlement one stop up the line to Manchester, they themselves were
looked down on by the elitist band even further out at Peover. Such
were the petty snobberies of the suburban world.

The 'Natural Leaders'

As we have seen, the residential segregation which had resulted by
1850 in the congested slums of central Manchester, the inner ring of

Afternoon tea on the lawn in a suburban garden, Cheetham Hill.

working-class terraces, the outer belt of middle-class suburbs and the far-flung retreats of the business aristocracy was further refined as the century progressed. For the middle class of all social grades the big change was the move from the city centre. But this process of 'withdrawal' gave rise to the objection that in removing themselves from its environs, the city's 'natural leaders' had severed all links with its civil life. The loss of their leadership was regarded as the cause of many social ills. Charles Rowley, writing in 1899 summed up the complaint:

> In the old days in Manchester, every leading trader, employer, and so forth, lived in or near to the town and was known to everybody. He was, as a rule, a chum in his own workshop or warehouse. He felt his corporate duty and obligations. Now, you do not know our leading merchants etc., and our city is represented, for the most part if not entirely, by strangers, who have no real touch with the work-a-day community.[4]

Rowley felt that if 'God made the country and man made the town', then 'the Devil made the suburbs'. The 'isolated conceit' of the 'suburb dweller', he maintained, had meant a loss of interest in the city's problems, its local government and its social needs. Thus the 'separation of the classes' was revived as an explanation for civil discord and once again, as they had done in the 1840s, reformers blamed an absence of middle-class leadership for the presumed faults of the masses. Was this oft-repeated complaint any more valid in the 1890s than it had been in the 1840s? What were the effects on Manchester's civic and social life of the rise of the suburb? Firstly, the matter of civic leadership.

Rowley's complaint appears to be substantiated by the observations of Beatrice Webb when she visited the city in 1899 as part of her research into local government. She was of the opinion that the municipal council she witnessed at work in Manchester was of poor quality, consisting largely of 'hard-headed shopkeepers'.[5] This has become an influential view amongst historians and has tended to characterise our view of local politics in late Victorian Manchester. But had Manchester's social leaders abandoned the management of the city to shopkeepers? In fact the withdrawal of the town's social elite from civic affairs should not be overdrawn. The early years of the Manchester council had been dominated by important local businessmen. Figures like the banker William Neild and wealthy merchant Thomas Potter, the first mayor, led the Liberal fraction of the business class into the municipal era. Although the appeal of national politics, especially of the Anti-Corn Law League, may have drawn many from the civic arena, manufacturers and merchants still made up around one third of the Council from the 1850s through till the 1880s. In fact, as a group, merchants and manufacturers had outnumbered shopkeepers at least for the first forty years of the council's existence, providing an average of 37% of council members over the 1838–1875 period.[6] There was a marked decline in the participation of manufacturers and merchants during the last quarter of the century, but the proportion of seats going to retailers was balanced by a process neither Rowley nor Webb may have recognised, the rise of professionals (lawyers, engineers, architects, journalists and the medical profession), who were to outnumber retailers on the City Council by 1914. As for the presumed decline in the quality of civic leadership, it should be remembered that this was the era in which Manchester Corporation had the imagination to underwrite the Ship Canal project. Hard-headed perhaps, but not without vision.

Charles Rowley's complaint against the suburbs was not confined to the matter of civic leadership but also involved a presumed lack of concern for the city's social problems. There is some truth in this, though it exaggerates the degree of involvement earlier in the century. It should not, however, suggest that a country estate or a public school education automatically destroyed all sense of affiliation with the old home town. While many did abandon the city for good, several eminent families stayed in touch and were highly regarded locally. Many put their energies into voluntary action. Moreover, enough of the city's rising professional middle class displayed a civic conscience which stretched beyond the worlds of the business district and the suburb. In the period before the Liberal welfare reforms of 1906–1914 (such as free school meals, old age pensions, labour exchanges and national insurance) most people with influence expected private action to contribute much to the solution of social problems. In this, Manchester's social leaders were no exception.

A good example of a Manchester businessman who devoted his energies to the city's social needs was Herbert Philips. The Philipses were one of the city's great mercantile families. Although Herbert Philips inherited an extensive estate in Staffordshire, he was a remarkably vigorous philanthropist in his home town. Retired early from business, he devoted himself to what might now be called urban renewal as well as to more traditional charities. He campaigned earnestly, if not always successfully, for open spaces in working-class districts. A Committee for Securing Open Spaces for Recreation came into being through his efforts. He founded the Noxious Vapours Abatement Association, acting as both its president and treasurer. His most prominent post was as president of the Manchester and Salford District Provident Society, a position he held for the twenty years up to his death in 1905. Other institutions which were part of his public work included the Young Men's Christian Association, the Manchester Warehousemen and Clerk's Orphan Schools and the Manchester and Salford Reformatory Schools for Juvenile Criminals. In 1897 the freedom of the city was conferred on him for his public service. Other philanthropic figures of comparable stature included Benjamin Armitage, Hugh Hornby Birley and Oliver Heywood. The importance of voluntary societies to the Victorian provincial bourgeoisie is often noted. Such endeavour was not only an outlet for personal concern but also an expression of social authority. By the mid-Victorian period there was already a long tradition of charitable provision in Manchester.

By 1850 the town already supported a variety of voluntary hospitals and medical charities. The most notable of the former was the Manchester Royal Infirmary, founded in 1752. This prime example of civic philanthropy dominated Piccadilly until its demolition in 1910 and subsequent relocation to its present buildings on Oxford Road. Other voluntary hospitals included Manchester Royal Eye Hospital begun in 1818 as the Manchester Institution for Curing Diseases of the Eye; St Mary's Hospital for Women and Sick Children (1854) and the Ancoats Hospital (1872). The two latter institutions had evolved from earlier charitable foundations, St Mary's from the Lying-In Hospital whose greatest benefactor had been Hugh Hornby Birley and Ancoats Hospital from the charitable dispensary which operated in this working-class district from 1828. Dispensaries were a common response to the medical needs of the poor in the early nineteenth century. Like voluntary hospitals they were funded by subscribers, served by unpaid physicians and surgeons and attended only to poor patients nominated by subscribers. Unlike hospitals, dispensaries had no beds and dealt only with out-patients. Although dispensaries were cheaper to fund, by 1900 most surviving institutions had evolved into infirmaries. Perception of the medical requirements of the needy had changed. Despite this, medical charities like these never reached more than a small proportion of the sick poor.

A huge variety of philanthropic societies operated in later Victorian Manchester, but it is difficult to assess how widespread was support. Casual giving generally leaves no record. The only guide is the annual reports of the charities themselves which listed contributors. A contemporary survey of 10,500 charity subscribers found that nearly 8,200 (78%) subscribed to only one society; 1,065 gave to two; whilst a minority of 420 (4%) supported more than five.[7] Charitable motives were mixed, often combining compassion with religious zeal, and inclined to favour the helpless (especially children in need), but also extending to alarm at the threat to public order arising from unemployment and homelessness. Whilst some gave or worked without thought of reward, for others philanthropy offered a route to status. The socially concerned and publicly prominent citizen was expected to be a patron of the poor and helpless. It was part of the civic duty, the obligation which 'the great and the good' owed the city which had made them rich or welcomed them as wealthy or talented acquisitions. Well-advertised support for a prominent charity (subscribers' names were always made public) was a most acceptable way of combining social authority and public spirit. Moreover, visible support for local charities could also be a pre-requisite for electoral success.[8] Many of Manchester's 'natural leaders' may have turned their backs on the city, but the vibrancy of local charities suggests that some at least had stayed to pay the debt of Dives.

From the 1860s to the 1890s there ensued a stream of charities for the poor, many of which provided institutions for the reform as well as the relief of particular categories of destitution such as orphans, street children, 'fallen women', 'girls in moral danger', discharged and juvenile criminals and the homeless. They were a response to the 'separation of the classes', precisely that problem which Charles Rowley had associated with the middle-class exodus to the suburbs. The Boys and Girls Welfare Society (founded in 1870) pioneered techniques later used by Dr Barnado in the rescue of 'street arabs'. The Manchester Ladies Association for the Protection and Reformation of Girls and Women (1882) established its own home to provide training for domestic service for 'girls in moral danger'. Employment was usually found in the houses of the wealthy ladies who ran the Society.

Charitable work, or social work as it was being called by the 1890s, provided one of the few paths into the sphere of public service for middle-class women. The Victorian woman was the 'angel in the house'. Her proper sphere was the domestic one. However, charity work, workhouse visiting and sanitary campaigning might each be acceptable outlets into the public sphere at a time when politics and other arenas of public life were generally barred to women. Some of the social work done or organised by Manchester women was of great significance. For example, the Manchester and Salford Ladies Sanitary Reform Association, formed in 1862, may justifiably claim the credit for inventing health-visiting. Working-class women were employed and trained by the Association to teach hygiene to poor women in their homes. In the early days this often consisted solely of a demonstration of the power of disinfectant and medicated soap against verminous insects. But the reputation of the Association's work grew, and from 1890 six of its fourteen health visitors were paid by the Manchester Corporation in response to panic about the city's persistently high infant mortality rate. By 1907 all the visitors were employed and supervised by the Corporation's Infant Life Protection sub-committee. As in many areas of social work, the voluntary sector pioneered activities later taken over by publicly funded bodies.

For most of the charitably-minded, involvement stopped short at fund-raising, but for a few charity work was central to their lives. A great many hours of committee work and fund-raising were put in by a dedicated minority of business and professional people. Often religion determined the charity supported. As with voluntary-funded schools, charitable effort was often divided along denominational lines. Roman Catholic and Jewish charities were especially active in Manchester, but the Methodists provided two of the city's most imaginative charitable fund-raisers of the Victorian period. Over one hundred years later both are still in operation: the Manchester and Salford Methodist Mission founded in 1886 and based in Central Hall on Oldham Street and the Wood Street Mission which began work in the slums of Deansgate in 1869.

The Wood Street Mission is an instance of the sometimes startling range of social work undertaken by some Victorian charities. The Manchester and Salford Street Children's Mission was popularly known as the Wood Street Mission after it moved in 1873 to its present site now in the shadow of the John Rylands' Library (the current Mission building was opened in 1905). Initially a workingmen's church and ragged school, its activities expanded to include a mission hall, a rescue society and home for destitute and neglected boys (plus holiday homes in Southport), a Sunday school, a temperance club and band of hope, and a soup kitchen and night shelter for the homeless. The driving force behind all this work was Alfred Alsop, a Primitive Methodist of humble origins who began street corner preaching at the age of sixteen. Alsop was a promotional genius whose publishing enterprises raised valuable funds. His semi-fictional accounts of slum life were intended to appeal to the conscience of the middle-class giver. Beginning with penny tracts boasting stark titles like *A Cry for Help*, *Hells of the City* and *Arabs of Deansgate*, he later ventured into the realm of novel and

Manchester and Salford Street Children's Mission, Wood Street. A tea party for the children of poor families, c. 1905. (*Courtesy of Manchester Central Library*)

short story writing, under the pseudonym of 'A Delver'. His were solemn and sentimental tales of drunkenness and cruelty to children with titles such as *Below the Surface or Down in the Slums* and *Street Children Sought and Found.* His monthly magazine *Delving and Diving* claimed a circulation of 60,000, though most copies were distributed in search of the charitable donation. Whilst Alsop's activities provided evangelical fervour the management of Wood Street was in other hands. Local businessmen like the engineer Charles J. Galloway and the clothing manufacturer Edward Tootal Broadhurst supported the Mission and John Rylands was a trustee, though most of the active management was done by prominent professionals notably the solicitor C. J. Needham who was a mainstay of Wood Street until his death in 1899.[9]

A small minority went further than committee work or home visiting and actually settled among the poor. Thus in 1889 the wealthy engineer and Salvation Army supporter, Francis Crossley, abandoned the comforts of his mansion in Bowden to live at a 'reclaimed' music hall, the Star in Ancoats, which he and his wife converted into a temperance mission. Also in Ancoats, the University Settlement began its work in 1895. Initially sharing accommodation with T. C. Horsfall's Art Museum in Ancoats Hall, the former home of the Mosley family, the Manchester University Settlement was to offer generations of idealistic young men and women the opportunity of collective residence amongst the poor so as the better to tackle educational and social work. For most of its life (it still exists) the Manchester Settlement was housed in Every Street. Neither of these locations was in the poorest quarters. The Settlement Movement's historian notes that it 'generally sought the respectable working class, ... settlement houses were set in dreary but decent streets, often with a sprinkling of white-collar workers, shopkeepers and small employers amongst their inhabitants'.[10] By 1900 charity work was becoming professionalised with training courses for social workers replacing the amateur voluntarism of the Victorian philanthropist. The expectation of social reform by central government may have contributed to the declining status attached to the performance of charitable duties. The city still commemorated its notable philanthropists – a statue of Oliver Heywood was erected in Albert Square in 1894 – but by then the great age of Victorian philanthropy had passed.

Municipal Achievements

Nineteenth-century Manchester was a symbol of economic individualism. It seemed natural that this product of the unplanned pursuit of wealth should have become the intellectual home of free trade. Until the late 1870s its chief public buildings were the Royal Exchange and the Free Trade Hall, homages in stone to unfettered commerce. Yet 1877 saw the completion of the huge gothic pile which is Manchester Town Hall. Nine years in the making and at the cost of £1m., it was a municipal monument grand in scale and imposing in presence (thanks to Albert Square). Manchester's Town Hall was meant to show the world that the city took its self-government seriously.

During the second half of the nineteenth century the Manchester Corporation organised a complex local administration encompassing social services and public utilities. Moreover, the municipal boundaries were successively extended between 1885 and 1913. The area covered by the new borough created in 1838 had been 4,293 acres. By 1913 the area had increased five-fold, and Corporation authority extended over 21,645 acres. As well as the Manchester township the original borough consisted of the townships of Chorlton-on-Medlock, Hulme, Ardwick, Beswick and Cheetham. In 1885 Harpurhey, Bradford and Rusholme were added, followed by Blackley, Moston, Crumpsall, Newton Heath, Openshaw, Kirkmanshulme and West Gorton in 1890. Moss Side, Withington, Burnage, Chorlton-cum-Hardy, Didsbury, Gorton and Levenshulme were incorporated in 1904 and 1909. The last phase of expansion was to come with the acquisition of Wythenshawe in 1930.

These extensions of the municipal boundary ushered in a period of rising rateable values, thus adding to the city's prosperity. The consequent increase in the value of the rate was crucial to the substantial capital projects undertaken by the city at the turn of the century. Quite apart from the Ship Canal, by 1905 Manchester had invested £7.4m. in water, £2.6m. in gas, £2.3m. in electricity supply and £2m. in tramways. Its municipal enterprise exceeded in capital scale and annual turnover many of the nation's leading manufacturers. How and why did the living symbol of free trade succumb to corporate provision on such a scale?

The motive of civic pride was probably less important than the practical advantage to be gained from effective sewage disposal, fresh water supplies, efficient public transport and reliable energy supplies. The business class of Manchester had realised that they could not rely on the market for their public utilities. Water is a case in point.[11] Fresh water supplies are an essential requisite of good public health. The lack of pure water, as we have seen, was a major cause of disease. A healthier workforce was one of the advantages to be gained from municipal enterprise. Moreover, the market had patently failed in this area. The

Manchester Town Hall, designed by Alfred Waterhouse. (*Photograph: Ian Beesley*)

Manchester Town Hall. *(Photograph: Ian Beesley)*

Manchester and Salford Waterworks Company supplied the town's water in the 1830s and 1840s. It had only short-term projects in mind, and its vision did not extend beyond the next meeting of the share-holders. Manchester Corporation bought out the private water company in 1847 and set about an ambitious programme to supply water to every house and business premise in the town. This took more than the next half-century to achieve. It involved huge capital investment in the digging of reservoirs and the piping of water. Thirlmere Aqueduct covered 96 miles from the Lake District and was completed by 1894. This was the culmination of almost fifty years of municipal water supply.

The benefits were many. The health factor aside, industry benefited from the availability of unpolluted water for the first time since the beginning of the industrial revolution. Pure water reduced industrial costs. Manchester's rivers ran like sewers, and even usable river water was too hard for textile processes such as chemical bleaching where soft water was required in large quantities. Improved supplies attracted printers, dyers and bleachers to the town. To the textile finishing trades, clean water was the equivalent in value to over half their energy costs. Thus municipal enterprise made sound economic sense.

Civic responsibility could gain a momentum all of its own. By the early twentieth century, Manchester's 'municipal socialism' extended not only to water and gas but to electricity supply, an electric tram system, the building of a Corporation housing estate at Blackley and the purchase of Heaton Park in 1903. Committees of the Council controlled civic amenities ranging from art galleries to abattoirs, from libraries and parks to sewage works, public baths and wash-houses. Corporation responsibilities even extended to the provision of public works for the unemployed. The local distress committee created under the Unemployed Workmen Act of 1905, although intended to be independent, soon became little more than a Council sub-committee. The city's Municipal Code drawn up between 1892 and 1901 extended to six fat volumes. Manchester Corporation had become one of the strongest and most extensive civic authorities ever known. Self-management had become part of the Manchester gospel, its civic identity offering valuable accompaniment to the persistent refrain of commercial viability.

A notable element of Manchester's municipal system was its provision of technical and further education. By the 1870s Manchester's Mechanics Institute (1824) and the School of Art (1838) were well-established institutions. Building on this legacy a system of technical and further education was developed by the same generation that built the Ship Canal and for much the same motive, the preservation of Manchester's economic supremacy. Under the influence of J. H. Reynolds, the Mechanics Institute was remodelled to conform more closely to the needs of industry and in 1882 became the Manchester Technical School. Technical education in the city was further advanced in the shape of the Whitworth legacy. Part of the huge fortune left by the engineering genius, Sir Joseph Whitworth, who died in 1887, was used to found the Whitworth Institute of Art and Industry. But these initiatives were superseded in 1892 by the creation of the Manchester Municipal Technical School under the Technical Instruction Act of 1889. This soon became one of the country's leading centres of technical and scientific education. Its prestigious new building in Sackville Street was officially opened by Prime Minister A. J. Balfour in 1902. The Technical School ran several courses of university standard, and when the Victoria

University of Manchester became an independent institution in 1902 it seemed obvious that its faculty of technology should be located in the Technical School. Thus began an educational relationship which was to evolve into the University of Manchester Institute of Science and Technology.

By 1914 the city had a variety of institutions of further education mostly supported by the municipal corporation. The Municipal School of Art at All Saints had earned a national reputation and played host to teachers of the quality of Walter Crane and Adolphe Valette who taught L. S. Lowry, a pupil at the School before the First World War. An Evening School of Commerce provided the commercial and office training which along with technical skills were considered essential for economic survival. Separate institutes for women existed in the municipal Central Evening School of Domestic Economy on Whitworth Street, teaching a variety of homemaking skills thought appropriate to womankind, and a voluntary institution, the School of Domestic Economy and Cookery which by 1914 had evolved into the city's first teacher-training college (later Elizabeth Gaskell College). By 1914 the system of technical education and vocational training available in Manchester, embracing evening schools, specialist institutes and university courses, was matched by few other English cities.

Electoral Politics

'Manchester School' economics, free trade and Liberalism: the economic and political identity of 'Manchester Man' seems secure. They talked of free trade and voted for the Liberal Party. Yet this is another of the myths about Manchester. As a description of the allegiances of Manchester's late-Victorian and Edwardian middle class it is only half true. They talked of free trade without doubt, but by the mid-1880s they were more likely to be voting Conservative. It is quite wrong to equate the Manchester middle class exclusively with Liberalism.

Manchester became an important arena for parliamentary politics during the last quarter of the nineteenth century and the first decade of the twentieth. The Reform Act of 1867 extended the franchise and reapportioned seats, dividing Manchester into three parliamentary constituencies. The Reform Act of 1884 granted the city six seats in parliament. Manchester became the centre of North West parliamentary politics and party organisation. It attracted prominent candidates such as A. J. Balfour, MP for Manchester East from 1885 to 1906 and Conservative Prime Minister between 1902 and 1905. The young Winston Churchill was Liberal MP for Manchester North West between 1906 and 1908.

Manchester was affected by the shift in voting allegiance between

the parties which gathered pace after the Liberal split over Home Rule
for Ireland in 1886, but which in fact ran much deeper. The business
class was losing faith in the Liberal Party and switching to the Conservatism of Benjamin Disraeli. Whereas Liberals were returned in each
of the electoral contests in Manchester between 1832 and 1867, the
extension of the vote from that date favoured the more populist Tories.
The election of Hugh Birley at the top of the poll in 1868 heralded a
Tory revival which saw them win four out of the nine seats available
in the general elections held between 1868 and 1880 and an astounding
21 of the 30 seats available in Manchester contests between 1885 and
1900. Much of this success was due to the votes of the working-class
Tory (more of which later), but there is little doubt that the politics
of the business community had shifted from 'Manchester School' to
'Tory Democracy'.

The rise of business Conservatism did not mean the abandonment
of free trade. On the contrary, until the tariff reform campaign of
Joseph Chamberlain in the early 1900s free trade and Conservative
politics appeared quite compatible. However, the Manchester businessman of the last century was not all he might seem. Despite a reputation
for radicalism acquired through the agitation against the Corn Laws in
the 1840s he was an inherently conservative and deferential creature.
Once the Manchester business community had secured the economic
benefits of a national policy of free trade they ditched their radical MP,
John Bright, and switched to the more conservative Palmerstonian wing
of the Liberal Party. At the same time many erstwhile Dissenting
families were making a judicious transfer of religious allegiance to the
Established Church so that a subsequent voting preference for the
Conservative Party was to set the seal on the unification of a class once
so split by religion and politics.

Until 1906 most successful parliamentary candidates were businessmen. Two examples will suffice. William Houldsworth, a paternalistic
cotton spinner, first contested a Manchester division in 1880 and was
elected in 1885 as MP for the new constituency of Manchester North
West, a seat he held for the next twenty years. Houldsworth was a
Conservative. His family had been Liberal, but he became attracted by
the new Toryism of the Disraeli era. He served on several Royal
Commissions but never held high political office. Born in Ardwick in
1834 and educated at St Andrews University, he was knighted in 1887
and had a house in Knutsford. Another Conservative, William J. Galloway of the celebrated Manchester engineering firm, won Manchester
South West from the Liberals in 1895. Born in Sale in 1868 and
educated at Wellington College, he had various business and philanthropic interests and was widely travelled. Galloway held his seat until
the 1906 election when he lost to George Kelly, trade unionist and
Labour Party candidate. The Liberal landslide in the 1906 general

election, a rejection of the now official Conservative policy of tariff reform, wiped out the Tories in Manchester, delivering four constituencies to the Liberals and two to Labour. But the Tories were far from finished, and the post-war collapse of the Liberal vote left the Conservatives and Labour as the only serious contenders in Manchester politics.

A Cosmopolitan Culture

Manchester had been the first of the industrially based cities of the nineteenth century to create a cultural identity distinct from that of the traditional London–Oxbridge axis. Its culture and intellectual life were products of the same energies which had generated the Anti-Corn Law League. The city became a cultural centre of international significance and a focus of national educational reform. Among the surviving cultural monuments from the Victorian age are the Hallé Orchestra, Owens College (now the Victoria University of Manchester) and the *Manchester Guardian* (now *The Guardian*), one of the world's most famous newspapers. It was also a great cosmopolitan city. What was exciting and noteworthy about Manchester's cultural life owed much to its heterogeneous range of immigrant business communities.

Owens College was effectively the first of the civic or 'redbrick' universities founded in the second half of the nineteenth century. Formed in 1851 from a legacy of £100,000 left by the Manchester merchant John Owens, the college which took his name was first housed in Richard Cobden's former residence in Quay Street. After some difficulties in the early years it was soon offering a full range of university subjects and attracting some talented students and staff. A new purpose-built campus on Oxford Road was opened in 1873. By then students were winning academic prizes at London and scholarships at Oxford and Cambridge. There was particular excellence in certain areas, notably chemistry. Among its staff were professors with international reputations such as the chemist H. E. Roscoe, the economist W. S. Jevons, the engineer and physicist Osborne Reynolds and the distinguished jurist and historian James Bryce. With 1,350 students in 1880, Owens College was a university in all but name. University status came two years later, although as a result of opposition from the older universities the initial charter was for a joint university of the northern towns. The Victoria University was intended to incorporate colleges from Leeds and Liverpool, with Owens as its first constituent element. Liverpool was admitted in 1884 and Leeds in 1887. The arrangement continued until 1902 when each of the three members received individual charters. The original University title was retained in the new designation, the Victoria University of Manchester.

For most of the 1850–1914 period the educated Mancunian had a choice of reading over breakfast. In that great age of the provincial press, Manchester could boast three quality morning newspapers, the *Courier*, the *Examiner* and the *Guardian*. Politically, the *Manchester Examiner* was to the left of the *Guardian*, and for forty years its chief rival, but it never recovered from an equivocal stand over Irish Home Rule in 1886 and folded ten years after. The *Guardian*'s other rival was the town's Tory paper the *Manchester Courier*, which survived until 1916. But in newspaper history as well as in size of readership the *Manchester Guardian* was Manchester's greatest paper. Under the editorship of the celebrated C. P. Scott from 1872 to 1925, a provincial paper was transformed into a national institution. Scott gathered round him some of the most talented writers of the day and greatly expanded the

The Free Trade Hall. (*Photograph: Ian Beesley*)

newspaper's coverage. Scott's Unitarianism ensured that *Guardian* journalism never extended to retrograde pastimes such as horse-racing, which encouraged gambling. His Liberalism defined the paper's political stance, although it was not shared by all its readers. Scott became the most important Liberal outside Parliament, but still cycled to work each day from his villa in Fallowfield.

The *Manchester Guardian* always reported the Hallé concerts. In the later nineteenth century Manchester became a centre of international renown in the performance of orchestral music. This owed most to the impact of one German emigrant, Charles Hallé, who came to Manchester from Paris during the Revolution of 1848 and stayed to transform the Gentlemen's Concert Society into the Hallé Orchestra. The Hallé Concerts became a Manchester institution. They survived their founder's death thanks to the Hallé Concerts Society, formed in 1898 largely through the efforts of Gustav Behrens. It was also Behrens who was instrumental in obtaining the services of Hans Richter, then acknowledged as the world's greatest conductor, who stayed with the orchestra till 1911. Manchester, in Richter's time, was internationally known as a great centre of symphonic music.

'Moving out' to the suburbs did not damage the Hallé Concerts. Every Thursday during the winter was Hallé night. The railways ran special trains, and countless carriages arrived from residential quarters to crowd the city thoroughfares. There were standing places at the back of the Free Trade Hall for the less well-off music lover, but generally this was a gathering of the rich and fashionable. Even 'the unmusical were obliged week by week to attend the Free Trade Hall, using the arts ... as a means to scale society'. All Manchester knew about the Hallé. At the sight of the carriages:

> The ordinary denizen of Manchester, clerk or artisan, or manager of a bank at £500 a year, remembered, if he ever chanced to forget, that this was Hallé Concert night. Not all of the population ... could have told you exactly what went on ... except that it was 'classical' music, mostly German.[12]

The Hallé Concerts were part of Manchester's inheritance from its pre-1914 German community. Manchester's position as the world's largest market for cotton goods had attracted successive settlements of foreign immigrants, especially German and Greek merchants. This, plus the growth of a vigorous Jewish community, made Manchester into a great cosmopolitan city. The Germans were perhaps the most important of the city's ethnic communities from mainland Europe. From the earliest years of industrialisation a number of foreign merchants had set up agencies in the town. The steady flow of business migrants was stimulated by the political repression of the 1830s and 1840s. The number of foreign export firms in Manchester rose from

78 in 1834 to 101 in 1837 (75 of them German). By 1870, there were about 150 German business houses in the city. The community was always small but dynamic. Around one thousand persons of German birth were recorded by the 1851 Census and according to that of 1911 there were about 1,500 German nationals residing in Manchester and Salford. That German influence was out of proportion to the size of the community was down to its wealthy elite. Together Manchester's German businessmen constituted a distinct ethnic and cultural group. Indeed, their contribution to Manchester's cultural life was not confined to the Hallé.

The wealthy among the German migrants were rapidly assimilated into the local elite, but as a community they retained their ethnic and cultural identity via a series of 'German' institutions, chief of which was the Schiller Anstalt. Founded in 1859 to mark the centenary of the birth of the poet, this club was both cultural and social centre and private space for the coming together of Manchester's German gentlemen. It contained a library, concert hall, gymnasium, skittle alley and billiard room, and boasted a male-voice choir, amateur dramatics society and regular programmes of lectures and chamber concerts. Membership covered the full range of middle-class German residents from Charles Hallé to Frederick Engels. Prominent members included the manufacturers Henry Gaddum and Salis Schwabe and the merchant banking Behrens family. Louis and Solomon Levi Behrens were also leading lights in Manchester's Jewish community.

Many among Manchester's German elite were Jewish and Manchester's Jews also played a prominent part in the cultural life of the city. For example, several of the academics at Owens College/Victoria University were Jewish, including Arthur Schuster, Professor of Physics, Julius Dreschfield, Professor of Pathology, Samuel Alexander, Professor of Philosophy and Chaim Weizmann, Israel's first president, who lectured in chemistry. Unlike the poorer Jewish immigrants of the late nineteenth century, Manchester's Jewish businessmen and professionals had faced little hostility from the indigenous community. They had chosen integration with the local society and culture. Settlement in the suburb of Cheetham Hill provided a community large enough by the 1850s to support two synagogues, one for the Orthodox and a second for the Reformed branches of the faith.

Chief among the other nationalities represented in Manchester's business community were the Greeks and the Armenians. Whereas in 1835 there were only four Greek merchants operating in the town, by the 1860s, with the growth of the Levantine trade, there were upwards of 150. As a community they were more tightly knit than the Germans, a commercial aristocracy living in the city but not of it. The main areas of residence were Kersal and Higher Broughton, and a Greek Orthodox Church opened on Bury New Road in 1860. Manchester's Armenian

The Manchester Jewish Museum. (*Photograph: Ian Beesley*)

businessmen were much fewer in number. By 1880 there were some thirty Armenian firms in the city. Nonetheless, their ancient Christian traditions encouraged them to construct the first Armenian Church in England on Upper Brook Street.

The cosmopolitan character of Manchester's cultural life can be overdrawn. Whilst the Hallé was 'German', Manchester's corresponding contribution to the history of the theatre could be classed as 'Lancastrian'. By the 1890s, Manchester's chief theatres were the Prince's, the Royal, the Queen's and the Gaiety; all within the Peter Street/Quay Street area that was Manchester's 'theatreland'. Manchester's theatrical tradition stretches back to the opening of the Theatre Royal in 1775, but its most notable era was that of Annie Horniman's Repertory Company at the Gaiety, the first of its kind in England. The Gaiety had had a chequered history as a music hall and even a circus when Miss Horniman bought it in 1907 to stage the modern drama of the age of Ibsen and Shaw. She stayed for 13 years, producing 200 plays, 100 of them original. Around her company evolved a Lancashire 'school' of dramatists; writers of locally-based realist dramas such as Stanley Houghton (*Hindle Wakes*), Harold Brighouse (*Hobson's Choice*) and Allan Monkhouse (*Mary Broome*). Among the actors to walk the boards at Miss Horniman's Gaiety were Sybil Thorndike, Lewis Casson, Basil Dean and Herbert Lomas. Most had first come together in 1894 in the Independent Theatre Committee producing short seasons of serious drama. Under Annie Horniman they became part of an experiment that was, for a while, the most dynamic force in the English theatre. Mancunians had every right to be proud of their far from provincial cultural life. Not only was their city the permanent home of one of the great orchestras of the world, they could also enjoy the benefit of the best of modern drama including numerous premiers of new plays. Thus continued Manchester's strong tradition in the performing arts.

Late Victorian Manchester enjoyed a vibrant and diverse cultural life dominated by the pursuits and pleasures of the propertied. But the sum of Manchester's intellectual, educational, artistic and musical culture was even greater than its component parts. Manchester had created a 'civilisation'. It had a cultural existence all its own. In England's cultural and intellectual history the nineteenth century was the era of the provinces and of the bourgeoisie. The gentry and nobility were in retreat and the new urban business class which challenged them found cultural expression in the numerous intellectual and artistic societies of the first half of the century and chiefly through the foundation of the new civic universities in the second. The symbolic act of independence from the traditional aristocratic culture embodied in Owens College was the heir to a provincial Dissenting culture stretching back to the eighteenth century. It is significant that Manchester's other cultural pillar, the Hallé, owed so much to the efforts of some other 'outsiders', this time the city's German immigrants. Manchester may have ceded political leadership of the provinces to Birmingham and the process of absorption into national or metropolitan culture may have already begun, but late Victorian Manchester still represented an independent-minded cultural force.

References

1. O. M. Westall (ed.), *Windermere in the Nineteenth Century*, University of Lancaster, Centre for North-West Regional Studies, Lancaster, 1976, p. 39.
2. Nancy Mitford, *The Ladies of Alderley*, Hamish Hamilton, London, 1967, p. 62.
3. K. Chorley, *Manchester Made Them*, Faber and Faber, London, 1950.
4. C. Rowley, *Fifty Years of Ancoats: Loss and Gain*, privately printed for the Ancoats Brotherhood, Manchester, 1899, p. 11.
5. B. Webb, *Our Partnership*, Longmans, London, 1948, p. 162.
6. See A. J. Kidd and K. W. Roberts (eds), *City, Class and Culture*, Manchester University Press, 1985, p. 14, for further details of council membership in these years.
7. F. Scott, 'The need for better organisation of charitable effort in Manchester and Salford', *Transactions of the Manchester Statistical Society* (1884/5), pp. 127–80.
8. P. Shapely, 'Charity, status and leadership: Charitable image and the Manchester Man', *Journal of Social History*, 32 (1998), pp. 175–7.
9. For the Wood Street Mission and Alfred Alsop, see A. J. Kidd, 'Outcast Manchester: voluntary charity, poor relief and the casual poor 1860–1905'

and T. Thomas, 'Representations of the Manchester working class in fiction 1850–1900', both in Kidd and Roberts, *City, Class and Culture*.

10. M. E. Rose, 'Settlement of university men in great towns: university settlements in Manchester and Liverpool', *Transactions of the Historic Society of Lancashire and Cheshire*, 139 (1989), pp. 143–4.

11. For what follows see J. A. Hassan, 'The growth and impact of the British water industry in the nineteenth century', *Economic History Review*, 38 (1985), pp. 531–47.

12. Neville Cardus, 'Music in Manchester' in W. H. Brindley (ed.), *The Soul of Manchester*, Manchester University Press, 1929, p. 179; *idem., Second Innings*, Collins, London, 1950, p. 8. For the Hallé concert as a bourgeois cultural rite see S. Gunn, *The Public Culture of the Victorian Middle Class: Ritual and Authority in the English Industrial City 1840–1914*, Manchester, 2000, ch. 6.

CHAPTER 9

England Arise! The Politics of Labour and Women's Suffrage

Chartism's mass appeal waned after the failures of 1848. New forces and new interests determined the path of organised labour. Whereas the first half of the nineteenth century had been characterised by the resistance of certain groups to industrialisation, such as the handloom weavers, after 1850 trade unions generally accepted the new industrial order to the extent that working-class industrial and political activity followed separate paths for forty years. They were content to negotiate over pay and conditions and leave politics to the established political parties. This remained true even after the extension of the vote to many working men in the Second Reform Act of 1867. It was not until the 1880s and 1890s that working-class political parties once more emerged and not till the new century that the Labour Party was formed. Manchester was to play a significant role in the early years of the new Labour politics and thus resume a tradition of independent working-class politics which dated back to the last lingering years of Chartism. Moreover, the city holds an important place in the history of women's rights, especially the right to vote in parliamentary elections. The public agitation for women's suffrage began in Manchester in the 1860s, and later its most prominent and controversial figures, Emmeline and Christabel Pankhurst, started their militant campaign in the city.

Chartism after 1848 had proved more resilient in Manchester than in most other places. It was also more radical. The socialist Ernest Jones, much admired by Marx and Engels, captured the Manchester Chartists in 1852. Although Chartism's mass appeal was declining, Jones could still attract thousands of supporters to public meetings. These were pale shadows of the monster demonstrations of earlier years, but they were enough to sustain the infrastructure of independent working-class politics into the third quarter of the century. The spirit of independence was kept alive by the Manchester Manhood Suffrage Association, formed in 1858 at a meeting of four thousand people. Jones initially used the Manchester Association and later the Northern Department of the Reform League to oppose any alliance with middle-class reformers who were campaigning for household rather than manhood suffrage. But declining popular support in the 1860s forced him to compromise, and during the 1866 campaign for a reform bill

Jones led the Reform League into an alliance with the Reform Union in a campaign for the household franchise. The Reform Act of 1867 created a new political map, and the erstwhile socialist Jones drifted to the political right, ending up as an unsuccessful Liberal candidate for Manchester in the 1868 elections, delivering speeches eulogising William Gladstone and John Bright. The dying pangs of Chartism in Manchester were over. The working class were to be without an independent political voice for a generation.

The increasing moderation of Ernest Jones' politics was a barometer of working-class political aspirations, enough to make Marx and Engels despair of the 'bourgeois' character of the English proletariat.[1] What frustrated them was the phenomenon which historians have come to characterise as the 'rise of working-class reformism' during the era of 'mid-Victorian stability' which replaced the social unrest of the first half of the century. In the post-Chartist era the working class appeared to accept the economics of industrial capitalism. During the Cotton Famine of the 1860s Lancashire's mill workers became a potent symbol of this 'new realism'. Although the passivity of the unemployed operatives should not be exaggerated,[2] the generally peaceful acceptance of mass unemployment for the duration of the American Civil War contrasted sharply with the riots and looting in the East End of London which accompanied economic distress during the bad winters of 1860/1 and 1866/7. The northern cotton towns with their friendly societies, cooperative stores and Sunday schools seemed the very epitome of Victorian self-help and respectability: a far cry indeed from the industrial disorder and mass protests of the Chartist era. Even Manchester's image benefited from this new aura of respectability. The city was no longer the focus of popular unrest it had been for much of the preceding half century. Political and economic protest parted company with the demise of Chartism. But political stability did not mean industrial harmony nor the demise of class conflict. Industrial unrest continued and occasionally turned to violence, but never again posed a serious threat to public order.

Trade Unions

During the second half of the nineteenth century, modern notions of 'collective bargaining' came to be accepted by trade unionists. Rising wages in certain skilled occupations encouraged the development of so-called 'New Model' unions. These too were a symbol of working-class reformism and respectability. They were national in organisation, exclusive to skilled men who had served an apprenticeship, charged high subscription rates and employed paid officials. There had been craft unions since the earliest days of trade unionism and attempts at national organisation in the 1820s and 1830s, but what was new in the 1850s was the successful and permanent nature of such endeavours.

The archetype of the 'New Model' appeared in the engineering industry. A variety of engineering unions had operated since the repeal of the Combination Laws in 1825. Confined to particular branches of the trade (millwrights, smiths and so on), they had been regional or local in scope. The largest and wealthiest was the Journeymen Steam Engine and Machine Makers, founded in Manchester in 1826. Known as the 'Old Mechanics', it played the leading part in the formation of the Amalgamated Society of Engineers (ASE), founded in 1851. There was initial rank and file resentment over ceding central control to London, but gradually the ASE came to represent the vast majority of engineering craftsmen. National organisation came rather more slowly to the unions of the cotton industry. After several attempts, a spinners' amalgamation emerged in 1870. Following a succession of industrial disputes, collective bargaining in the cotton industry was eventually institutionalised by the Brooklands Agreement of 1893. 'Brooklands' ended a six-month lock-out and introduced a system of conciliation and annual wage settlements which established relative industrial peace in the industry for twenty years.

Even during the era of 'mid-Victorian stability' craft unions were quite prepared to take strike action. In exceptional circumstances this involved a degree of violence which undermined the image of growing union respectability. The peaceful advance of trade unionism was disrupted by the infamous 'Sheffield Outrages' of 1866 in which the intimidation of blacklegs in the cutlery trade extended to the use of gunpowder to bomb a workman's house. Such excesses led to the appointment of a Royal Commission to investigate the whole subject of trade unionism. Less well known are the parallel disturbances which occurred in the Manchester brick trade and which were also investigated by the Royal Commission.

A wave of strikes swept Manchester in the mid-1860s, of which disputes in the brick trade were the most violent. The brickmasters wanted to mechanise the manufacture of bricks, a development opposed by the brickmakers' trade union. The hand making of bricks by 'moulder' and 'temperer' was a craft skill keenly protected by a union which had successfully imposed strict controls on the production and even the distribution of locally made bricks. The industry had a history of violent disputes which has already been referred to (see Chapter 5). Union control was strongest in the vicinity of central Manchester and disputes affected several firms. The Ardwick Brick Company went out of business after its brick-making machines were sabotaged. Other masters faced similar acts of Luddism and worse, especially if they tried to operate machines with non-union labour. In 1862 William Atkins used non-union members to work his new machines and promptly found his engine room destroyed. After two years of repeated threats and 'brick-spoiling' he gave up his business. John Ashworth followed a similar path but returned to the hand-making of bricks with union labour after a man, mistaken for his son, was badly beaten. The initial success of these craft workers in defending traditional work-practices owed much to sympathetic action by the bricklayers. But this was short-lived, and ultimately brick-making was mechanised. Although the scale of the violence was less than in Sheffield, these Luddite-style attacks in the Manchester brick trade are a feature of the other face of trade-union respectability in the mid-Victorian period.

Manchester's leading trade unionists abhorred such violence. At the height of the strike wave of 1866–7 the Manchester and Salford Trades Council was formed to assist member unions in the pursuit of industrial claims. But its purpose was neither radical nor revolutionary. The political views of its early leaders were moderate to say the least. William Wood and Samuel Nicholson, the Trades Council's first secretary and president, were both enthusiastic Conservatives. In 1869 Wood became secretary of the Conservative Workingmen's Association. But organised skilled labour was much more likely to be Liberal than Tory, and in 1870, with the exception of Wood and Nicholson, all members of the Trades Council were Liberals. After Wood, the secretaryship fell to Peter Shorrocks, an executive council member of the Manchester Liberal Union. The Manchester body was one of several permanent trades councils formed between 1858 and 1867 in the major cities, but unique among them it was responsible for a step of the utmost importance in trade union organisation and the history of the Labour movement.

The Manchester and Salford Trades Council convened the first ever Trades Union Congress (TUC). In February 1868 a circular addressed to 'fellow-unionists' was issued which cited 'the profound ignorance which prevails in the public mind' about trade unions and the imminence of legislation as reasons for a permanent national organisation. The assembled union delegates duly met in the Mechanics Institute (now the National Museum of Labour History) during Whit week in June 1868. Recognising the important role played by Manchester in all this, William Wood was elected President and Peter Shorrocks was Secretary. The trades councils and the TUC represented the respectable face of trade unionism. But the public had been influenced by the 'Sheffield Outrages' and the violence in the Manchester brick trade. In the event, government policy was swayed by the arguments of leading unionists (through, for example, the Parliamentary Committee of the TUC formed at the third annual Congress in London in 1871) and several pieces of legislation in the 1870s ensured the legal position of trades unionism. So whilst the Manchester brickmakers contributed to the image of trades unionism as dangerous and violent, other

Manchester unionists were publicising the respectable face of organised
Labour by founding the Trades Union Congress.

During the last quarter of the nineteenth century trade unionism
spread beyond the skilled working class to the unskilled worker. This
was the so-called 'new unionism'. Rising real wages and the increasing

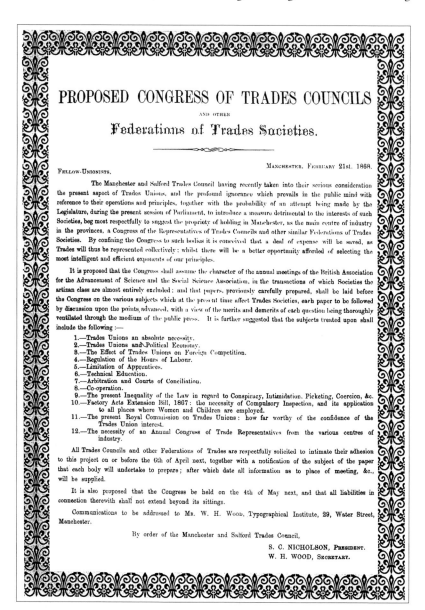

The Manchester and Salford Trades Council circular which led to the convening of the first
Trades Union Congress in 1868.

size of many firms made possible trade union organisation among the lower paid, including women. The 'new unions' were marked by their aggressive attitude towards employers, and their leaders were influenced by ideas from outside the conventional political spectrum, notably by the revival of socialism in the 1880s. Starting in London with successful and well-publicised strike action in 1888 and 1889 by the gasworkers, the dockers and the Bryant and May match-girls, the 'new unionism' soon spread throughout the industrial centres. A branch of the Gasworkers and General Labourers Union was the first to be formed in Manchester, and during the autumn and winter of 1889–90 the city's tram guards and drivers, shop assistants and railwaymen were also unionised. Jewish workers in Manchester's tailoring sweatshops were also among the first wave of 'new unionists'. The early nineties saw unions formed in a variety of previously unorganised occupations: from porters and carters in the city's railway stations, docks, warehouses and markets to construction workers such as navvies, paviours and quarrymen and service workers like hairdressers. By 1900 the principal new unions in the Manchester area were branches of the Dock Labourers Union and the Tramway Employees, and the specifically Manchester-based unions, the Quay and Railway Porters and the British Labour Amalgamation organised by Tom Fox. Although several of the leaders of these new unions were socialist in politics, there is little to suggest that the rank and file followed suit. The voting preferences of union members remains largely a mystery, but many must have voted Conservative.

Working-Class Toryism

Many male workers became voters by virtue of the 1867 and 1884 Reform Acts. How did they use this opportunity? The radicalism of the Chartist era had evolved into the Liberalism of most trade union leaders by 1867. But the leaders of organised Labour were not typical of their class. For the majority of the new working-class voters of Manchester and the other Lancashire boroughs enfranchisement meant the chance to vote Tory. In the 1880s and 1890s the Liberal Party in the North West was squeezed between a loss of middle-class support (see Chapter 8) and the emergence of popular Toryism. As a result, Lancashire became a Conservative Party stronghold. The Tory revival which had begun in Manchester in 1868 was so complete that by 1895 only one of the city's six parliamentary seats remained in Liberal hands. That the working class should have adjusted to the existing economic and political system is one thing. Why they should have opted so overwhelmingly for one rather than another of the established parties is far from certain. No doubt many voters were convinced by political argument, but other factors were also at work.

Possibly the greatest single factor in the working-class Toryism of northern towns like Manchester was antagonism towards the Irish migrant and his Roman Catholic religion. A strain of militant Protestantism ran through many working-class communities in nineteenth-century Lancashire. It sometimes found expression in membership of Protestant bodies such as the English Orange Order which had originated in Manchester.[3] Working-class 'Orangemen' were attracted by the practical benefits of membership such as job opportunities in firms with Protestant masters and enhanced status in their communities, not to mention the conviviality of lodge meetings held in pubs. The Orange Order was a respectable body, patriotic and emphatically Tory. It brought master and men together. In the Manchester organisation, the trade unionist Samuel Nicholson, co-founder of the Trades Council, rubbed shoulders with the cotton manufacturer, leading Lancashire Conservative and Manchester MP W. Romaine Callender. Nicholson was responsible for organising a mass demonstration to greet Benjamin Disraeli when he visited the city in 1872. Twenty thousand marched through the Manchester rain, the Orangemen parading with oranges spiked on their umbrellas. During his visit Disraeli graciously accepted honorary membership of local lodges.

The English working class were generally not church-goers. Nevertheless, the Church of England was successfully promoted by the Tories, along with the Monarchy, as twin symbols of English national pride. Patriotism, Protestantism and the Conservative Party were united in an ideology with great popular appeal. The Tories and Liberals vied for popular support after 1867, each arranging mass political rallies at election time. The Tories outstripped the Liberals, however, both in their appeal to the working-class voter and in the patriotic ritual of their rallies. The Liberals met in the sedate comfort of the Free Trade Hall, but the Tories generally hired the vast Pomona Gardens for meetings preceded by organised processions tens of thousand strong, through the streets of Manchester, 'fighting with the Irish along the way'. Bands played and banners waved in the most stage-managed of occasions. Patriotic symbolism was never far away. After the passing of a resolution on the Eastern Question at a Pomona rally in 1878:

> 'Rule Britannia' was heartily sung. A gentleman at the rear of the hall then held up a portrait of the Queen. This was the signal for another outburst of cheering and 'God Save the Queen' was sung with thrilling effect, all the heads being uncovered and those on the platform rising from their seats. The sight from the platform at this moment was something to be remembered. Veteran politicians remarked as they looked down upon that sea of upturned faces, that they had not witnessed anything like it for many a day.[4]

The Liberals could not compete with this kind of political theatre.

The outer fringes of Orangeism could be violent. A 'patriotic' hostility to Irish migrants and towards the Catholic faith caused friction between working-class communities who otherwise shared similar life experiences. Drunken brawls and the occasional serious assault or murder were the everyday incidents of English–Irish conflict in the slums. The pressures of slum life, a fear of Irish competition in the labour market and plain xenophobia provided fertile ground for the propaganda of Tory and Protestant agitators. Riots directed against Irish districts and Catholic clergy accompanied election campaigns from the 1850s onwards. The cry of 'No Popery' was the excuse for riots such as those which occurred at Stockport in 1852 in which two Catholic churches were destroyed. Matters reached a head in 1868 when public hostility was heightened by the activities of the Fenians.

The Fenians, or the Irish Republican Brotherhood, were an independence movement that had taken up arms against British rule in Ireland. In the late 1860s they took the struggle to the mainland. An abortive attempt to seize the arms depot at Chester Castle in February 1867, preparatory to an armed uprising, was followed by a campaign of sabotage and incendiarism throughout the summer, striking at gas works, railways and other public facilities. Quite by chance two Fenian organisers, Thomas Kelly and Timothy Deasy, were arrested in Oak Street, Shudehill, in September 1867. A week later, as the two prisoners were being removed to Bellevue Gaol after formal identification as Fenians, a daring escape was effected near the railway arch on Hyde Road not far from the prison. Thirty to forty armed men, mostly drawn from Fenian supporters in Manchester's Irish districts, supplied with

The armed attack on the van which released the Fenian prisoners, 1867.

revolvers purchased in Birmingham so as not to arouse local suspicion, stormed the van carrying the prisoners. Kelly and Deasy were rescued and made good their escape, never to be recaptured. But in the process a police sergeant was unintentionally shot and died: among the charges laid against the 28 men subsequently arrested was that of murder. At the trial in November 1867 five of the accused were sentenced to death by hanging. One was pardoned and the sentence of another commuted, but three, William Allen, Michael Larkin and Michael O'Brien, were publicly hanged at Salford Gaol.

To the Irish the executed were the 'Manchester Martyrs': to the majority of the host population they had been guilty of the 'Manchester Outrages'. Despite the opposition of the Catholic hierarchy (Cardinal Vaughan forbade any commemoration of the 'Martyrs' in a Catholic Church) Fenianism did enjoy significant support among the Lancashire Irish. The Fenian connection enabled demagogues, like William Murphy, to exploit anti-Catholic sentiments and strengthen the view of the Irish as subversive aliens. The so-called 'Murphy riots' at Manchester during the election campaign of 1868 were really noisy demonstrations of anti-Catholicism. Murphy addressed a gathering of six thousand on open ground in Chorlton about the need to vote for Protestantism. The assembled crowd gave three cheers for the Queen, three more for William, Prince of Orange and three groans for the Pope.[5] Murphy was a self-publicist with no Conservative connections who spoke in several south-east Lancashire constituencies in 1868, but not surprisingly the Conservative Party's election campaign in 1868 was aggressively Protestant. The Tory candidates in Manchester, Birley and Hoare, exploited working-class prejudices by claiming that dis-establishing the Irish Church would be a prelude to dis-establishment of the Church in England and religious equality with Roman Catholics. 1868 was the first ever election success for the Tories in Manchester and heralded the Tory revival in the city. The *Manchester Guardian* was of the opinion that William Gladstone, the Liberal leader, had been 'kicked out of Lancashire for not being a Protestant'.[6]

Labour and Socialist Politics

Manchester was one of the key centres in the early years of modern British Labour politics. By 1914 the Manchester Labour Party was one of the most effective in the country with significant representation in municipal and parliamentary arenas. Moreover, the Manchester region has an important place in the history of the Labour and Socialist movement in the period before the formation of the national Labour Representation Committee (Labour Party) in 1900. The Social Democratic Federation (SDF), formed in London in 1884, was the first Marxist political party to emerge in Britain. By the 1890s the Lancashire branches of the SDF were the most important Socialist clubs outside London. Another left-wing political party actually drew its first breath in Manchester. The Independent Labour Party (ILP) was 'born' at a meeting in St James Hall in May 1892, although its formal existence as a national party came a year later in Bradford. Add to all this the Socialist journalism of Robert Blatchford and the Clarion movement he inspired and Manchester emerges as one of the heartlands of British Labour.

The Social Democratic Federation was a party of direct action rather than electoral politics. In theory it was a revolutionary party, and the energies of its members were typically channelled into activities designed to raise the 'revolutionary consciousness' of the workers. Additionally members organised demonstrations and public meetings to pressurise local and central authorities into making concessions on issues such as unemployment and housing. Much effort was put into agitation amongst the unemployed. It was, however, a very small party indeed. The Lancashire membership (1,089 at its peak in 1897 but down to 709 by 1902) outstripped that of London although the number of branches was fewer. Easily the largest local branch and one of the oldest in the country was South Salford with around 200 members. Beginning in 1884 with weekly meetings at the Black Horse on the Crescent, the branch grew until it acquired larger premises in Trafford Road and went on to play an active part in Socialist organisation in the region for over twenty years. The Manchester branches were much more ephemeral in character, coming and going as economic conditions fluctuated. The most important were Hulme (renamed the South-West Manchester branch in 1901) and Manchester Central (formed in 1903).

The Independent Labour Party also had its strongholds in the north of England. Of 305 branches listed in 1895, 102 were in Yorkshire and 73 in Lancashire. Its strength in Lancashire was in towns like Nelson, Colne, Preston, Oldham, Ashton and in the Manchester branches. The ILP's Manchester origins were relatively humble. Sylvia Pankhurst, one of its early members, described the first regular meeting place of Central branch as 'a poorly lit, evil-smelling room over a stable, in a side-street off Oxford Road'.[7] But things improved during the 1890s until party membership surpassed that of the older SDF. Branch returns in 1897 listed 693 members in Manchester and district. However, in the following year only 268 were listed as having paid their membership fee to the Manchester and Salford branches. The number of active members may have been very small. The ILP could not lay claims to a mass membership, but it did come to enjoy some public support and electoral success.

Manchester's first independent Labour councillors were elected in 1894. Previously 'Labour' members had entered the municipal chamber under the auspices of one of the established parties (generally the Liberals). But when Jack Sutton headed the poll in Bradford and Jesse Butler won Openshaw in November 1894 a new chapter in political history had been opened. Subsequent electoral success was steady rather than spectacular. Two more seats were won in 1897 and another in 1898. But support for an independent party for Labour was expressed in well-attended public meetings. An estimated 40,000 gathered at Boggart Hole Clough in July 1896 to hear Keir Hardie, the ILP's first ever MP. In national terms events were moving towards independent Labour representation free from the constraints of Liberal or Conservative Party membership. A major catalyst was the need of trade unionists for an independent political voice in their struggle over legal rights. Over a decade of discussion within the Labour movement culminated in 1900 with the emergence of the Labour Representation Committee (LRC) which in 1906 was renamed the Labour Party.

The Manchester and Salford Labour Representation Committee was formed early in 1903 largely at the behest of the Trades Council which was already affiliated to the national LRC. The Manchester and Salford Trades and Labour Council ('Labour' had been added in 1894) was no longer the 'conservative' body of the 1860s. During the 1890s SDF and ILP members had transformed it into a campaigning force issuing resolutions supporting an eight-hour day, land nationalisation, public works for the unemployed and the independent representation of Labour. The executive committee of the Manchester and Salford LRC consisted of nine trade union delegates and three each from the Trades Council and the ILP. Whilst trade-union subscriptions underwrote LRC finances it was the ILP which provided most of the municipal candidates. Manchester Central branch claimed 56 members including the Labour councillors Elijah Hart, Tom Fox, Tom Cook, James Johnstone and J. Mclachlan. The LRC enjoyed its first parliamentary success at the General Election of 1906 when the trade unionist and former Liberal G. D. Kelly overturned a large Conservative majority to take South-West Manchester; future government ministers, J. R. Clynes and John Hodge, won Manchester North-East and Gorton respectively. A pact with the Liberals avoided three-way contests in all three seats. When the LRC became the Labour Party in 1906, in addition to its three Manchester district MPs there were thirteen Labour members of Manchester City Council and six Labour representatives on Salford Town Council. These were early days, but the new Labour politics had arrived.

There had been a history of cooperation in Manchester between the SDF and ILP but this was undermined by the formation of the LRC. Whilst most ILP branches became affiliated to the new electoral body, the SDF pursued a separate path in which direct action was generally preferred to electoral politics. The only SDF venture into parliamentary

A demonstration of the unemployed storms Manchester Cathedral, 1908. This SDF-inspired protest was in response to some derogatory remarks about the unemployed made by Dean Welldon.

politics was Dan Irving's disastrous failure in the Manchester North West bye-election of 1908, coming bottom of the poll with only 276 votes. In electoral terms the Labour Party in alliance with the Liberals was the way forward. SDF energies went in another direction. Unemployment was among the major social issues of the day. From the mid-1880s SDF activists had carried on a campaign of demonstrations among and on behalf of the unemployed. These intensified during the Edwardian years as the public authorities tried various strategies for employing out-of-work males on public works programmes. SDF agitators were able to exploit the inadequacy of these measures in a series of demonstrations in major cities.

In Manchester the SDF campaign resulted in a number of disturbances the like of which had not been seen for more than a generation and which sometimes caught the national eye. One such occasion was the outcome of a demonstration in Manchester on 31 July 1905 over the Conservative government's unemployment policy. A mass meeting in Albert Square was followed by an unscheduled demonstration in which a large body of men were led by two local SDF activists in a march up Market Street blocking it to traffic. Police used a series of baton charges to disperse the crowd and the leaders were arrested. The scenes of riot were said to have 'no parallel in the history of the city since the dreadful days of Peterloo'.[8] The Conservative Government, led by Manchester MP Arthur Balfour, may have been sufficiently alarmed by this incident into reviving the Unemployed Workmen Bill and appointing a Royal Commission on the Poor Laws to defuse Labour protest.[9] At any rate, as a result of SDF organised demonstrations during these years there were further battles over the control of the streets between the police and the unemployed. The police did not always manage to keep the peace.

In September 1908 several thousand gathered outside the Town Hall in Albert Square awaiting the outcome of a Town Meeting (public forum) on the unemployed question. The authorities had feared an 'invasion' of the Town Hall by the unemployed. The Ford Madox Brown murals in the Great Hall were covered to protect them and outside 800 policemen guarded the entrances. These fears were justified for at the sound of a bugle the crowd rushed the Town Hall steps. Police drove the demonstrators from Albert Square but the crowd simply dispersed into surrounding streets. Windows were smashed in Cross Street and Deansgate and the Midland Hotel narrowly escaped attack. Isolated policemen were assaulted. But the police faced a further humiliation when the crowd were able to regroup in Albert Square. An attempt to arrest their leader, Leopold Fleetwood of the SDF, an engineer at the GEC works in Salford, ended in fiasco. As he addressed the crowd from the steps of the Albert Memorial a formation of fifty officers broke through and captured him. But the crowd almost immediately seized him back. A baton charge failed to prevent Fleetwood being carried away to Stevenson Square where he continued his address. Ultimately the police restored their authority, breaking up all street gatherings on sight.[10]

Such disturbances have been overshadowed by the strike riots of 1911 in which a nationwide sequence of industrial action hit the docks and transport industries. In fact these industrial disputes occasioned less violence in Manchester than in many other places. In Liverpool, for example, troops fired on rioting strikers in August 1911, killing two of the demonstrators. The earlier unemployed riots in Manchester are part of an under-researched element in the increasingly violent character of protest in Edwardian England. However, the SDF campaign can be said to have achieved very little. Certainly Socialism was never going to be built upon the unemployed alone, and the campaign became a question of public order rather than public policy. Twenty years later in 1931 further unemployed demonstrations, against reductions in benefit during the Depression, were once more broken up by police and the leaders arrested. Political protest by the unemployed generally gave rise to public disturbance, not to political change. Moreover, many felt that Socialism was about self-education and building a Socialist culture as much as political agitation of any sort. The chief influence in this direction was the *Clarion* newspaper.

The *Clarion* was the most widely read Socialist newspaper of its day. Its founder, ex-army sergeant turned journalist Robert Blatchford, made his reputation under the pseudonym of 'Nunquam' in articles for the *Sunday Chronicle*. But when the paper's star journalist became a Socialist its proprietor, Edward Hulton, sacked him. After a brief spell writing for Joseph Burgess's *Workman's Times*, 'Nunquam' resurfaced in 1891 with his own paper, the *Clarion*, based in Manchester. There were many Labour and Socialist papers, the SDF's journal, *Justice*, was well produced and the ILP's *Labour Leader* was informative, but none had the impact of the *Clarion*. After William Cobbett, Blatchford was arguably the most important popular political journalist of the nineteenth century. His collected journalism sold well, especially *Merrie England*, his savage indictment of industrial capitalism, published in 1893. Blatchford had been the first president of the Manchester and Salford ILP but soon severed his links with the party to concentrate on his own blend of Socialism and patriotic rhetoric. But Blatchford's journalism did more than sell books about Socialism; it inspired the Clarion movement with its network of social, recreational and political groups.

The Clarion banner was a rallying point for Socialists who belonged to any or no political party, but mostly for young lower-middle-class professionals who saw Socialism as a question of recreation and culture as well as political doctrine. The Manchester and Salford area was the heartland of the Clarion movement with its choirs, scouts, rambling and cycling clubs and its proselytising Clarion vans. The Clarion movement did much to broaden the appeal of Socialism beyond the trade union movement and reached out to the office workers and shop assistants who became the typical *Clarion* reader. It earned many new recruits for the Labour movement, especially the ILP. Many of its members felt they were building a Socialist culture which absorbed their leisure time and anticipated a harmonious future. Stella Davies, then working as a switchboard telephonist in Manchester, joined the Clarion Cycle Club which had acquired club houses at Bucklow Hill and Handforth. Clarion outings were social as well as Socialist, and members were uniformly young.

> The Clarionets, as we called ourselves, met at appointed places on the outskirts of Manchester ... furnished with stacks of leaflets, pamphlets and the Clarion ... Arriving at some village in Derbyshire or Cheshire we held an open air meeting trying to catch the

people as they came out of church or chapel. We were young and given to buffoonery ... we scrawled slogans in chalk on barns and farmhouse walls ... We sang 'England arise, the long, long night is over' outside pubs and on village greens.[11]

The Clarion movement's role as a focus for Socialist activity in the city is best exemplified by the Clarion Cafe at 50A Market Street. Opened in 1908 and not closed down till 1936, the Clarion Cafe was a rendezvous for Socialists and trade unionists of all persuasions. The Fellowship Press and the Manchester branch of the Fabian Society shared the premises. Weekly debates were held and speakers included the likes of Tom Mann and Ben Tillett. The *Clarion* preached the equality of the sexes, and generally the Socialist movement was sympathetic to women's suffrage. As with Labour history, the North West and Manchester in particular played an important role in the cause of votes for women.

Women's Suffrage

The 1918 election was the first to include women (albeit over thirty) on the parliamentary electoral register: full voting rights for women over twenty-one did not arrive till 1928. Yet women had voted in various local elections for some time. From 1834 women householders had the right to vote in elections for Poor Law guardians; by the mid-1880s they were successfully standing as candidates in Poor Law elections. They were eligible for election to the school boards created by the Education Act of 1870, and women were being elected to municipal councils from 1907. But the prize of full civil rights was a long time in the winning. This is not the place to tell that story but to point out

Police escort a women's suffrage demonstration in Manchester.

the important role played by women from the Manchester region in the struggle for equal rights.

The women's suffrage movement had its origins in Manchester. The National Society for Women's Suffrage was formed in the city when the Second Reform Bill of 1867 failed to include women. Lydia Becker was the Society's organising secretary from 1867 until her death in 1890, when the leadership passed to Millicent Fawcett. Born in Manchester in 1827, Becker had become the first woman elected to a provincial school board, and through the suffrage campaign she was the first Victorian woman to enter successfully the male sphere of public speaking on political matters. She organised the first ever public meeting in this country to be addressed by women, which was also the first ever public meeting about women's suffrage, in the Assembly Room of the new Free Trade Hall in April 1868. She spoke alongside other local 'ladies' and went on to address numerous suffrage meetings up and down the country. Becker conducted a highly respectable campaign, cultivating parliamentary support for the succession of bills for women's suffrage which were presented to the Commons in the 1870s. Through her leadership of a national movement and her power of oratory she became an eminent Manchester figure, apparently sufficient to grant her honorary male status since a local periodical condescendingly dubbed her 'A public man of whom Manchester has reason to be proud'.[12]

The suffragists of Lydia Becker's generation were predominantly middle-class women, the vast majority of whom merely wanted a share in a limited franchise with property qualifications. By the mid-1890s, after almost thirty years of polite campaigning, they seemed no nearer their goal. A younger generation of suffragists were more prepared to reach out to working-class women in their campaign and some turned to the high profile militancy which was to earn the title 'Suffragette'. Manchester and Manchester women were central to both these developments.

The suffrage movement in Manchester was revived from the doldrums it entered after Becker's death by the efforts of Esther Roper. As secretary of the Manchester Suffrage Society from 1893, this young but exceptional middle-class woman (she was a graduate of Owens College at a time when it was still unusual for women to enter higher education) made a direct appeal to working-class women to enter the campaign. Women were leafleted at the factory gate and invited to suffrage meetings in all the major cotton towns. Working women were already organised as workers. The Women's Co-operative Guild, formed in 1883, held a grand 'festival' in Manchester in 1892 and the Women's Trade Union League organised a thousand strong meeting in Manchester in 1893. Roper's initiative was strengthened by the arrival in Manchester of Eva Gore-Booth who, despite her background as an

Anglo-Irish aristocrat (her sister was Countess Markievicz, later the first woman elected to Parliament), successfully bridged the class barrier becoming co-secretary of the newly-formed Manchester and Salford Women's Trade Union Council. After 1900 a new generation of working-class women of the cotton district made the link between the claims of the Labour movement and the campaign for women's rights including the vote. The call for equal pay and child benefit joined the cry for electoral reform.[13]

Manchester was also the home of the Suffragette movement, a campaign for women's suffrage which left the gentility of the Becker era far behind. The term 'Suffragette' is inevitably linked with the name Pankhurst. Mrs Pankhurst, christened Emmeline Goulden, was born in Manchester in 1858 into a wealthy manufacturing and Liberal family. At the age of twelve she had accompanied her mother to hear Lydia Becker speak at a suffrage meeting. Her marriage in 1879 to the Manchester barrister Richard Pankhurst brought entry into the world of Radical and then Labour politics. Although a supporter of women's suffrage, she took no part in the campaign until after her husband's death in 1898, preferring to work through the Independent Labour Party for him and as an ILP member on the Chorlton Board of Guardians. It was not until 1903 that she, and her daughters Christabel and Sylvia, formed the Women's Social and Political Union (WSPU) at a meeting in the Pankhursts' home in Nelson Street not far from the Victoria Park villa they had had to abandon after the death of Dr Pankhurst.

At first the WSPU recruited its members from the ILP and the trade union movement but after 1906 Christabel Pankhurst led the WSPU

Emmeline Pankhurst and her daughters outside Central Station, Manchester.

on a separate path as a single issue lobby for votes for women as distinct from the broader campaigns for adult suffrage pursued within the Labour movement. Thereafter, the WSPU campaign moved to London and its militancy regularly caught the headlines. The origins of the militant stance of the Suffragettes, however, were in Manchester in 1905. Christabel had been impressed by the merits of direct action when the Manchester unemployed demonstration of 31 July appeared to frighten the Government into introducing legislation. She hoped to do the same for the women's suffrage issue. She determined to get arrested in the most public of ways to draw attention to the WSPU campaign. The opportunity arose when Winston Churchill and Sir Edward Grey, two prominent Liberals likely to be in a Liberal Cabinet if the party won the forthcoming general election, addressed a meeting at the Free Trade Hall on 13 October. Christabel and her devoted follower Annie Kenney interrupted the meeting demanding votes for women and refusing to be silenced. To ensure her arrest Christabel spat at one of the policemen called to eject the protesters, and the magistrate sentenced her to seven days in Strangeways Prison. Thus began the militant campaign of the Suffragettes.

The attention subsequently given to the WSPU may be out of all proportion to its significance. It may even have delayed women's suffrage by its militant tactics. Certainly it split from the rest of the suffrage movement as early as 1906. The Pankhursts' authoritarian style as much as the increasing violence of their tactics put off potential supporters, until on the eve of the First World War the small band of Pankhurst followers, who had by now even resorted to arson, were almost a guerrilla group. After 1906 the WSPU had virtually abandoned Manchester, which left the field to the respectable suffragists, heirs of the Becker tradition, who belonged to the North of England Society for Women's Suffrage, and the radical suffragists, who worked through the several organisations which mobilised working and professional women. However, in national terms, they were overshadowed in public consciousness by the Suffragettes, especially when the authorities resorted to the brutal policy of forcible feeding to deal with the hunger strikes pursued by WSPU prisoners. But despite the prominence of the militant Suffragettes, it was largely the arguments of suffragists over generations plus the experience of the war years that broke the mould and gave the vote to women.

References

1. See K. Marx and F. Engels, *On Britain*, 2nd edn, Foreign Languages Publishing House, Moscow, 1962, pp. 537–8.
2. See M. E. Rose, 'Rochdale man and the Stalybridge riot' in A. P. Donaj-

grodski (ed.), *Social Control in Nineteenth-century Britain*, Croom Helm, London, 1977.

3. See F. Neal, 'The Manchester origins of the English Orange Order', *Manchester Region History Review*, IV:ii (1990–1), pp. 12–24.

4. Quoted in P. Joyce, *Work, Society and Politics: The Culture of the Factory in Late Victorian England*, Methuen, London, 1980, p. 281.

5. *Manchester City News*, 19 September, 1868 cited in H. J. Hanham, *Elections and Party Management: Politics in the Time of Gladstone and Disraeli*, Longmans, London, 1959, p. 307.

6. *Manchester Guardian*, 16 February 1869, cited in N. Kirk, *The Growth of Working-Class Reformism in Mid-Victorian England*, Croom Helm, London, 1985, p. 341.

7. E. Sylvia Pankhurst, *The Suffragette Movement*, Longmans, London, 1931, p. 128.

8. *Manchester Evening Chronicle*, 31 July 1905.

9. This is the claim made in K. D. Brown, *Labour and Unemployment 1900–1914*, David and Charles, Newton Abbot, 1971, pp. 59–62.

10. For the SDF campaign see A. J. Kidd, 'The Social Democratic Federation and popular agitation amongst the unemployed in Edwardian Manchester', *International Review of Social History*, XXIX (1984), pp. 336–58.

11. C. Stella Davies, *North-Country Bred: A Working-Class Family Chronicle*, Routledge and Kegan Paul, London, 1963, pp. 84–5.

12. *City Jackdaw*, 31 December 1875, cited in J. Parker, 'Lydia Becker: pioneer orator of the women's movement', *Manchester Region History Review*, V:ii (1991), p. 18.

13. For Lancashire's working-class suffragists see, J. Liddington and J. Norris, *One Hand Tied Behind Us: The Rise of the Women's Suffrage Movement*, Virago, London, 1978.

Part III

Within Living Memory:
Manchester Since 1914

CHAPTER 10

In the Face of Industrial Decline

Nineteen thirteen was a record year for the Lancashire cotton industry. Cloth exports totalled over 7,000 million linear yards, comprising 80% of the industry's total output. Over 65% of the world's cotton cloth was the produce of Lancashire's looms. But beneath this position of supremacy the industry was vulnerable. There had been little recent investment in new technology and 45% of exports went to one market, India. The First World War cut off the supply of British-made cloth and left the Indian market open to the Japanese and the Indian producers themselves. After a brief post-war boom Lancashire's mills began to feel the pinch. Prices fell in the face of foreign competition throughout the 1920s. The Slump of 1929–31 further exacerbated the situation.

The chief problem was the development of textile industries in former British markets. The British cotton industry was suffering the common fate of industrial pioneers faced with the advantages enjoyed by 'late-comers', in this case cheap labour and newer plant and machinery. By 1939 the decline had become catastrophic. Cloth exports had plummeted to less than one fifth the 1913 level. Furthermore, short-sighted management in the face of the challenge of overseas competition left the industry ill-equipped to survive. The home market was still intact in 1939, but this also went in the successive mill closures and final collapse of the industry in the 1950s. The failure to bring in new technology, despite the obvious success enjoyed by the American use of ring-spinning in place of the older mules, and the persistence of restrictive work practices in the interwar years ensured the fate of Lancashire textiles. The forced rationalisation and modernisation introduced by the Cotton Industry Act of 1959 came too late to reverse the trend, and by the 1960s it was no longer strictly accurate even to talk of a 'cotton' industry since 'man-made' (synthetic) fibres developed by ICI and Courtaulds now accounted for most of the raw materials used. British production of the cotton cloth that had once generated an industrial revolution was now effectively dead.

Trafford Park

How did the decline in cotton affect Manchester? The impact was dramatic for Lancashire as a whole but the damage was unevenly distributed. Manchester's more complex industrial base protected it against the worst effects of the Depression, and the Ship Canal and Trafford Park helped Manchester weather the storm better than most. The city's unemployment figures were consistently below the national average throughout the interwar years. The Port of Manchester was ranked the third or fourth most important custom port in the UK on the basis of the value of import and export trade for 39 out of the 55 years for which figures exist between 1904 and 1964. The 'Ship Canal Zone' was an industrial magnet even during the Depression, cushioning the Manchester economy against its worst effects and benefiting the whole of south Lancashire at the expense of the north. As we have seen in Chapter 6, from the early years the Trafford Park Industrial Estate was the emblem of the Ship Canal's importance to Manchester; a new manufacturing 'Manchester' on the doorstep of the parent city. Trafford Park was entirely without cotton mills. Even in the 1890s it symbolised the alternative to 'Cottonopolis'. Its most characteristic industries were in the oil trade, engineering, chemicals and foodstuffs. The very existence of Trafford Park had served further to diversify Manchester's industrial structure and helped it to cope with the decline of cotton.[1]

An example of diversification is the fact that Trafford Park became an important centre of the food industry, relying on the Ship Canal for imports of grain, fruit, provisions, tea and, to a lesser extent, meat and sugar. The grain trade alone stimulated industrial development. Amongst long-term residents in the Park, CWS and Hovis had both opened flour mills at Trafford Wharf before 1914, Kemp's biscuits were being produced by 1923, and the establishment of Kellogg's new European factory on the Barton Dock Estate in 1938 contributed greatly to the post-1948 boom in maize imports. Among other foodstuffs, tea became a major imported commodity with Brook Bond based in Trafford Park and their rivals, the CWS, across the Canal in Ordsall.

The Port of Manchester's trading importance had attracted foreign, especially American, firms to Trafford Park from the earliest years. British Westinghouse (reorganised in 1919 as Metropolitan Vickers) had begun the trend which led, by 1933, to the presence of over 200 American firms. The Ford Motor Company came in 1910, and by 1913 mass production had made the Model T the cheapest car in Britain and Ford the country's largest car manufacturer. Ford's plant at Trafford Park was at its peak in the early 1920s, but competition from Austin and Morris forced it to seek further markets and the company left Manchester for Dagenham in 1931 so as to be nearer the European buyer. It was the 1914–18 war which brought the Port and the Park into full use for the first time, especially for the manufacture of munitions, chemicals and aircraft for the war effort. Trafford Park firms generally survived the Crash of 1929/31 without bankruptcies, which was not the case elsewhere in Lancashire.

The return of war between 1939 and 1945 once more benefited Manchester engineering. Even prior to the outbreak of hostilities local firms were the beneficiaries of rearmament. Factories and production lines were converted to war needs. For example, Metropolitan Vickers (MetroVicks) adapted plant to aircraft construction, making 'Manchester' and then 'Lancaster' bombers (with engines from A. V. Roe of Hollinwood, near Oldham). A thousand 'Lancaster' bombers were completed by the end of the war. The most spectacular item of MetroVicks war work was the development and manufacture of radar equipment. MetroVicks made the first radar transmitter ever commercially produced. The firm manufactured many other war items on a large scale, including controls and parts for anti-aircraft and naval guns, automatic pilots and compasses for aircraft, equipment for dealing with unexploded bombs and mobile power stations for despatch to the Soviet Union. Other Trafford Park firms involved in war work included Ford Motors who returned to the Park to adapt their mass production techniques to the manufacture of Rolls Royce Merlin XX aero engines. By 1944 over 17,000 Ford workers were turning out 900 engines every month. During the Second World War Trafford Park was the greatest of Britain's arsenals and a prime target for the German bombers.

The Second World War, however, proved to be the summit of Trafford Park's importance. The Port of Manchester had been the country's second most important oil port since the early twentieth century, reaching a peak in 1946 of 24.5% of the nation's imports of crude oil, and maintaining an average of nearly 16% between 1946 and 1960. Yet the benefits drifted away from Manchester as the industrial focus of the Canal shifted to its western end. Trafford Park gradually ceded economic first place to Ellesmere Port and Runcorn. Employment in the Park declined from a peak of 75,000 in 1945 to 50,000 by 1967. But the sharpest fall in the workforce came in the early 1970s. The Manchester Docks had remained prosperous into the mid-1960s. But during the next decade trade declined dramatically in the face of containerisation. Only the ports which could handle the huge container ships and had the storage space for bulk container traffic were going to survive the 'container revolution'. Manchester was not one of them. Felixstowe, Tilbury and Southampton took over Manchester's shipping trade.

The motorway revolution and the decline of rail freight-carrying further contributed to Trafford Park's decline by spreading the industrial zone along the Ship Canal banks and away from the focal point of Manchester. Trading estates were springing up everywhere and container lorries increasingly headed for the newer rivals of the world's first industrial estate. In the face of these challenges the workforce plummeted to 15,000 by 1976. Firm by firm there were savage cut backs. For example, GEC (manufacturing turbines, switchgear and traction control gear at Trafford Park) reduced their workforce from 22,000 in 1964 to just 3,000 by 1976. Ironically GEC had traded successfully over these years, but its expansion was in electronics rather than heavy engineering and any new jobs had gone to the South.

The Ship Canal and the Manchester Docks had been a vital success story for the city and of great significance for the economy of much of south Lancashire. Trafford Park was the dynamo of Manchester industry during the first half of the twentieth century. But the Manchester Docks have now closed for business. Trade had all but disappeared by the early 1980s. Since then the Docks have been reborn as Salford Quays, a complex of leisure facilities and commercial offices, and an example of the kind of dockland redevelopment scheme which

An advertisement for the Port of Manchester, 1920s.

Trafford Park in 1936, the Sunflour Mills. *(Courtesy of Manchester Central Library)*

had also been tried on the old Liverpool rival. The decline of Trafford Park since the 1960s was part of a general malaise in local manufacturing which made Manchester, the one-time powerhouse of the industrial revolution, into one of the weakest industrial cities in Britain. The sorry state of the world's first industrial estate by the early 1980s epitomised the situation. However, the work of the Trafford Park Development Corporation between 1987 and 1998 has reversed the process of decline. The TPDC channelled public money into the creation of the transport infrastructure necessary for its redevelopment as a site of leisure activity as well as commercial use. Private investment followed this groundwork and in the 1990s jobs were being created rather than lost in Trafford Park. Equally, the availability of land so close to the city centre makes it a suitable location for leisure and tourist attractions such as the Lowry Centre and the Imperial War Museum in the North. The future may be brighter for Trafford Park than could have been hoped in the early 1980s, but it is a different kind of future. Manufacturing has long since ceased to be a sector of strength in the world's first industrial city.

From Manufacturing to a Service Economy

The poor performance of the North West in national terms has been a consistent feature of post-1945 industrial development. Yet the

Manchester region has sometimes seemed to offer the basis for optimism. Unfortunately, in manufacturing terms, this has been generally
misplaced. In the early 1960s there was hope that a second 'industrial
revolution' was on the horizon and would ensure the future prospects
of the region. The older heavy engineering trades were declining, but
electrical engineering looked more promising with firms like Metro-
Vicks and Ferranti's, and the potential of pharmaceuticals through ICI
suggested future strength not weakness. Even the stagnant textile
industry was being rejuvenated by ICI and Courtaulds' manufacture of
synthetic fibres. All this linked in with the emerging motorway network
and the phenomenon of virtually full employment to generate a climate
of optimism. In the event this was a false dawn. The 1970s and 1980s
were decades of national industrial decline in which the Manchester
region more than played its part. Moreover, Manchester's performance
was worse and its decline earlier than that of the region as a whole.

The greatest change in the economic structure of Manchester since
the industrial revolution took place after the Second World War. The
half-century and more since 1945 has seen a restructuring of the local
economy away from manufacturing and towards the service sector. As
we have seen, the late 1960s and early 1970s were a period of dramatic
industrial decline, beginning a trend in unemployment and job losses
which continued through to the mid-1980s. Over the period 1961–1983
Manchester lost over 150,000 jobs in manufacturing. Trends in male
employment figures, a crucial economic indicator, tell a dismal tale. If
the 1961 figures for Greater Manchester are taken as 100, the index
had fallen to 97 by 1966, 89 by 1970 and 84 by 1975. The inner core
of the conurbation was worst hit. Between 1966 and 1972 one in three
manual jobs in manufacturing were lost and one quarter of all factories
and workshops closed.[2] The inner industrial belt of factories, workshops,
canals, railway depots and row upon row of terraced housing, which
had once been a lively, dirty but exciting place, betrayed the symptoms
of inner-city decay.

Losses in manufacturing employment, however, were accompanied
(although not replaced in the same numbers) by a growth in service
occupations. The regional trend towards service employment was already apparent in the 1950s. It has been particularly marked in
Manchester. By 1985 only 23% of the workforce of the Manchester
metropolitan district were employed in manufacturing, compared to
figures of over 40% for the nearby towns of Bolton, Oldham and
Rochdale. Manchester's much reduced manufacturing sector included
the engineering, electrical, chemical, food, clothing and textile industries. In addition, a further 4% were involved in construction. Of
the 73% employed in the service sector the single most important
element was the public and scientific services (e.g. health and education),
providing 22% of all service occupations; other large elements were

'Sooty' Manchester: Ancoats in the 1930s.

the distributive trades (14%), the financial institutions (11%) and transport and communications (9%).[3] But even the service sector was under pressure. For example, Manchester's central business district suffered from the decentralisation of office development from the 1960s through to the 1980s. Put off by the problems of inner-city parking and attracted by better motorway access and lower rents, new office blocks rose across the southern suburbs. The city centre's share of commercial offices fell from approximately 40% of the total for Greater Manchester in 1974 to 33% in 1982.

Despite the demise of cotton and decades of manufacturing decline, Manchester continued to dominate its region. Manchester's role as a commercial centre was weakened after 1914 by the decline of its major commodity, but nonetheless, throughout the interwar Depression, the city continued to provide commercial, financial, insurance and transport services for industrial Lancashire. Manchester retained its nineteenth-century ranking as the leading financial centre outside London. For many years it held on to its handful of local banks. Local firms, even the larger ones, could obtain comprehensive financial services in Manchester without recourse to London. All this gave the place an air of independence and helped to keep Manchester's bankers' clearings larger than those of any other provincial city. In 1936, the total was over £533m. or 38% of the total provincial clearings, exceeding the amounts cleared at the three next largest centres combined.

However, the constantly growing power of the City of London meant that Manchester's independent banks were eventually absorbed by national concerns. Thus Williams Deacon's (begun in Manchester as the Manchester and Salford Bank in 1836) became part of the Royal Bank of Scotland group in 1930, and the District Bank (originally the Manchester and Liverpool District Banking Company) was absorbed into the National Provincial group in 1962. Despite such developments, Manchester has retained its position as the second largest financial centre in the country. Since the mid-1980s there has been an explosion of financial and consultancy services which has revived the prospects of Manchester's central business district.

Twentieth-century Manchester also remained a distribution centre of some note. The wholesale trade dominated until the 1950s. Apart from the distribution of manufactured goods, Manchester was the most important market for foodstuffs outside London. Between the wars it was the principal market in England for Danish butter and the regional entrepôt for cereals, meat and fruit. The national headquarters of the Cooperative Wholesale Society (CWS), developed with various construction projects between the 1860s and the 1930s, formed a community of buildings at the northern end of Corporation Street, between Miller Street and Withy Grove. Good communications in general and the Ship Canal in particular were crucial to CWS operations. Granaries and warehouses at the Ship Canal Docks were supplemented by cold stores and ordinary warehouses in the city. The CWS was continuously represented on the board of directors of the Ship Canal Company from 1893 to 1945.

Wholesale distribution was overtaken by the retail sector in the 1950s. The numbers in shop work grew while the warehouse sector contracted. Independent stores like Lewis's, Paulden's, Affleck and Brown's, and multiples like Marks & Spencer (who opened their Cross Street store in 1961), were joined in the 1960s by the supermarkets which revolutionised British shopping habits in a generation. In the 1960s the most popular shopping areas were around Market Street and Oldham Street. Smaller retailers clustered in the side streets, spilling out along Princess Street and Cross Street. There was a degree of specialisation: for example Peter Street was lined by car showrooms whilst Tib Street was cluttered with the cages of its innumerable pet shops. Oxford Street displayed a characteristic mixture of cafes, restaurants, cinemas, newsagents and tobacconists. St Ann's Square and King Street remained fashionable shopping quarters, and Deansgate boasted the upmarket stores of Kendal Milne and Marshall & Snellgrove. The increasing relative importance of shopping to the local economy revealed itself in adventurous plans for a covered shopping centre for the city. The shopping streets of Manchester were transformed in the 1970s by the massive scale and indoor malls of the Arndale Centre, the city centre's answer to increasing competition from the region's other retail centres.

This, plus pedestrianisation, has saved Market Street but at the expense of other traditional shopping thoroughfares like Oldham Street. Nonetheless it may have gone some way to preserving Manchester's role as a retail centre.

Its distributive function and excellent communications for a time made Manchester the most important centre of the newspaper industry outside London, with national newspapers establishing complete printing, publishing and editorial offices in the city. Manchester's newspaper industry was probably at its zenith in the early 1960s, but a portent for the future was the removal of *The Guardian* to London. In 1959 the *Manchester Guardian* had assumed its modern title in recognition of its status as a national newspaper. London printing was begun in 1961 and the editor moved to the capital three years later. The loss of *The Guardian* was an event of symbolic importance, but more significant changes were to come two decades later. New printing machinery, new work practices and computerisation transformed the newspaper industry during the 1980s. The impact on London's Fleet Street is well known, but the industry's decentralisation also hit the economy of central Manchester. The recently converted *Daily Express* building on Great Ancoats Street is a visible reminder of the city's former role as the newspaper capital of the North. Manchester, however, remains the

Air raid precautions, 1939. In anticipation of a gas attack, regular drills were undertaken in the use of gas masks.

home of the country's most important provincial daily, the *Manchester Evening News*, and the city's importance in other branches of the media seems secure. Manchester has enjoyed a high profile in the fields of radio and television. The BBC chose the city for its Northern Regional headquarters as early as 1922. Since the 1950s, Granada Television, based in Manchester, has been among the most imaginative and successful producers of programmes in the country: its flagship series, 'Coronation Street', has taken a fictional 'North' to viewers across the world. Moreover, in the 1980s and 1990s Granada's hugely popular Studio Tours made the city a focus for 'media tourism'.

Moreover, the industrial heritage of the region became a strength of the city's growing tourist trade. For example, the Manchester Museum of Science and Industry is an attraction of international significance. Work was what once brought people to Manchester in their thousands; now it is the leisure industry. Local economic planners recognise this only too well. Mills have been converted as museums and shopping outlets across the old industrial heartlands of the North, but the past need not be put into a museum to preserve it. The Museum of Science and Industry was part of the reclamation of the formerly derelict Castlefield Basin (the site of the Roman fort, the terminus of the Bridgewater Canal, and once the cradle of Manchester's industrial revolution) as Britain's first urban heritage park. Today it is promoted as a series of visitor attractions, including The People's History Museum, the Science Museum, the Roman Fort and the leisure use of the restored Bridgewater and Rochdale canals.

At the beginning of the twenty-first century Manchester's central business district is enjoying a period of revival. It is the single largest concentration in the North West of offices, shops, warehouses, hotels and theatres. Part of the area's attraction is its built environment. It may seem odd to comment thus about 'sooty' Manchester, which until the 1950s was a byword for dreariness and gloom. The products of industrial pollution and the unrestricted use of the domestic coal fire were fog, smog and blackened buildings which together with an infamous climate (more permanently damp than actually wet) contrived to give Manchester its grey visage. In the mid-twentieth century its image also had something to do with a prevalent distaste for all things Victorian. The Clean Air Act of 1956, which effectively doubled winter sunshine, and a policy of sandblasting in the 1970s dispelled much of the gloom, removing the grime from atmosphere and buildings alike to reveal the architectural flourish of the latter, now more readily appreciated.

There are those who claim that most of Manchester's Georgian and Victorian character has gone, destroyed either by the German bombers of 1940 or the retail complexes of the 1970s. In the 1930s the city was still dominated by its nineteenth-century buildings, its distinctive

The Manchester blitz, December 1940. Warehouses ablaze at Piccadilly, on the site of today's Piccadilly Plaza.

commercial streets were 'canyons, walled in by cotton warehouses'.[4] The Manchester Blitz undoubtedly destroyed much of the Victorian character of the central business district. The devastation permanently disfigured the face of Manchester. For three nights prior to Christmas 1940 the Luftwaffe dropped their incendiary bombs. Before dawn on Christmas Eve, after a second night of aerial bombardment, the whole city was lit by the inferno that ignited the magnificent warehouses of Portland Street and Mosley Street. Onlookers saw bales of cotton cloth shoot skywards as explosions came from within the blazing buildings, engulfed by a great wall of fire raging out of control. The fire services could not cope and the Royal Engineers were called in to blast fire breaks. Much of the old Market Place had been hit on the previous night. Within a mile of Albert Square 165 warehouses, 150 offices, five banks and 200 other business premises were destroyed or severely damaged.

The urban planners of the 1960s further eroded the Victorian character of the city. The purlieus of Market Street and Corporation Street, an unglamorous but atmospheric rabbit warren of alleyways and back streets, were demolished to make way for the Arndale Centre and other urban embellishments. Yet enough remains of the city's Georgian and Victorian architecture to make Manchester an interesting place to walk through, at least to those prepared to look above and beyond the shop windows. Twentieth-century additions of note include E. Vincent Harris' impressive Central Library and Town Hall Extension, standing between Albert and St Peter's Squares. The classical style and striking curve of the Central Library, opened in 1934, are linked to Waterhouse's original neo-Gothic Town Hall by the Extension of 1937, a halfway house between Victorian and modern styles. Additions since the Second World War generally excite less enthusiasm, although the 25-storey CIS building on Miller Street, erected in 1962, is standing the test of time better than most.

Communication by Road and Air

An improved communications network to match changing industrial conditions, residential patterns and new forms of transport required a coordinated policy across the conurbation as a whole. This was recognised as early as 1926 in the recommendation of 65 projects for regional and main district roads by the Manchester and District Joint Town Planning Advisory Committee.[5] Even at that early stage of the motor age they spoke of the need for bypasses and widened arterial roads and of the necessity of inter-regional routes. The existing road connection to Liverpool was clearly out of date. At one stage it passed through a stretch of road only 15ft 4ins wide at Sankey Street in the centre of Warrington. The new East Lancs Road of the 1930s met the call for improved motor routes to the west, but the connection to Yorkshire had to wait till the 1960s when the M62 was constructed, broadly following the route recommended in 1926. The road network boldly envisaged in 1926 has taken some time to come about. The post-war *City of Manchester Plan* (1945) included well thought through proposals for regional road communications involving inner, intermediate and outer ring orbital routes to ease the chronic congestion arising from the 900% increase in road traffic since 1919. Since the 1940s national priorities have determined the progress of the region's network of major roads. The outer orbit envisaged in 1945 was finally completed by 2000 and the Manchester region now has more miles of motorway than any other conurbation outside London. There has been less improvement in the city centre. Apart from the Mancunian Way, the central Manchester road pattern is in large part the one laid down during the nineteenth century.

If rail was the revolutionary new transport of the nineteenth century, then air travel was the most successful at contracting distance in the twentieth century. Manchester's air traffic has grown considerably since the prospect of an 'air station' was first mooted in the 1920s, and the decision was taken in 1929 by the City Council to give Manchester a municipal aerodrome. It soon outgrew its location at Barton near Eccles and, on land acquired adjacent to the Wythenshawe estate, the larger Ringway Airport was built. Ringway opened in 1938 to its first arrival, a KLM DC–2 from Amsterdam. KLM provided the only international service operating out of Ringway before the Second World War and, quaintly, offered passengers a 'request stop' at Doncaster! The great expansion of air travel came after 1945. In 1953 Manchester was already handling 200,000 passengers a year; by 1999 the figure had risen to 17 million. Ringway was renamed Manchester Airport in 1962, and today is the country's third largest airport. In the contest with the protagonists of Stansted over the siting of 'London's' new airport (paralleling nineteenth-century tensions over transport between Manchester and Liverpool?) Manchester lost. Manchester Airport is expanding nonetheless, with a second terminal and a new runway to cope with the increasing number of flights. It advertises itself as the 'Gateway to England's North Country' and has over 60% of the country's manufacturing industry within a radius of 100 miles. Manchester Airport arguably does for the region what the Manchester Ship Canal did almost a hundred years ago: it links it directly with the commerce and industry of the world.

Governing the Modern City

The building of the country's first municipal airport was the tip of an iceberg of corporate activity wholly in keeping for the city which had sponsored the Ship Canal a generation earlier. In 1926 Ernest Simon (former Lord Mayor, authority on local government, housing campaigner and much more) observed how few people realised that Manchester's annual budget exceeded that of some of the smaller European states. In fact, Corporation expenditure for the previous year had approached £5m. The country's great municipal corporations had become major employers of labour. Manchester City Council employed more than 25,000 people in 1926, and Simon estimated that one tenth of the city's population lived in the households of Council employees. By 1939 annual expenditure topped £9m. and the Corporation had assets in land, buildings, stocks and investments of over £88m.[6] Trading undertakings included the city's waterworks, gas and electricity supply, transport (electric tramcars and motor buses) and markets. A full list of Corporation responsibilities at that time would include several that are familiar but others that have disappeared with time, such as public assistance,

Manchester: the core city of the modern conurbation. The 'two-tower' CIS building is seen to the left in this view. (*Photograph: Ian Beesley*)

inherited from the Poor Law authorities in 1929, relief works for the unemployed and the preparation of air raid precautions.

Since 1939 municipal responsibilities have diminished in some areas and been transformed in others. During the second half of the twentieth century municipal authorities like Manchester had legal responsibilities in the areas of housing, education, libraries and art galleries, personal and social services, engineering and public services, pollution, sewerage and environmental health. During its short life the Greater Manchester County Council (1974–1985) took on responsibility for passenger transport, police, fire service, consumer protection, refuse disposal, housing and planning. But despite the brief episode of the GMC (see below), the trend in finance and responsibility over the last thirty years has been away from local to central government. In the 1980s central government restricted and reformed local government finance and put pressure on local authorities to 'privatise' existing services, obliging them, for example, to sell off council houses and introduce competition in public transport.

In the twentieth century regional planning for urban development and transport infrastructure had a varied history. In this context Manchester was treated as a city-region or conurbation, incorporating towns with strong traditions of their own, Bolton, Bury, Oldham, Rochdale, Stockport and so on. Even this was not as all-encompassing as the urban Lancashire unconvincingly designated 'Lancaston' by Patrick Geddes, the man who first coined the word 'conurbation'.[7] Geddes recognised a process of 'agglomeration' which had come about since 1850. The suburban diaspora of the late nineteenth century, aided by transport improvements, spread 'Greater' Manchester over surrounding villages and townships, an outward dispersal of population which continued through the twentieth century. Accompanying a largely unplanned suburban growth was a more directed development towards rehousing the inner-city population often far outside the municipal boundary (see Chapter 11). The economic interdependence of such city-regions led by 1951 to the official (and misleading) designation of the region as the South-East Lancashire Conurbation, despite the fact that the chosen area reached deep into Cheshire.

Administrative reform follows economic reality tempered by historical precedent, but in a very real sense the boundaries mean little. The various elements of the conurbation had grown into one another long before they were united by local government reform. Economic reality rarely balks at municipal boundaries. For example, 'industrial Manchester' cannot be confined within the administrative areas shown on a map. This can confuse the unwary. Thus the major docks of the Manchester Ship Canal were in fact to be found in Salford, and Trafford Park industrial estate occupied land in Stretford and Urmston. Finding the physical 'heart' of Manchester has never been easy. The visitor in search of it may cross and recross the boundary with Salford without realising it. The 'twin cities', linked by more than the bridges across the Irwell, are divided by a boundary which has no basis in physical or economic fact. To the outsider amalgamation may seem rational, but Salford has nurtured its separate identity over the years and any prospect of absorption by its wealthier neighbour was effectively blocked when Salford became a city by letters patent in 1926.

The administrative relationship between municipal Manchester and its immediate neighbours fluctuated during the twentieth century. In terms of territorial expansion, Manchester's 'imperial' phase was over by 1914, although the addition of Wythenshawe in 1930 accounts for the elongated shape of the municipal borough (see map on page 202). Despite economic inter-dependence within the region, surrounding towns such as Salford, Stockport, Oldham and Rochdale jealously guarded their independence. Local government reform tended to strengthen their position whilst recognising the dominance of Manchester. For example, the Local Government Act of 1972 created Greater Manchester as one of six new metropolitan counties. Following Greater London and the West Midlands it was the third largest of the new giants of local government and the only one in the provinces to be named after its core city.

Greater Manchester County (which narrowly escaped being designated 'Selnec', an acronym formed from the initials of its catchment area, south-east Lancashire and north-east Cheshire) stretched over almost 500 square miles and included a population of 2.7 million. As well as the borough of Manchester it included a cluster of newly created

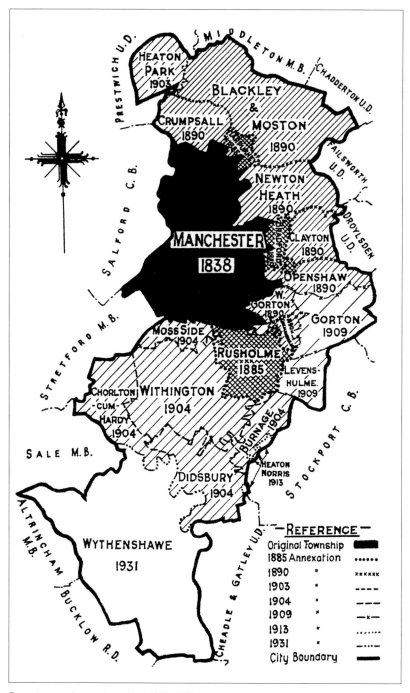

Extensions to the city boundary, 1838–1938.

metropolitan authorities. These were focused on the crescent of industrial towns to the north (Wigan, Bolton, Bury, Rochdale and Oldham) and the adjacent boroughs of Salford and Stockport, to which were added new administrative inventions: Trafford (incorporating Altrincham, Bowden, Bucklow, Hale, Sale, Stretford and Urmston) to the south of Manchester and Tameside (Ashton-under-Lyne, Audenshaw, Denton, Droylsden, Dukinfield, Hyde, Longendale and Mossley) to the east. As a unit of local government the Greater Manchester County had a short life but the metropolitan boroughs have survived. The existence of these modern metropolitan authorities surrounding the borough of Manchester (the boundaries of which remained unchanged in 1972) reflect the limits to expansion reached by Manchester much earlier in the century.

Industrial Unrest and Unemployment, 1914–1939

After 1914 Manchester no longer occupied the centre stage in Labour history as it had done ever since the industrial revolution. Manchester played only a supporting role in the industrial unrest and popular politics of the 1920s and 1930s as the Labour Party's parliamentary rise focused attention on Westminster. Against a background of rising unemployment in the early 1920s, heavy engineering and textiles, amongst other industries, experienced a number of trade disputes over wage reductions and management strategies to increase productivity. These disputes culminated in the greatest industrial confrontation of the interwar years, the General Strike of 1926. Finally, the unemployment problem dominated domestic politics between the wars, and reignited the politics of protest in Manchester and Salford in dramatic fashion.

The most serious labour unrest of the First World War had originated in the textile-machine making factories of the Manchester region. In the spring of 1917, the issue of 'dilution' (paying women a lower rate to do jobs traditionally reserved for skilled men) combined with price rises and war-weariness to produce a wave of strikes which spread from Lancashire to engineering works in Sheffield, the West Midlands and London. This was a rank and file action coordinated by a Joint Engineering Shop Stewards Committee and not official trade union leaders. The Shop Stewards Movement negotiated directly with government, but strike leaders, including delegates from Manchester, were arrested at a meeting in London and the government were able to break the strike by forcing the shop stewards under threat of imprisonment to accept a settlement agreed with officials of the engineering union.

After the brief post-war boom of 1919–20, industrial relations entered an unsettled phase in which groups of workers sought to preserve

The General Strike in Manchester. A meeting in Albert Square.

wartime gains in the face of rising unemployment and employer pressure
for wage-reductions. A lock-out in the engineering industry seriously
affected Manchester in 1922, and after a bitter 13-week dispute the
men returned to work on the employers' terms. Disputes also occurred
in the cotton mills over the introduction of more machines per operative
as employers tried to combat the technical superiorities and lower wage
costs of their overseas competitors. Similar conflicts over wage reductions and work rates affected a number of industries across the country,
most notably coal mining, and culminated in the General Strike.

The General Strike of 1926 was called by the TUC in support of
the miners' fight against a 20% wage cut. The TUC feared that success
for the coal-owners might signal a more general attack on working-class
living standards across all major industries. For nine days in May, a
national stoppage was conducted in support of the miners. It ended on
12 May in an effective capitulation by the TUC. Manchester was not
at the forefront of the Strike: there were fewer than a thousand miners
employed locally, but the city was virtually closed down by the dispute.
Transport workers acted first: the trams stopped running and work
ceased at the Manchester Docks. The Ship Canal was quiet, although
grain and other supplies were unloaded by strike-breakers after the
arrival of the Royal Navy destroyer *HMS Wessex*. Among the city's
newspapers, the *Manchester Guardian* had to be printed by editorial staff
on one or two sheets and the *Manchester Evening Chronicle* appeared on

a single sheet. On the other hand, a Manchester edition of the TUC paper, the *British Worker*, was edited by Fenner Brockway and distributed by transport workers across the country. The aftermath of the General Strike and the final defeat of the miners six months later was a prolonged period of industrial peace in which wages fell, unemployment rose and trade union membership plummeted. Moreover, industrial action became depoliticised, partly through the perceived ineffectiveness of trade union activity but also through the rise of Labour as a party which aspired to govern not just to act as an agency of protest. However, the politics of protest were ignited in another quarter during the height of the Depression in 1931.

Unemployment reached its peak between 1931 and 1933, but popular protest was muted largely due to the absence of Labour Party or TUC support for street demonstrations and hunger marches. Such unemployed agitation that did occur was organised by the Communist-inspired National Unemployed Workers Movement (NUWM). The motives were similar to those of the Social Democratic Federation (SDF) in the years before 1914, to advance the cause of the unemployed by pressurising central and local authorities into making concessions, and to forward the cause of Socialism by turning the unemployed into a revolutionary force. The NUWM was no more successful than the SDF on either count, although it did produce a better coordinated national campaign.

The climax of the NUWM's agitation came in 1931 with protests against cuts in unemployment insurance benefit and the introduction of the hated Means Test by Ramsay MacDonald's National Government. Among the largest demonstrations, and most serious clashes with police, took place in Manchester and Salford. As before 1914, the police were prepared to use force to clear unemployed protesters from the city streets. On 1 October a huge march against the Means Test blocked Chapel Street, Salford. A deputation met the Lord Mayor, but as the body of the marchers approached Salford Town Hall it was met by a police baton charge in Bexley Square. Several arrests ensued and police prevented the demonstrators reaching the Town Hall. The incident was made famous when it was used as the factual basis for a fictional scene by Salford writer Walter Greenwood in *Love on the Dole* (1933), the most important and influential novel of working-class life to come out of the Depression years.[8]

But the largest and most violently dispersed of the Lancashire demonstrations against the Means Test came seven days later in Manchester. Tens of thousands of men and women, with nine Labour councillors at their head, set out from Ardwick Green with the intention of escorting a deputation to the City Council, requesting non-implementation of the cuts and the Means Test. The police denied the marchers access to Albert Square, the scene of serious clashes between police and unemployed 23 years before. But the organisers were not to be deflected from their target and the march set out. Their way was barred by police at the junction of London Road and Whitworth Street. The demonstrators response was to sit in the road. After a few minutes the police began a series of baton charges to clear the road, and fire hoses from the Whitworth Street Fire Station which overlooked the scene spouted tons of water onto the protesters. After some time the march was broken up and several arrests were made. There were further protests by the unemployed in the city during the 1930s, for example against the dole cuts of 1935, but police action and lack of parliamentary support marginalised such street politics, born of desperation as much as hope. The recurrence of mass unemployment fifty years later in the 1980s did not produce the same degree of organised protest, although it can be held as indirectly responsible for the riots which sporadically affected Manchester and other big cities.

Politics and Elections since 1918

British politics entered the modern era in the decade after the First World War, with voting rights extended to all adult males in 1918 and to females in two stages, for those over thirty in 1918 and for all over twenty-one in 1928. Thus the Parliament of 1929 was the first in Britain elected according to the principle of universal suffrage. We have already seen how the advent of the working-class voter since 1867 had had surprising results. The rise of a party of Labour was perhaps no surprise. But the success of the Conservative Party in gaining the working-class vote was less predictable and equally significant. After 1918 the Liberal Party was squeezed out of the political race, playing a diminishing role in Parliamentary politics during the interwar years and generally occupying a marginal position between 1945 and the 1980s, with a revival in its fortunes (as the Liberal Democrats) since then.

How has the balance between party politics and political power worked out in Manchester since 1918? Major themes in the story have been the absence of Liberal MPs for the city since 1929 followed by a virtual wipe-out of the Liberal Party from the municipal arena after 1945; a steady but unspectacular rise of the Labour Party in parliamentary and local politics during the interwar years, but much more success since 1945; and a significant part for the Conservative Party in terms of parliamentary representation of the city up to the 1960s and an equally important role in municipal politics until the late 1970s when they suffered a spectacular fall in favour.

The last great Liberal success in Manchester was in 1923 when the Party won five of the city's ten parliamentary seats (Blackley, Exchange, Moss Side, Rusholme and Withington) in the general election which brought the first Labour government to power and saw the Liberals reunited after the divisions of the post-war years. But these seats were all lost to the Conservatives less than a year later as the tide of national opinion shifted against the Liberal Party. The Liberals won Blackley and Withington once more in 1929 but this was their swan song. No Liberal has represented a Manchester constituency since 1931. The Liberals fared little better in municipal politics. Whilst individual Liberal councillors like Ernest Simon were a major influence on the direction of policy, his party was rapidly marginalised. By the 1930s it was already the 'also ran' in an essentially two party system. The key factor in the national decline of the Liberal Party was an increasing (although never complete) polarisation of politics along class lines. The Liberals lost out to the Conservatives in middle-class constituencies and wards, and were squeezed between Conservative and Labour in the struggle for working-class votes. This was as clear in Manchester as anywhere else.

The new working-class constituencies were barren territory for the Liberals. They did not even join the contest in Ardwick, Clayton or Gorton until 1929, when they came a poor third. Contests at Miles Platting in 1922 and 1924 were equally humiliating. Municipal elections in the 1920s also revealed Liberal weakness in working-class areas. Research on Manchester's municipal elections between 1919 and 1928 reveals average party support across the ten-year period as follows: Conservatives 44%, Labour 32%, Liberal 21.5%. But Liberal support was concentrated in certain suburban residential wards mostly to the south of the city centre. By contrast the inner industrial wards were neglected. For example, only one Liberal ever contested a council seat in any of the wards within the boundaries of the Gorton constituency between 1919 and 1929, and all ten municipal contests in Ardwick ward for these years were straight fights between Labour and Conservative. Liberal organisation had collapsed in industrial Manchester. Meanwhile Labour steadily eroded Conservative strength in working-class wards. Between 1919 and 1923 honours were even with 47 victories each in identifiably working-class wards, but the 1924–1928 period saw Labour success in 65 contests as opposed to a tally of 34 for the Conservatives.[9] By the 1930s the Tories were replacing Liberals in the city's suburban wards and a steady Liberal decline turned into a collapse. Liberal councillors in post-1945 Manchester had the rarity value of an endangered species.

In contrast to the Liberals, the Conservatives in Manchester enjoyed remarkable electoral success until the Labour landslide of 1945. Between 1918 and 1937 Conservative and Unionist candidates won 43 of the 74 parliamentary electoral contests which took place in Manchester constituencies compared to the 24 won by Labour and seven which went to the Liberals. Tory victories included several in the largely working-class constituency of Hulme, which was represented by Lt. Col. Joseph

Nall for most of the interwar period. It was not until 1945 that Labour took a majority of Manchester's parliamentary seats, winning nine of the available ten with only Withington going to the Tories. Elections between 1950 and 1959 saw the parties more evenly balanced in the city but with Labour always in the ascendent. Of the 48 contests between 1945 and 1959, 31 were won by Labour candidates whilst 17 went to the Tories. Reliable Conservative constituencies at this time were Blackley, Moss Side, Withington and Wythenshawe. The election of 1964, however, witnessed a seachange in Manchester politics: the Conservatives were reduced to two seats when they lost Wythenshawe and Blackley as Labour came to power nationally. Moss Side also fell to Labour ten years later. This was more than a passing trend.

The flow of votes away from the Tories in the larger cities of the North was a feature of urban politics from the 1960s to the 1990s. In the 1983 election, despite a national victory, the Conservative Party won less than half the number of seats it had won in the larger cities in 1959, the previous election when a Conservative government had been returned with a three-figure majority. Manchester was among the cities in which the decline was most marked. In the 1959 election the Conservatives had won a total of 15 seats in Glasgow, Liverpool and Manchester. In the same three cities in 1983, they held only one (Withington). This was against the national trend in 1983 which saw a swing away from Labour, especially in rural areas and the South. But despite the national pattern the drift to Labour in the big cities of the North continued during the 1980s. The last Conservative seat in Manchester was lost when Withington fell to the Labour candidate in the 1987 general election. Manchester had joined Glasgow and Liverpool in having no Conservative-held parliamentary seats, a situation which was confirmed in the general elections of 1992, 1997 and 2001.

The consolidation of Labour support in the big cities of the North was a striking phenomenon in an era of Conservative success nationally. It may owe something to disillusion generated by industrial decline and government policies, but the continued loss of population from cities such as Manchester may be affecting the social composition of its constituencies, with electoral consequences for the Tories. In municipal politics Manchester followed a similar path with a steady attrition of Tory seats in the 1960s and early 1970s turning into a rout by the 1980s. Tory representation on Manchester City Council has become miniscule in recent years. In view of current Labour predominance, the local parallel which springs to mind is with the mid-Victorian period at the height of Liberal Party hegemony over Manchester politics when local Tories had been similarly marginalised.

Education and the Arts

During the twentieth century Manchester's position as a major centre of higher education and learning has been enhanced. The culmination of the free library system came in 1934 with the opening of the Central Reference Library building in St Peter's Square, once regarded as the 'British Museum of the North'. The various specialist departments of the Central Library (Social Sciences, Technical, Language and Literature, Archives, Arts, Music, Local History, Jewish, Commercial and Patents) and its massive collections made it one of the most important public libraries in the country. Today it remains one of the city's unremarked cultural treasures. It is a resource of regional importance and (in the case of some collections) of national significance. Another element in Manchester's library inheritance from the Victorian era is the John Rylands Library. The purchase of rare books and manuscripts by the great merchant's widow, plus the building of the neo-Gothic edifice on Deansgate which houses them, is a fine endowment to the city. 'John Rylands' remained independent until 1972 when it merged with the library of Manchester University to form what is now called the John Rylands University Library of Manchester, the third largest academic library in the United Kingdom.

Further education was a key area of municipal activity in Manchester for most of the twentieth century. Carrying on the tradition established before the First World War of encouraging post-school education related to the world of work (see Chapter 8), interwar Manchester could boast an impressive range of municipal provision. This was most important in view of the paucity of secondary school places. Although the city was proud of the ancient traditions of the Manchester Grammar School (founded by Hugh Oldham in 1515) and possessed several private secondary schools, the Council had been slow to provide municipal secondary education. By 1924 there were 1,400 free places available, but six candidates for every place. The vast majority of pupils left elementary school at fourteen. Although a number of 'senior' schools were opened during the 1930s, the city's further education sector offered the only opportunity for many to further their education beyond the elementary stage. The College of Technology (as the Technical School was renamed in 1918), the Municipal School of Art, the High School of Commerce and the Central Evening School of Domestic Economy were responsible for the more advanced courses. Lower level instruction was offered by a number of continuation schools and evening institutes, providing a ladder of educational opportunity which in theory stretched upwards to university level. By the mid-1930s some 26,000 students were enrolled on farther education courses in the city.

The 1944 Education Act required secondary provision in grammar, secondary modern and technical schools, selection being made at the age of eleven. The raising of the school-leaving age to 15 in 1947, and the increased birth rate of the post-war years, put pressure on local education authorities like Manchester. Nevertheless, a great advance in provision was made. In the 1920s only one in 30 pupils received a full-time secondary education beyond 14, but by the early 1960s one in three were staying on voluntarily to attend full-time classes for a year beyond the statutory leaving age of 15.

However, the single most striking change in the schools system in the 1960s was the introduction of non-selective or comprehensive schools. The government circular 10/65 encouraged local education authorities to end the eleven-plus examination and to eliminate the division between secondary modern and grammar schools. Some authorities, like Manchester, had already introduced a few comprehensive schools in the late 1950s and early 1960s, and in 1967 the city was one of the first to reorganise its secondary schools. Although the change to comprehensives was broadly welcomed it was not without acrimony, especially when the government made non-selective secondary education compulsory in 1976 and removed direct grant status from maintained grammar schools. Comprehensive education was introduced comparatively smoothly in Manchester, with the city's Catholic schools making the change in 1977. But the reform met severe resistance in the neighbouring authority of Trafford, and through successful court cases and a change of government in 1979, it has proved possible for some areas in the Manchester region to retain the older selective system. Moreover, the ending of direct grant status has caused some of the formerly maintained schools to leave the state system altogether, and the number of independent schools in the Greater Manchester area doubled in the 1970s and 1980s to around 25. Government policy in the 1990s which enabled schools to 'opt out' of local education authority control, could be seen as a return of grant-maintained status.

The years since the Second World War have seen dramatic developments in Manchester's further and higher education sector, in which the groundwork provided by local authority control enabled newly independent institutions to emerge. In the mid-1950s the highly successful College of Technology emerged from municipal control to assume full university status as the University of Manchester Institute of Science and Technology. This left the city without a central technical college, a situation that was amended in 1964 with the opening of the John Dalton College of Technology on Chester Street near what was to become the Mancunian Way. Other new colleges at this time included the Domestic and Trades College (Hollings College) which opened its distinctive 'Toast Rack' building at the junction of Old Hall Lane and Wilmslow Road in 1960.

But the most dramatic educational change of the post-war years was the expansion of teacher training. Before the Second World War

Manchester Education Committee had held only limited responsibilities for the training of teachers. A post-war national teacher shortage and the government's emergency training programme gave Manchester four major training colleges (Manchester, Mather, Elizabeth Gaskell and Didsbury colleges of education) as well as teacher education departments in two of the city's central colleges. A declining birth rate since the 1960s and changed government priorities have seen a correspondingly sharp contraction in the teacher education sector and none of these colleges has retained their independence; only Didsbury College survived intact as a faculty of Manchester Polytechnic, now the Manchester Metropolitan University.

As part of a further central government initiative in higher education, Manchester Polytechnic was formed in 1970 from an amalgamation of the John Dalton College of Technology, the College of Commerce (former High School of Commerce) and the College of Art and Design (former School of Art). In 1977 Didsbury and Hollings colleges became part of this growing institution, under local authority control and providing a range of advanced courses including an increasing range of degrees. Manchester Polytechnic, having taken in the remaining teacher-training colleges in 1983, soon became the largest institution of its kind in the country and, with a certain air of inevitability, was removed from local authority control in 1990. Under the Further and Higher Education Act of 1992 it assumed university status as the Manchester Metropolitan University.

Since 1902 the Victoria University of Manchester has been one of the country's leading institutions of higher education. In terms of leadership in research its greatest days came earlier in the century and were concentrated in the Natural Sciences. Since 1906 no fewer than 14 scientists who had been students, research fellows or members of academic staff were Nobel Prize winners for Physics or Chemistry (although this number includes only four since 1950). Undoubtedly its most significant twentieth-century scholar was Ernest Rutherford. Between 1907 and 1919 Rutherford held a chair in Physics and, working with scientists of the calibre of Ernest Marsden, Niels Bohr and others, he originated the modern science of nuclear physics, culminating in 1919 with his achievement of the first artificial nuclear disintegration. In the first half of the century Manchester University's reputation extended beyond the Sciences into such areas as History with professors like the medievalists, J. Tait and F. M. Powicke, the economic historians George Unwin and Arthur Redford, and J. E. Neale and L. B. Namier in modern history. A. J. P. Taylor's lectures at Manchester before the Second World War were legendary, although the historian who contributed most to the development of Manchester University was T. F. Tout. Since the Second World War the University of Manchester has been an important although less distinctive institution. However, it did pioneering work in the field of computer science after 1945, and the Jodrell Bank Telescopes, under the direction of Bernard Lovell, have made a vital contribution to the development of the new science of radio astronomy since the 1950s. Moreover, Manchester University remains one of the largest universities in the UK. It forms part of a huge, if geographically scattered, higher education precinct, which along with the University of Salford, the University of Manchester Institute of Science and Technology and the Manchester Metropolitan University, gives Manchester and Salford the largest concentration of students in Western Europe.

As the city's Victorian era had demonstrated, 'Manchester Man' was a great collector of art. In the twentieth century this has been represented in public rather than private collections. Manchester possesses one of the best municipal art galleries in Britain. The collections of the Manchester City Art Gallery, including its justly famous pre-Raphaelites, are chiefly the result of nineteenth-century purchases and donations. Even the building itself was a free gift from the governors of the Royal Manchester Institution in 1882. Another Victorian benefactor (Joseph Whitworth) gave Manchester its other major gallery. The Whitworth Art Gallery has consistently acquired twentieth-century works, although its most notable specialism has been English water-colours. Benefiting from the donation of 154 water-colours in the 1890s by J. E. Taylor, Director of the *Manchester Guardian*, and purchases made before 1914, the Whitworth has built a collection of English water-colours which today can only be paralleled in the Victoria and Albert and British Museums. The other strength of the Whitworth lies in its collection of textiles, an appropriate collection for Manchester and one which is second only to that in the Victoria and Albert Museum.

In terms of artistic production, Manchester can lay claim to being the home of a distinctive school of industrial landscape painters of whom L. S. Lowry is only the best known. The Manchester Academy of Fine Arts annual exhibitions were the focal point for the display of work by local artists. Lowry's works were often the outstanding feature of the Academy list. Successful Manchester artists inevitably turned to London, Lowry's first London exhibition was in 1939: nevertheless, in the same year, the president of the Academy could justifiably claim that: 'Manchester was the art centre of the north of England',[10] and as if to support his boast, the Academy exhibition of 1939 ran to 350 works by over 80 artists. However, the stark quality evident in Lowry's industrial landscapes was generally absent from other exhibits at the Academy. Lowry's vision was not always to local taste. Many felt he misrepresented the North to the rest of the country. But Lowry was not the only local artist willing to portray the contemporary North. After 1945 a younger generation of artists formed their own 'salon' at Margo Ingham's Midday Studios directly opposite the City Art Gallery on Mosley Street. Since then the Manchester region has been the home of several important painters of the urban industrial scene such as William Turner (born in Chorlton-upon-Medlock), Roger Hampson (Bolton) and Harold Riley (Salford).

Manchester's reputation as a centre of musical performance established during the nineteenth century survived into the twentieth. The Hallé Concerts Society continued to provide the core of this reputation. Despite some uncertain times between the world wars, the Hallé Orchestra, under the leadership of Sir John Barbirolli from 1943 to 1959, went from strength to strength. Its traditional venue, the Free Trade Hall, was virtually destroyed in the Manchester blitz of December 1940 with only its outer walls left standing, but the building's careful reconstruction in the later 1940s restored the Hallé to its traditional home. Continued success (both commercial and artistic) since Barbirolli's time culminated in removal to the purpose-built Bridgewater Concert Hall on a site opposite the Greater Manchester Exhibition Centre (G-Mex).

Manchester's musical reputation also depends on its role in tuition. Part of the inheritance from Charles Hallé is the college of music which he founded in 1893. The Royal Manchester College of Music developed a formidable reputation for the quality of its tutors and the calibre of its students. The latter have included the violinist Arthur Catterall and the pianist John Ogdon. In 1972 it amalgamated with the Northern School of Music (formed in 1942 as a municipal-aided institution from the school of music originally founded in 1920 by Tobias Matthay in small premises on Deansgate) to become the Royal Northern College of Music, one of the leading music colleges in Europe. Add to this the transformation in 1969 of Chetham's Hospital School from a boys' boarding establishment into a co-educational school offering a curriculum geared to the needs of musically gifted children and modern Manchester emerges as a city endowed with an impressive array of musical institutions.

Modern Manchester is also a centre of musical excellence of a quite different sort. Since the 1950s, the city has been an important location for the performance of popular music, with numerous local bands and lively clubs. Although Liverpool may have been in the ascendant during the 1960s, the 1980s was the decade of 'Manchester music'. With famous figures in the pop world such as Morrissey and Happy Mondays and well-known dance clubs such as the controversial Haçienda, Manchester gained an international reputation in the world of popular music culture. Appropriately, Salford College of Technology was the first in the country to offer a degree course in popular music.

Manchester's place in the history of the English theatre is less secure than is its musical pre-eminence. The golden age of the Manchester drama was during the Horniman era at the Gaiety Theatre before the

First World War. But the Gaiety had become a cinema by 1921 and serious drama in Manchester entered the doldrums. Audiences turned up in droves for popular musicals and revues by C. B. Cochrane and Noel Coward at the Palace or the Opera House but these were touring productions. Repertory drama was revived in the shape of the Library Theatre built into the basement of the Central Library in the 1930s. But despite this municipal initiative, the city played only a minor part in the provincial theatre. Improvement had to wait till the 1960s, firstly when the Manchester University Theatre (now the Contact Theatre) opened in 1965, but chiefly in the shape of the 69 Theatre Company which evolved into the Royal Exchange Company. The choice of the redundant Royal Exchange as the venue for a purpose-built theatre-in-the-round was more than a particularly apposite use of an integral Manchester building: it heralded a revival of drama in the city which has once more given Manchester a leading dramatic role amongst the larger provincial cities.

References

1. There is no satisfactory history of Trafford Park, but much can be gleaned from D. A. Farnie, *The Manchester Ship Canal and the Rise of the Port of Manchester 1894–1975*, Manchester University Press, 1980, ch. 6 and passim. The development of the Park can be followed through various promotional publications, such as *Trafford Park: Britain's Workshop and Storehouse*, Trafford Park Estates, Manchester, 1923; *The Trafford Park Handbook*, Trafford Park Estates, Manchester, 1962.

2. P. E. Lloyd and C. M. Mason, 'Manufacturing in the inner city: a case study of Greater Manchester', *Transactions of the Institute of British Geographers*, n.s. 3 (1978), pp. 66–90.

3. *Trends in Employment and Unemployment in Manchester*, Manchester Employment Research Group Ltd, Manchester Polytechnic, 1987.

4. *A Pictorial and Descriptive Guide to Manchester*, Manchester City News, 1937, p. 36.

5. Manchester and District Joint Town Planning Advisory Committee, *Report on the Regional Scheme*, Manchester, 1926, pp. 37–62.

6. E. Simon, *A City Council From Within*, 1926, p. 1; *How Manchester is Managed*, Manchester City Council, 1926 and 1939. For Simon see, M. Stocks, *Ernest Simon of Manchester*, Manchester University Press, 1963.

7. P. Geddes, *Cities in Evolution*, Benn, London, 1968, pp. 31–2, 34. First published in 1915. 'Lancaston' included Liverpool.

8. S. Constantine, '*Love on the Dole* and its reception in the 1930s', *Literature and History*, 8 (1982), pp. 232–47.

9. See C. Cook, *The Age of Alignment: Electoral Politics in Britain 1922–1929*, Macmillan, London, 1975, esp. pp. 52–3, 83–5.

10. Quoted in R. Davies, *A Northern School: Lancashire Artists of the Twentieth Century*, Redcliffe Press, Bristol, 1989, p. 117.

CHAPTER 11

Living in Modern Manchester

The vigorous population growth of the Victorian era came to an end in the early twentieth century. Population increase in the region[1] had already slowed to less than 1% per annum between 1901 and 1911 to around a total of 2.3m. Growth slowed even farther over the next 20 years to reach a shade over 2.4m. by 1931, a figure which remained stable for the following 30 years. Since then population decline has been the pattern. Ironically, the years between 1921 and 1951 were a period of the most rapid physical expansion of the built-up area in the region's history. Whilst the pressure of numbers eased, the character of the population altered in the new age of the smaller family with rising expectations of adequate living space. Thus the number of households in the region grew by 22% between 1931 and 1951 despite zero population growth. Correspondingly, the housing stock rose by 24% over the same period.

Within this overall picture there was a submerged pattern of decentralisation, suburban growth paralleling inner-city decline. After reaching a peak of 766,300 in 1931, the population of the borough of Manchester fell by 8% between 1931 and 1951, and a further drop of 6% to 661,800 by 1961 meant a loss of over 100,000 in thirty years. The decline intensified over the next twenty years due to manufacturing decay and a policy of rehousing outside the municipal boundary. The figure of 404,861 for 1991 was little more than half the 1931 peak. Along with Liverpool and Glasgow, Manchester sustained the greatest population loss since 1951 of any of the large cities in the UK (although there is evidence that city centre population is on the rise – see Chapter 12).

By contrast, the populations of several neighbouring districts were hugely increased during the second quarter of the century. Between 1921 and 1951 the population of Prestwich had risen by 82%, Wilmslow by 90%, Hazel Grove and Bramhall by 100%, Urmston by 156% and Cheadle by 186%. Such figures represent, in part, the trend towards owner-occupation which has come to characterise residential tenure in twentieth-century Britain, but also the advent of the council-owned suburban housing estate. Both developments, in different ways, have extended further down the social scale a pattern of suburban living pioneered by the Victorian upper middle class. The scale and impact of these changes justify the term a 'housing revolution'.

The Housing Revolution

The housing revolution was a national phenomenon and, although encouraged by the state, largely unplanned. Between 1919 and 1939, 4m. new houses (or one third of the total housing stock in 1939) were built across the country, of which 2.5m. were private and 1.5m. were government subsidised (1.1m. council-owned and 400,000 in private ownership). The voluntary resettlement of the better-off in the private sector after 1914 was accompanied by growth in the public sector housing stock, largely got under way by Addison's Housing Act of 1919 and only brought to a serious halt, sixty years later, by changed central government priorities since 1979. The outflow to the suburbs left behind generation after generation of inner-city poor, ill-housed and poorly supplied with amenities but constantly replenished with immigrants, most recently by West Indians and Asians since the 1950s. Successive rehousing schemes have, sometimes imaginatively, too often inadequately, relocated some of those who could not afford entry to the owner-occupier 'club'. The growth in the number of council house tenants paralleled the rise of the mortgage holder, but perpetuated a social geography inherited from the Victorians.

Manchester's suburban increase after 1914 continued the nineteenth-century pattern of southwards expansion into Cheshire. The private housing boom of the 1920s and 1930s refashioned villages and fields into residential suburbs. Existing towns and settlements contributed to an expansion which was more than a mere growth outwards from the centre. Falling house prices – around £400 in the 1930s bought a three bedroom semi – created a revolution in home ownership. The suburban frontier at Altrincham, Alderley Edge and Wilmslow had been established as early as 1850, courtesy of the first commuter lines of the railway era. Along the line into Manchester there was still much green space. Residential development in the interwar years filled in the gaps between outer suburb and town. Thus the infill of bricks and mortar in Brooklands and Timperley physically joined the towns of Altrincham and Sale. Cheshire villages like Gatley, Cheadle, Cheadle Hulme and Handforth were each absorbed into the continuous suburban belt of South Manchester. Independent-minded Stockport was swamped in the process, forming part of an uninterrupted townscape which had taken on most of its present dimensions by 1939. The north of the city was less affected by the interwar building boom, except for the Prestwich–Whitefield–Bury corridor. A further housing boom in the 1960s and preferential tax relief for the mortgage holder set the seal on half a century of private development.

Manchester City Council was among the first to respond positively to the 1919 Housing Act. The next twenty years saw the construction of Corporation estates, mainly on suburban sites, and the planning, on a visionary scale, of Manchester's own 'garden town' at Wythenshawe, which has been described as 'perhaps the most ambitious programme of civic restructuring that any British city has ever undertaken'.[2] Planning for healthy homes was the impetus behind what Ernest Simon, the chief advocate of the Wythenshawe scheme, styled the 'rebuilding of Manchester'. He felt that the lesson of history had shown *laissez-faire* in housing to be 'nothing less than a calamity'. In 1935 Simon applauded the change in public opinion over the previous hundred years which he believed had led to corporate housing policy.

> The condition of the slums a century ago was the result of leaving the provision of housing for the working classes to private enterprise without any control ... In 1835 the slums might be as bad as they liked, nobody thought of interference by the city authorities or by the Government.[3]

Later in the nineteenth century Manchester Corporation had developed a housing policy which focused on the reconditioning of existing properties (see Chapter 7). However, after 1919 the pre-war policy of reconditioning was abandoned in favour of the building of new houses, either directly by the Corporation or, from 1925, via subsidy or loan to private contractors. Hindsight suggests that rehousing and reconditioning were complementary not competing policies. Whilst many tenants were rehoused in superior accommodation, the existing housing stock of the inner city was unfortunately neglected. The chief efforts were put into the newer policy of house building. After a slow start in the early 1920s, due largely to the stop-start policies of changing central governments, the pace quickened to well over a thousand new Corporation houses a year. Between 1920 and 1938 a total of 27,447 council houses were erected, plus a further 8,315 built by private contractors with Corporation financial assistance. These numbers exceeded by far the 15,845 private houses built locally without subsidy between 1925 and 1938, a ratio of public to private construction well above the national average.[4] Manchester's council houses of the interwar years were planned to meet the latest requirements in health and convenience, and with considerable attention to detail. House styles varied, but the most common Corporation home consisted of a living room, kitchen and scullery, plus two or three bedrooms. Upstairs bathrooms were to be standard, and instructions were even given that mouldings and skirtings were to be without ledges to prevent the accumulation of dust.

Manchester's Slums in the 1930s

By 1929 Corporation building was just about keeping pace with housing demand. The degree of overcrowding in Manchester was below the national average, and the city was ahead of Birmingham, Liverpool and London in its slum-clearance programme. Yet there remained significant numbers of inner-city poor who carried on their daily life in circumstances of depressing squalor, little improved since Victorian times. It is true that most of the deplorable sanitary conditions of the nineteenth

Women were the main protagonists in the battle against poverty.

century had gone and housing densities had been reduced by the policy of reconditioning, but social investigations in the 1930s revealed pockets of quite desperate poverty and bad housing. The highest unemployment figures and the worst housing conditions prevailed in the inner residential ring, in the districts of Miles Platting, Chorlton-on-Medlock, Hulme, Ancoats, Angel Meadow and Redbank.

Although Manchester's interwar unemployment rate was below the national average there were parts of the city with much worse figures. Investigators from Manchester University in 1934 found a quarter of all households contacted in Miles Platting had no earned income from any family member. Amongst adult males in the sample no less than 42.5% were unemployed at the time of the survey. The investigators estimated that half the district's families existed at or below the 'poverty line'. Two years earlier, an investigation on behalf of the Manchester and Salford Better Housing Council of 326 houses in Hulme had discovered 165 to be in 'indifferent' or 'bad' condition, and only 66 were regarded as 'satisfactory'. A 'satisfactory' house was one which required no major repairs, had a drip-free roof and was 'fairly free' from vermin. Conditions of life could be very demoralising. As well as obvious deficiencies, such as the uniform absence of bathrooms and inside toilets, many of the dwellings had damp walls, peeling plaster and were infested with vermin. Keeping the body clean and food hygienic was a constant battle in the domestic life of the slums, a contest in which women were the main protagonists. Of the Hulme sample mentioned above, almost 80% had to manage without a food store in their homes. A survey of an area of Chorlton-on-Medlock, bounded by Grosvenor Street, Oxford Road, Charles Street and London Road (an area now including the BBC studios and UMIST) reported similar conditions. The Report concluded that life here was:

> a constant fight against vermin firmly entrenched in the old and crumbling walls. In the whole district there is hardly a pantry or any similar cool, airy place in which the housekeeper could store food. The few cupboards ... are invariably in a recess at the side of the kitchen fire. Of necessity the family fire must burn from about 6 a.m. to 10 p.m. in many homes. Even if the food is not exposed to the attacks of bugs and beetles, it cannot withstand the heat of the kitchen fire. Added to this there is the weekly discomfort of the family wash which, if the weather is damp, must be hung in the only living room.

This was close to where Dr McKeand had reported the dreadful conditions in which the cholera epidemic of 1849 had arisen. Over eighty years later houses of that era were still inhabited. Originally back-to-backs built between 1794 and 1820, they had been reconditioned by the demolition of every third dwelling to allow ventilation

and space for backyards. The investigators stressed these were not the
worst streets they could find, nor were their conditions unique. 'There
are acres and acres of similar property in the belt of slums surrounding
the centre of Manchester.' They were certainly not the oldest working-
class properties still inhabited. An investigation of the slums behind
London Road (Piccadilly) Station in the Store Street area found families
in housing dating back to the 1740s.[5]

Such slums as these ought not to have survived. The foundations of
modern slum clearance were laid in the 1930s. The Greenwood Act of
1930 (the implementation of which was delayed two years by the
economic crisis of 1931) gave a central government subsidy to each
local authority which developed a slum-clearance scheme of demolition
and rehousing. But disappointingly few properties were replaced under
this legislation up to 1939. The Manchester authorities condemned
only 15,000 houses out of a total stock of around 180,000. In 1942,
the city's medical officer of health estimated that Manchester still had
approaching 69,000 unfit properties, and over a third of all houses
remained below 'reasonable' standards of sanitation.

Whilst the remaining inner-city housing continued to decay,
Corporation estates contributed to filling in the gaps around Manchester. Mary Stocks describes the impact of the Corporation development
at Wilbraham Road, still in the early 1920s an 'unadopted' country
lane running westwards into open fields from the main road out of
Manchester to the south, near the once sleepy village of Fallowfield.

> Manchester had in earlier years expanded starfish-wise along its
> main exits, the intervening spaces remaining unbuilt, except for
> old established country cottages and farms. Into such an area Wil-
> braham Road ... led ... Its road surface was primitively rural, and
> on exceptionally clear days it offered long views to the south ...
> But with the operation of the post-war Addison Housing Act in
> full swing, these amenities soon gave place to others. Wilbraham
> Road was 'adopted'; Corporation trams began to run on smooth
> concrete; the dirty little Platt Brook which crossed it was incarcer-
> ated in a tidy sewer ... and on the fields through which Wilbraham
> Road ran a large new Corporation housing estate ... arose. In due
> course it was furnished with a church, a chapel, a school, ... [and]
> a branch public library.[6]

But were the houses on the first council estates going to those most in
need? Were people able to escape the slums in sufficient numbers? Of
the Manchester Corporation houses built by 1924 over half had gone
to clerks or others from lower middle-class employments and by no
means all the manual workers who occupied the rest had come from
the slums. The poorest workers could not afford to pay council house
rents of up to 15s. (75p) a week at a time when slum tenants paid around

8*s*. (40p). But the Corporation were in a cleft stick. Building costs had multiplied five times since prewar days and an economic rent, it was estimated, would have had to be nearer 30*s*. (£1.50) per week.[7]

However, rents were not the only problem. In 1926 inner-city residents from the Medlock Street area were offered houses at Wilbraham Road in an attempt at the transference of slum tenants. But only a small proportion of the 134 households involved made the move and stayed. Either the journey to work proved too expensive or the new council rents too high. The unsuitability of 'remote' estates far from traditional places of work without local employment possibilities was to confound all but the best efforts of those who wished to rehouse the slum dweller. In the event the Wilbraham development, one of the earliest and largest of Manchester's interwar Corporation estates, attracted only the most prosperous tenants. Meanwhile, the problem of bridging the gap between work and home whilst rehousing the city's congested population in new and viable communities was being tackled in visionary fashion, in the concept of Wythenshawe.

Wythenshawe Garden City

Wythenshawe Garden City was planned by the Corporation in the early years after the First World War. By 1926 farmland was being cheaply purchased on a grand scale eight miles to the south of the city, and in 1931 Wythenshawe was incorporated within the municipal boundary. It was not the size of Wythenshawe which made it exceptional (Becontree in Essex was much larger with a population of 90,000 by 1934) but the original conception behind it. A product of the garden city movement, it was conceived as a 'satellite garden town ... deliberately planned ... to cover a large district including not only houses and parks but also a factory area ... the population working partly in the area and partly in the mother city'.[8] This was a new town before its time, planned from scratch around the focal point of Wythenshawe Hall and Park, a gift to the city from Ernest and Sheena Simon who had so much to do with the early development of Wythenshawe. Bisected by the breadth of Princess Parkway it was to include industrial zones and civic amenities and to house a target population of 100,000.

Houses went up quickly. By 1939 nearly 40,000 people inhabited 8,145 homes. Rents ranged from 9*s*. (45p) to 15*s*. 9*d*. (78p), a total which included general and water rates as well as electricity. This was at a time when a skilled factory worker would expect to earn around £2 15*s*. 0*d*. (£2.75) a week. Wythenshawe was soon the most popular destination among applicants for Corporation housing. But most Wythenshawe tenants came from the better-off working class not from the slums. A survey in 1935 by the Manchester and Salford Better

Housing Council found that the majority of new residents were not slum clearance cases. Only one in five households had previously paid less than 10*s*. (50p) in rent. Few slum properties had cost that much.[9] There is evidence that the authorities exploited Wythenshawe's popularity to maintain high standards. A resident recalled the early years.

> Not everyone could get a house in Wythenshawe. Before we got one an official from the Town Hall wanted to know all about us: our parents had a nursery in Northenden and my husband had steady employment and a fair wage. We had to prove we would be good tenants ... We ... heard that some people were from the slums but we never met any of them.[10]

It was not until the 1960s that Wythenshawe reached full capacity. Although factories for the production of electrical goods, embroidery, hosiery, biscuits and other products were established early on, the economic depression of the 1930s was not the most propitious time for expanding new businesses. It was not till the 1950s that Wythenshawe's three industrial zones (at Sharston, Roundthorn and Moss Nook) took proper shape. Equally the much awaited civic centre was not completed till the 1960s. In the event Wythenshawe became a garden suburb rather than a satellite town. It was too close to its parent

A Manchester street between the wars. Only a minority were rehoused in twentieth-century dwellings before 1945.

to be independent, and residential priorities meant the proportion of industry to housing was too low for a self-contained community to develop. Nonetheless it had been a brave conception.

Housing and Poverty Since 1945

Despite all the best efforts of the interwar years Manchester entered the second half of the twentieth century with its housing problem still not solved. As late as 1959 the city still possessed up to 68,000 houses described as 'grossly unfit'; a decaying housing stock of nineteenth-century properties often lacking the basic amenities which had been standard in modern private and Corporation homes since 1919. Wythenshawe was full and the search was on for a successor. In the absence of a coherent plan for the region in the 1950s and 1960s, Manchester opted for overspill estates outside the city limits. Between 1954 and 1976 Manchester Corporation demolished some 90,000 dwellings and erected 71,000 new council houses and flats. Approaching half of these were on large overspill estates like those at Heywood and Langley (Middleton) in the north, Hyde in the east and Worsley in the west. These were not mini-Wythenshawes. There was no planned industry to accompany them and social amenities were notable by their absence. These estates were generally of traditional design, made up of semis and short terraces of 'garden city' style.

Although Manchester had experimented with 'high rise' dwellings as early as the 1890s (Victoria Buildings, Oldham Road) and had constructed 9,000 council flats between the wars it was not until the late 1960s that the Corporation turned to the tower blocks so popular with other metropolitan authorities. When they did, the results, although sometimes architecturally innovative, as in the 'Crescents' in Hulme, more often proved socially disastrous. The living problems created by some designs were so severe that demolition was considered the only solution less than two decades after construction. Despite these problems, by the late 1970s approaching half of the borough of Manchester's inhabitants lived in accommodation rented from the City Council, well above the national average of 29%. However, the era of massive public rehousing programmes may be over for good. At any rate, government policy after 1979 acted as a restraint. Cut-backs in local authority housing finance reduced the number of properties built by the city from 2,200 in 1977/8 to just 77 in 1986/7.

Slum clearance brought other problems. Communities were broken up, local facilities such as shops and community services removed and local employment lost. Social problems were conveyed to the new estates and often became worse in the new environment. Rehousing had not proved the social panacea some had expected. As in the

The John Nash Crescent, Hulme, in 1971. (*Copyright © Manchester Evening News*)

nineteenth century, social advance depended on improving living standards, effective education policies and raised expectations; housing was
only part of the equation. In fact, since the 1970s the trend in housing
policy has been towards conservation of existing stock. Perhaps this
could be seen as a return to what pre-1914 housing reformers would
have recognised as reconditioning, a policy which at least had the
benefits of preserving communities and of not disrupting work patterns.

Despite the policy of rehousing, the connection between inner-city
living and poverty, so patent to the investigators of the 1930s, continued
into the later twentieth century. During the recession of the early 1980s
unemployment reached crisis proportions in certain inner-city districts
of Manchester. In 1986 59% of adult males in Hulme were unemployed.
In Miles Platting the figure was 46%, and Cheetham Hill and Moss
Side both registered male unemployment rates of 44%. Unlike in the
1930s, the brunt of unemployment in the 1980s fell on the young, and
the two areas with the highest youth unemployment were Hulme (68%)
and Cheetham Hill (59%). Hulme had the highest concentration of
young people in the city, a significant proportion of whom were almost
permanently unemployed.[11] As in the later nineteenth century and the
interwar period, unemployment and poverty were therefore concentrated in certain inner-city districts. And as in the past, these were the
areas with significant concentrations of new immigrants.

Manchester's cosmopolitan past reaches forward into the present with
an increasingly diverse ethnic mix emerging since the 1950s, largely

due to immigration from the New Commonwealth and Pakistan. According to the Census of 1991, 12.6% of Manchester's population were part of the ethnic group other than white (Indian/Pakistani/Bangladeshi 5.4%; Black groups 4.7%; Chinese and other groups 2.6%). In reality, Manchester's ethnic minorities represent a relatively small proportion of the total population as compared to cities like Bradford and Birmingham and several inner-London boroughs. They are, however, generally concentrated in the inner city. In the 1980s inner-city districts contained half the city's total inhabitants, but housed 95% of the West Indian community and 79% of those from the Indian sub-continent. According to the 1991 Census, Moss Side had the greatest number of West Indian households, whilst the largest Asian community was in Longsight. Hulme, Cheetham and Rusholme all had sizeable ethnic populations.[12] In addition, by the 1980s Manchester had become the regional centre for other immigrant communities whose residence was more evenly spread across the Manchester region. Most notably, the Chinese community, which has banks, shops, community centres and restaurants in a distinctive quarter of the city centre, now known as 'Chinatown' (George Street, Princess Street area).

Despite the rising living standards of the post-war years and the massive policy of rehousing followed through in Manchester, poverty has not been abolished, although our notion of what constitutes deprivation has changed. A survey of poverty in Manchester in 1987 found about 30,000 people living in homes without essential heating; 20,000 homes affected by damp; 80,000 people unable to afford a roast joint or its equivalent once a week; 20,000 households with at least one person who lacked a warm, waterproof coat; and nearly half of Manchester's residents too poor to afford an annual week's holiday. The survey identified the unemployed, one-parent families, large families, pensioners, the disabled and West Indian and Asian households as among those most 'at risk' of being poor. Manchester was a low wage area. The Greater Manchester Low Pay Unit estimated that over 48% of employees in the Greater Manchester region were low paid; two-thirds were women and 43% worked part-time. In February 1987, at least a third of Manchester's entire population was dependent upon Supplementary Benefits. Rehousing had not solved the social problem of poverty. The investigators in 1987 found council tenants three times more likely to be in poverty than owner-occupiers.[13] In the early twenty-first century the city remains scarred by economic deprivation (see Chapter 12).

The modern geography of wealth and poverty in the Manchester region follows the historic patterns of housing policy and suburban growth laid down since 1918. The poorest are concentrated not only in the traditionally impoverished inner city but also in the post-war overspill council estates that surround it to the north, east and west.

The more affluent mostly live within the broad swathe of suburbs to the south and in the smaller suburban belt which links Prestwich and Bury to the north. Additionally there are a few isolated pockets of middle-class housing such as Bamford in Rochdale and Alkrington in Middleton. The pattern of residential segregation is more complex than in the nineteenth century but, despite a resettlement of the better-off in the city centre it remains a significant feature of life in the Manchester region of today.

The Leisure Revolution

Despite the persistence of social inequalities, for most people the twentieth century was an era of advancing living standards, shorter working hours and increased leisure. In 1914 the average working-class family spent three-quarters of its income on food and housing, by 1938 this had fallen to under half. Purchasing power was growing and leisure and its uses had become big business. The increasing control of popular recreations by commercial organisations, which was already a feature of the later nineteenth century, has developed into a massive leisure industry.'Evils' such as gambling and drinking which so troubled the Victorian moral reformers have been transformed into consumer 'goods'. Mass audiences flocked to football matches and newer sports like greyhound racing and speedway; the cinema went through a 'golden age' of popular appeal between the wars only to be overhauled by television since the 1950s; and since the 1960s the motor car has increased the range of leisure pursuits available to many.

The heyday of the music hall was over by the 1920s, although the final demise of the 'halls' came after the Second World War in the television age. The Ardwick Empire, temporarily a cinema in the 1930s, reopened in 1937 as the New Manchester Hippodrome. The final curtain did not fall till 1961, long after the music hall had ceased to be profitable. The big money was to be made in the cinema industry, and the interwar years saw the advent of the Odeon and Gaumont cinema chains. In the late 1930s Manchester boasted 129 cinemas, the largest number of any city outside London. By 1951 the figure was still large at 91 cinemas with 99,000 seats between them, an even higher ratio of seats to population than that available to Londoners. Yet by the mid-1960s the total had fallen to 33 and the decline continued. The golden era of the 'picture house' was gone.

Cinemas had become larger and grander during the 1920s and 1930s. The Piccadilly, built in 1922, was the first of the new large scale 'picture palaces' in the North West. Overlooking the new Piccadilly Gardens, it contained a restaurant, cafe and dance hall as well as a cinema. Afternoon tea dances were popular. Such 'pleasure palaces' employed small armies of uniformed staff, from commissionaires to usherettes and pageboys, not forgetting the essential technician, the projectionist. The New Oxford Picture house screened the first 'talkie' in Manchester, 'Uncle Tom's Cabin', in November 1928. The 'talkies' encouraged the trend towards grandeur in cinema design and decoration. The larger city centre houses created an alternative world of glamour and opulence to contrast with the grimness of the Depression years. The Paramount (now the Odeon) in Oxford Road was the premier establishment of the 1930s. It opened in October 1930 with a stage show starring the Tiller Girls (a dance group) to precede the main feature, Maurice Chevalier and Jeanette McDonald in 'Love Parade'. The Paramount's souvenir brochure enthused over the cinema's interior decoration.

> The general scheme of the theatre is a harmonious assembly of lighter tints such as gold, silver, grey and tones that please the sub-conscious eye ... the whole spirit is one of repose-content-one might almost say a caress to the senses to soothe the nerves and prepare it for a show ... The decoration of the auditorium is ... a free treatment of the Baroque period.[14]

Not all cinemas were so grand. Local houses could be much more basic, like the Rex and the Electric which faced each other across Queens Road in Miles Platting, and which Anthony Burgess remembers in his autobiography. Here:

> The cinemagoer's criteria had more to do with hygiene than the quality of the entertainment offered. The Rex was called a bughouse and the Electric was not. The Electric used a superior disinfectant like a grudging perfume; the Rex smelt of its patrons and its lavatories. With the Rex, it was said, you went in with a blouse and came out with a jumper.[15]

There were few northern accents in the films of the era. Northern characters did appear, notably George Formby and Gracie Fields, but the diet of most Manchester cinemagoers was Hollywood and British movies generally devoid of heroes and heroines with regional accents. A post-war exception to this were the films produced by Film Studios (Manchester) Ltd between 1947 and 1954, the only feature film studio operating outside London. Based in a converted Wesleyan church in Dickenson Road, Rusholme, Film Studios made northern comedies using popular music hall stars like Sandy Powell, Norman Evans and Jimmy James, but chiefly Frank Randle. With titles such as 'Holidays with Pay', 'Somewhere in Politics' and 'School for Randle', these films were great box office hits in the North but did not go down well in the South. Film Studios succumbed to the declining trend in cinema audiences in the 1950s as television overtook the 'pictures' in popular appeal. Appropriately it was the BBC who inherited the Dickenson

Road studios. Manchester is also notable in the history of film produc-
tion in that it was the first city in Britain to commission a civic film,
'A City Speaks', sponsored by the Corporation and directed by Paul
Rotha in 1946.

As cinemas closed in the 1950s and 1960s some were converted to
serve as ten pin bowling alleys and bingo halls. Others, with good site
value, were replaced by garages, supermarkets and petrol stations,
victims not only of the television but of the wider range of recreations
available in the later twentieth century. A few became ballrooms for a
short while, reflecting the fashion for popular dancing venues run by
commercial organisations like the Locarno group. But the first 'dance
craze' had been in the 1920s, popularised by the radio broadcasting of
dance music from the ballrooms of some of the big London hotels.

Manchester's top dance halls in the 1920s and 1930s were the Ritz
on Whitworth Street and the Plaza on Oxford Street. Here, those
without a partner could hire one of the professional dancers by the
dance. The essential social skill of ballroom dancing could be learned
at local dance halls or at one of several academies such as Tommy
Rogers Dancing Studios on Oxford Road. Among the larger local bands
was Jack McCormack's playing in Lewis's Restaurant during the afternoon and in the ballroom on the top floor in the evening. Band concerts
were regularly given at Manchester venues. The bands of Jack Hylton,
Jack Payne, Harry Roy and Billy Cotton paid regular visits to the Palace
and the Manchester Hippodrome. Although the big band music of the
interwar years was another example of commercial enterprise, there
was a strong element of popular involvement in music making. Often
young men who had mastered the rudiments of the bugle, cornet or
drums in the boy scouts, boys brigade or Salvation Army would come
together with friends to form three- to six-piece dance bands. Most
were part-time, supplementing their wages from day jobs.

Cinema-going and ballroom dancing generally involved both sexes
and a mixture of social classes; by contrast attendance at most spectator
sports was overwhelmingly working class and male. Association football
was the biggest of the spectator sports by 1918. First Division attendances averaged 25,364 in 1927/8, rising to 30,659 by 1938/9 and peaking
at 40,702 in 1949/50. In 1938/9 an average of 36,250 watched
Manchester United even though they languished near the bottom of
the table. In fact the interwar years were lean decades for United with
most seasons spent in the Second Division. Manchester City did better,
reaching three Wembley finals and winning the First Division
championship in 1936/7. Football clubs embarked on major capital
improvement programmes to meet rising attendances; City's (then) new
ground at Maine Road was opened in 1923.

Although national crowd figures have declined since 1950, the
two Manchester clubs are better supported than most. United attracts

Manchester City players meet King George V at the F.A. Cup Final, 1926.

followers across the world, but City is said to be more popular with Mancunians. In contrast with the interwar years, it is United's fortunes which have been in the ascendant since 1945. During the post-war decades, Manchester United became one of the 'glamour' clubs of international football. First (and then Premier) Division champions and F.A. Cup winners on numerous occasions, the club's crowning achievements were winning the European Cup in 1968 and 1999. However it was the Munich aircrash in 1958 (in which eight players died), and the way in which the club recovered from the tragedy under the guidance of Matt Busby, which has earned Manchester United a particular place in the city's memory.

Professional boxing was another major spectator sport. Title fights and other top matches took place at the Free Trade Hall, or the New King's Hall at Belle Vue, the leading boxing venue in Europe. A host of lesser venues included the likes of Smithfield Market Boxing Club and Churnett Street Public Hall in Collyhurst. Out of Manchester's back street gyms and boxing booths of the Depression years came several top class boxers, notably Jackie Brown, flyweight world champion, 1926–39. Racial prejudice prevented another notable Manchester fighter from achieving the recognition he deserved. A black man was not allowed to fight for a British title until 1948, even if he had been born in this country. Thus, Len Johnson, born in Manchester in 1902 to a West African father and a local mother, was barred from boxing for the national title even though he was probably the best welterweight in Europe at his prime. Johnson became the proprietor of a travelling boxing booth after his retirement in 1933. The 1930s were the 'golden age' of Manchester boxing.

New spectator sports which attracted large crowds after 1914, and more women than football or boxing, were speedway and greyhound racing. There were 28,000 covered seats at the Belle Vue Speedway Track and 40,000 at White City in Stretford in the 1930s. In 1926 Alfred Critchley opened the first Greyhound Racing Track in Britain, opposite Belle Vue Gardens. The sustained popularity of the 'Dogs' was in large part due to the opportunities it offered for gambling. Greyhound racing was a predominantly working-class alternative to the 'on track' betting of horse racing. The number of bookmakers in Manchester rose from 108 in 1921 to 367 in 1931. Despite a growth in legalised gambling, street betting remained popular, organised around the 'bookies' runner'. The daily bet became a way of life for both men and women, with punters handing in betting slip and stake money in the back entries of terraced streets out of the gaze of the 'boys in blue'. The number of prosecutions for betting offences was consistently higher in Manchester and Salford than in towns with police districts of comparable size, including Liverpool. Why was this? Was gambling 'more rife' in Manchester than elsewhere, as some contemporaries believed? Or were the police simply more vigilant in the city which housed one of only three offices of the National Anti-Gambling League (the others were in London and York). The evidence is unclear.[16] In the event, the legalisation of 'off course' gambling and the advent of the betting shop in the 1960s has made redundant this particular outdoor pursuit.

In any case, betting is a fringe activity of the sporting world. Attendance at a sporting event betokens more serious interest, and since 1914 the big spectator sports were within the reach of many pockets. One shilling (5p) would gain entry to Old Trafford, Belle Vue, White City and most other sporting venues in the 1930s. However, not everyone was able to afford attendance at professional football matches. Even the better-off manual workers who lived in outlying Corporation estates like Wythenshawe could not always find the travel costs involved in watching City or United. But it was the casualised character of some Manchester occupations, plus the pockets of unemployment already referred to, which excluded individuals, families and neighbourhoods from much popular leisure. For example, the increasing popularity of the annual seaside holiday for the better-off working family was not a privilege extended to all. The annual holiday without pay amounted to a 'lock out' for the considerable section of the local working class who could afford to go no farther than their own backyard. However, there were always the free recreations of the streets, from the organised festivities of the Whit Walk and May Day, to the spontaneous dances generated as small crowds gathered round the Italian organ grinders who provided a popular and cheap form of entertainment in the streets of Ancoats, Hulme, Collyhurst and other working-class districts of the city.[17]

Many sports were geared to participation rather than spectating and a large proportion of these were run by non-commercial bodies. There were 37 billiard rooms in Manchester in 1929, a popular enough pastime to support the city's six billiard and bagatelle table manufacturers. More energetic tastes were catered for in the parks and open spaces owned by the Corporation. By 1938 municipal provision extended to 35 swimming baths, 398 tennis courts, 201 football and hockey pitches, 76 cricket pitches, 79 bowling greens, 24 children's playgrounds, a golf course at Heaton Park and 16 putting greens. These were outstanding facilities by any standard. In addition there was a wide range of self-organised groups in the interwar period. Football leagues abounded. The Rusholme and District League had seven divisions with about 15 teams in each. Similar leagues operated in most districts. Various bodies organised leagues, including the Cooperative Wholesale Society (CWS), the Sunday School Union and the Catholic Church. Organised amateur sport was not confined to men. The Sunday School Union Women's Hockey League had six divisions with an average of 11 teams in each.

As the nineteenth century had opposed rational recreations to popular pastimes so, in the first half of the twentieth century, leisure and its organisation were contested terrain between the gathering forces of commercialisation and those who wished to resist the rise of the leisure consumer. For various and sometimes overlapping reasons, both the voluntary sector and the Labour movement opposed the commercialisation of leisure. Moreover, the phenomenon of enforced idleness in the Depression, in which mass unemployment disrupted the normal pattern of worktime interspersed with short intervals of leisure, focussed attention on the broader relationship between labour and recreation.

There were a number of recreational initiatives in and around Manchester during the interwar decades. The CWS was particularly active in the organisation of sports in opposition to commercialised leisure. In 1928 it formed the Manchester Sports Association. This acquired its own sports grounds, formed two football leagues and sponsored competitions in bowls, swimming and ladies' cricket. Working-class rambling was strong in the North West. The Communist Party-inspired British Workers Sports Federation was responsible for the mass trespass on Kinder Scout in April 1932. There were over 100 clubs in the Manchester and District Federation of Ramblers. Voluntary endeavours included the summer holidays in the Lake District for the unemployed run by the National Council of Social Service (NCSS). The School Camps Association organised holidays for poor children. The recreational work of the NCSS extended to music, drama and art. Left-wing drama groups included the Salford Red Megaphones which Joan Littlewood and Ewen MacColl transformed into the Manchester Theatre of Action. In practice the voluntary sector and organised labour found it hard to resist the rising tide of commercialised leisure. Since the 1950s, with the growth of a mass youth culture and the personal mobility of the car age, the task has become impossible.

Mass participation in a bewildering variety of sports and pastimes became a feature of popular leisure during the 1960s and 1970s. A directory of sports in the Greater Manchester area for 1978 listed 66 participant sports for the borough of Manchester alone, from angling and darts to aikido and volleyball. By the late twentieth century, the age of mass car ownership had opened up an even wider world of participant sports, for those who could afford it, from dry-skiing at Rossendale to windsurfing at Sale. Moreover, Manchester can lay claim to being a major world centre for spectator sports. Apart from its famous soccer clubs, the city can boast one of the great cricket grounds of the world. As well as being home to Lancashire county cricket, Old Trafford is a regular test match venue. Rugby is also a popular sport with several Rugby Union clubs in the city, although the professional game, Rugby League, attracts more spectators with several top teams coming from the region. The prestige sporting projects of the 1990s and after were able to build upon this strong sports tradition.

References

1. Defining the region to be the South East Lancashire Conurbation as designated in 1951, see Chapter 10.
2. B. Rodgers, in G. Gordon (ed.), *Regional Cities in the United Kingdom 1890–1980*, Harper and Row, London, 1986, p. 44.
3. E. D. Simon and J. Inman, *The Rebuilding of Manchester*, Longmans, London, 1935, pp. 73–4.
4. A. Redford and I. Russell, *The History of Local Government in Manchester*, Vol. III, Longmans, London, 1939–40, p. 246.
5. The reports cited are J. Inman, *Poverty and Housing Conditions in a Manchester Ward*, Manchester University Economics Research Section, 1934; and three publications of the Manchester and Salford Better Housing Council, *Housing in Hulme*, 1932; *Some Housing Conditions in Chorlton-on-Medlock*, 1931; *Under the Arches: Behind London Road Station*, 1931.
6. M. Stocks, *Fifty Years in Every Street: The Story of the Manchester University Settlement*, Manchester University Press, 2nd edn, 1956, pp. 86–7.
7. Simon and Inman, *Rebuilding*, p. 26; E. D. Simon, *The Anti Slum Campaign*, Longmans, London, 1931, p. 11.
8. Sheena Simon in Simon and Inman, *Rebuilding*, p. 36.
9. *Wythenshawe: The Report of an Investigation*, Manchester and Salford Better Housing Council, 1935.
10. Quoted in D. Deakin, *Wythenshawe: The Story of a Garden City*, Phillimore, Chichester, 1989, p. 58.

11. *Trends in Employment and Unemployment in Manchester*, Manchester Employment Research Group Ltd, Manchester Polytechnic, 1987.

12. Population Census 1991: Ward profiles, Manchester; *Manchester's Population and Housing*, Manchester City Planning Department, 1980, p. 74.

13. *Poverty in Manchester: The Third Investigation*, Manchester City Council, 1988. See also G. Williams, *Metropolitan Manchester: A Social Atlas*, University of Manchester, 1975.

14. Quoted in M. Gomes, *The Picture House*, North West Film Archive, Manchester Polytechnic, 1988, p. 46.

15. Anthony Burgess, *Little Wilson and Big God*, Heinemann, London, 1987, p. 30.

16. See M. Clapson, *A Bit of a Flutter: Popular Gambling and British Society, c. 1823–1961*, Manchester University Press, 1992, pp. 45–6.

17. For the impact of poverty on leisure see A. Davies, *Leisure, Gender and Poverty: Working-Class Culture in Salford and Manchester, 1900–1939*, Open University Press, Buckingham, 1992, pp. 32–48 and passim. Study of the informal patterns of daily life and leisure in the twentieth century can be assisted by oral history, which is especially informative on women's lives. For Manchester and Salford see the work of Davies, and also M. Tebbutt, '"You couldn't help but know": public and private in the lives of working-class women, 1918–39', *Manchester Region History Review*, VI (1992), pp. 72–9.

CHAPTER 12

Manchester in Prospect

Manchester is surging ahead on a flood tide of economic and cultural innovations ... We are sweeping into the new millennium with a city region almost bulging with new facilities and new ideas ... The world needs to know all about these developments if Manchester is to take its rightful place on the world centre stage and command its share of global investment.

Sir David Trippier launching the 'Manchester is Up and Going' campaign, at the Bridgewater Hall. *Manchester Evening News*, 15 May 1997.

Manchester has never been about boundaries, never been about lines on the map or about local authority bureaucracy. Manchester is not so much a city as a state of mind.

From an article in *United We Stand* (football fanzine), 1996.

This has been a study of a city in retrospect. What can be said of Manchester over the last decade and into the future? It is now two hundred years since the place first came to the notice of outsiders as the 'boom town' of the early industrial era. In terms of historical importance Manchester's greatest days are undoubtedly over. It is unlikely that the city will ever be as significant economically or politically as it was in the nineteenth century. Then its industry and commerce had a global reach. Today Manchester is more 'globalised' than 'globalising'. This chapter will examine the Manchester of today. Although Manchester may now follow others rather than offer the lead, these are times of great change and may be marking out a path for the future.

Like many cities in the older industrial nations of the world, Manchester faced a dual challenge in the later twentieth century. The rapid decline in employment and investment in manufacturing of the 1960s and 1970s was further exacerbated by developments in the 1980s and 1990s. The impact of the new information technology and the advent of the 'network society', accompanied by more liberal economic policies, together have facilitated the almost instantaneous flow of information, communication and capital across the globe. This emergence of a global economy, and the declining significance of nation-states, have forced a new agenda on the major metropolitan regions of Europe. In the current competition for capital investment, globalisation places a premium on cities that are perceived as innovative, imaginative and entrepreneurial.

The new age of economic globalisation and the information revolution has forced cities around the world to become protagonists in their own cause. In addition, the process of globalisation has eroded the economic influence of national governments and (often following the example of the UK) many states have adopted less interventionist industrial policies than during the 1945–79 period. In the ensuing competition between urban centres for resources, cities have evolved less managerial and more pluralistic management systems, mixing public and private agencies and revolving around entrepreneurial strategies. Thus in Manchester, since the late 1980s, there has developed a 'partnership' between local council and non-governmental agencies such as the Central Manchester Development Corporation and later the constellation of bodies which co-operated during and after the Olympic Games bid. The intention was to develop a series of projects and policies to promote the city and the region. As elsewhere in the world, this process began with a number of prestige projects and was soon accompanied by the rhetoric of re-imaging. Manchester was promoted locally and internationally as a major European city-regional capital. This was portrayed as the only solution to the loss of manufacturing status. The rationale was summed up by one of its chief architects, Graham Stringer, city council leader from the early 1980s to the mid-1990s. 'About a dozen of [Europe's 40 or 50 second-tier cities] will become the cities where decisions are made ... We have to try and get there, because the alternative is to gradually decline.'[1] In practical terms the purpose was to win private investment and public grants for a city that was seen to have a vision, a sense of purpose and to offer an attractive environment. Thus, after more than a generation of decline, Manchester was to be re-branded.

The revival of Manchester has revolved around a startling sequence of prestige projects focused on leisure, culture and lifestyle. Arguably, the process began in the early 1980s. Castlefield, GMEX, the Metrolink were all under way or were planned well before the rhetoric of re-branding was defined. However, the trend was greatly reinforced by the Conservative Party's domination of national government whilst, locally, municipal politics had made Manchester virtually a one-party state (see Chapter 10). Labour's third general election defeat in a row in 1987 is seen by some as the spark that led one of the most left-wing city councils of the 1980s to downplay 'welfare'-oriented objectives and instead to adopt vigorously market-orientated economic strategies in the 1990s.[2] In fact the path to urban transformation followed in Manchester is common to a number of cities which seek to become 'global'. Firstly, it involves an awareness of the relationship of the local to the global in an era of economic globalisation. Secondly, it requires a

Manchester United: the procession through the streets of the city after the European Cup victory of 1999. (*Photograph: picturesofmanchester.com/Len Grant*)

coming together of the urban public and private agents and the existence of local leadership (political, business and civic). And thirdly, it needs a consensus in the city (and its region) about the direction of change.[3] Manchester has been foremost among UK cities in conceiving a local regional strategy in global terms.

Since 1987 the stream of prestige projects has been continuous. Sporting, leisure, cultural and heritage projects predominate. Manchester already enjoyed worldwide sporting recognition through the brand name 'Manchester United'. Thus it was in some ways a logical step to embark on the building of high-profile sports arenas. Sporting and leisure ventures in the 1990s included the Velodrome (the National Indoor Cycling Centre), the Manchester Aquatics Centre and other sporting arenas built in connection with the unsuccessful bids to host the Olympic Games of 1996 and 2000 and the successful bid for the Commonwealth Games of 2002. Equally, the qualitative value of a city's cultural life has been correctly linked to its competitive advantage. This observation and the knowledge that other cities have successfully trodden the same path (Barcelona is the oft-vaunted model to imitate) led to the development of a cultural strategy for Manchester in which big projects were to the fore. Major cultural and heritage projects since 1990 include: the Bridgewater Concert Hall (new home for the Hallé Orchestra), opened in 1997; the Manchester Evening News Arena (opened as the Nynex Arena in 1996); PrintWorks (an arts and leisure complex opened in former newspaper offices in 2000); and a major extension of the Manchester City Art Gallery and the new Urbis Centre, both due for completion in 2002. The Lowry Centre (an award-winning building housing two theatres and galleries devoted to the paintings of L. S. Lowry, 2000) and the Imperial War Museum in the North (2002), both in Salford, can be added to the list. These are each part of a massive arts and leisure-led regeneration of the urban core.

A key element has been what one might call the international games bidding process. In particular, the city's – ultimately unsuccessful – bids to host the Olympic Games were the catalyst for policies designed to raise the international profile of the city. More than anything else, the Olympic competition symbolised the extent to which the city's local politics had adapted to the phenomenon of globalisation. The Games were seen as a vehicle whereby Manchester could achieve its global aims. A promotional document of the time expressed it in the most optimistic terms:

> A targeted and managed economic and social programme of urban regeneration linked to Olympic sporting and multi-cultural investment could bring Manchester and the region a handsome and irrevocable dividend in the next century. Indeed by 2001, Manchester has the opportunity to emerge and remain unchallenged as: Britain's second city – the capital of the northern region; a European regional capital – a centre of investment growth not regional aid; an international city of outstanding commercial, cultural and creative potential.[4]

As an analysis of the bidding process has observed, going for gold becomes synonymous with going for growth.[5]

In the event growth has been most closely related to success in the winning of grant aid rather than private investment. Although both have played their part, it has been the remarkable success of City Council-inspired initiatives and its ability to build, and lead, coalitions

The Bridgewater Concert Hall (*top*) and the Lowry Centre.
(*Photographs: picturesofmanchester.com/Len Grant*)

of public and private forces that has been at the heart of the regeneration process. Indeed, in the 1990s, Manchester came to epitomise the entrepreneurial local state. Is it too much to cast Council leaders (Graham Stringer and Richard Leese) and the chief executive, Howard Bernstein, as the modern counterparts of those corporate entrepreneurs who created the Manchester Ship Canal project in the 1880s and 1890s? Moreover, the involvement of businessmen in public projects (Sir Bob Scott and the Olympic bid being the classic example) invites comparison with the role of the city's Victorian business leaders in local governance. After a century of exclusion from the public sphere, have we witnessed a return of the 'Manchester men'?

Whatever its structures or personnel, the potential of the regeneration process in Manchester was nationally recognised when, in 1994, along with Birmingham and London, the city was invited by central government to prepare prospectuses for development over the next decade. A result was Manchester's City Pride Prospectus (1994, enlarged in 1998) which envisaged a vibrant and cosmopolitan European city and concentrated on measures to attract both investment and business and tourist visitors. It was a self-consciously metropolitan, and regional, prospectus, bearing the signatures of the political leaders of Salford and Trafford as well as Manchester councils. But most significantly, it was also signed by the leaders of two Urban Development Corporations appointed by the Conservative central government, and by 150 other private and voluntary bodies.[6]

A major theme in the City Pride Prospectus was the need for a new organisation to market the city, one that would co-ordinate existing marketing strategies so as to capitalise on the international profile created by the Olympic Games bid. The outcome was the launch, in May 1997, of 'Marketing Manchester' formed by a combination of local bodies and agencies, including the Association of Greater Manchester Authorities, Manchester Airport, and a handful of private companies including British Airways and the National Westminster Bank. 'Marketing Manchester' used the notion of the city as the regional core and linked the economic success of the region to the performance of the core city. At the same time the formation of the Manchester Investment and Development Agency (MIDAS) put the city at the heart of strategies for the regeneration of the region. None of this was uncontroversial. There were sharp criticisms from within the city to 'Marketing Manchester's' slogans and strategies. Additionally, the city-region notion behind both it and MIDAS revealed tensions within the North West regarding the balance of interest (local, metropolitan and regional). This included resistance to the idea of Manchester as the super-city which subsumes the region.[7] However, in the new global economy it is important to have a clearly established identity. This is why cities are so important. Manchester will have to make good its claim to regional capital status. Its principal metropolitan competitor, Liverpool, is already the clear core of the Merseyside metropolitan area. Liverpool could aspire to broader regional leadership. But whilst the economic trajectory of both cities depends much upon the winning of grants from national government and the European Union, the award by the latter of Object 1 status to Liverpool in 1994 (a mixed blessing if there ever was one) effectively removed that city from such a contest. It is likely that Manchester's pre-eminence in business services and through Manchester Airport, as the international gateway to the North of England, will bring long-term benefits to the entire region.

Apart from the Olympic bid, the single most reported event of the 1990s was the bombing of the city centre by the IRA on Saturday 15 June 1996. At 1500kg (or 3,300lb), this was the largest bomb to be detonated in Britain since the Second World War. It was tremendous good fortune that there were no fatalities. This was due chiefly to the well-organised evacuation of 80,000 people. However, over 200 people were injured and the physical damage to buildings in the retail and commercial core of the city was extensive. Commercially, 672 businesses were displaced and 49,000 square metres of retail space and 57,000 square metres of office space were lost. The Arndale Shopping Centre was badly damaged, closing the city's largest bus station and two multi-storey car parks, and key routes through the city centre were shut for months afterwards. The commercial impact was marked. Trade in the city centre, already vulnerable to out of town shopping malls (the largest of these and one of the biggest in the United Kingdom, the Trafford Centre, was then under construction) was down a tenth even six months later. The direct insurance loss cover topped £100m. and the eventual costs of the rebuilding programme are likely to be over £500m.

However, it is the city's response to the bombing that has been most striking and has become symbolic of the process of regeneration which has been taking place since the 1980s. The coalition of public and private interests responsible for that regenerative process swung into action within forty-eight hours of the blast, with the City Council becoming the catalyst for a range of initiatives for re-occupancy and recovery. A Lord Mayor's Appeal Fund raised £2.5m. within twelve months and affected businesses were given financial aid and assisted with recovery or relocation. However, from the outset the disaster was treated as an opportunity and the aim was not merely restoration but reinvigoration. An International Urban Design Competition invited architects to redesign the heart of the city and a Task Force (Manchester Millennium Ltd) was appointed to co-ordinate what was regarded as a programme of renewal. The competition brief asked for 'an architec-turally distinctive core ... physically and socially integrated with the

Corporation Street (looking south) after the IRA bomb on Saturday 15 June 1996. (*Photograph: picturesofmanchester.com/Len Grant*)

rest of the city [which] stimulates economic activity ... minimises risk and fear of crime ... and where activity can take place at most times of day and night.' A consultation process, in which the comments of the public focused on environmental provision, particularly pedestrian access and traffic and transport issues, followed an exhibition of the five short-listed submissions.[8]

In the event the chosen scheme offered a redesigned city centre whilst restoring the spatial link to the Cathedral removed in the 1960s and the creation of new green space in the heart of the city. Since the IRA bomb, an urban renewal programme of remarkable speed has seen a number of high-profile projects. These include the restoration and enhancement of the retail core in an attempt to reinstate Manchester as the shopping heart of the region. This involves, among other things, the largest Marks & Spencer store in the world (23,000 square metres), a reconfigured and enlarged Arndale Centre redesigned so as to make it more visually integrated with its surroundings, plus the fashionable boutiques of The Triangle (a restored and recast Corn Exchange building). The ability to attract 'up-market' stores such as Harvey Nicholls is evidence of the city's recent retailing revival.

This renewal of the city-centre shopping district is accompanied by the creation of new open spaces (Exchange Square, Cathedral Gardens) in a newly designated Millennium Quarter. The intention throughout is to make the heart of Manchester as attractive and accessible as that of any European city. The plans for Cathedral Gardens, situated between Chetham's School of Music, the Cathedral and the Corn

Exchange, at the historic heart of the medieval town, include rolling sculpted lawns and trees. At the other end of the central area the Piccadilly area is being renewed through the auspices of the Piccadilly Regeneration Partnership, a classic combination of public sector agencies and private sector companies. As well as the refurbishment of existing buildings such as the Piccadilly Plaza complex and Piccadilly Train Station, there are controversial plans for a multi-storey office block on the Portland Street side of Piccadilly Gardens. This latter development is part of a radical re-landscaping of Piccadilly Gardens due for completion late in 2002.

It is impossible to exaggerate the scale of the renewal programme. Manchester's central area has been redesigned in record time. This is arguably the most dramatic (and rapid) restructuring of its landscape and architecture that the city centre has ever undergone (the work of the Luftwaffe and 1960s planners notwithstanding). Throughout the 1990s the urban skyline seemed permanently punctuated by cranes, the signal that building work was underway. The aspiration behind such projects was to make Manchester visually important, an attractive place to be in for workers, shoppers and tourists alike. Much of the debate over the renewal of the city centre in the 1980s and 1990s revolved around the necessity to create a modern urban environment likely to appeal to professionals and office workers. The retention of existing firms and the attraction of new employers are central to the economic

The old reflected in the new. The Corn Exchange and the Marks & Spencer building.
(*Photograph: picturesofmanchester.com/Len Grant*)

The Urbis Centre. (*Picture courtesy of Manchester City Council*)

health of the city. The heritage tourism, which the city has sought since the 1970s (as witness Castlefield), is also important to present plans. Moreover, its attractions have been enhanced by a reinvigorated cultural infrastructure, including the reopening and enhancement of the Royal Exchange Theatre (badly damaged by the IRA bomb), plus ambitious new projects, chiefly PrintWorks, a Cathedral Visitor Centre and most striking of all, the Urbis Centre. The Urbis Centre, in the officially designated 'Millennium Quarter', is symbolic both of the ambition behind the regeneration of Manchester's urban core since the 1980s and also of its ability to convince the holders of public money of the city's capacity to realise its objectives. Jointly funded by central government (the Millennium Commission and the Department of the Environment, Transport and the Regions), Manchester City Council and the European Regional Development Fund, Urbis is Manchester's new museum of the modern city.

In most of its major schemes the city has respected the architectural integrity of its valuable historical buildings (the Wellington Inn/ Sinclairs, the Royal Exchange, the Corn Exchange, PrintWorks and so on). However it is unfortunate, to say the least, that the same discretion has not been extended to arguably the city's most historically important structure and a building of national historical significance, the Free Trade Hall. Sensitively restored in the late 1940s after considerable war damage, the instantly recognisable façade was regarded by Pevsner in the 1960s as 'a monument of which Manchester can be as proud, both architecturally and civically, as of the Town Hall.'[9] The removal of the Hallé Orchestra to the Bridgewater Hall left the Free Trade Hall ostensibly redundant. In 1998 Manchester City Council sold it to a private developer who had plans for its incorporation into a luxury hotel complex. In the event, an original proposal for a cylindrical-shaped tower on the roof met with strong protests from conservation groups

Corporation Street in 2001, looking north. (*Photograph: picturesofmanchester.com/Len Grant*)

and was rejected by the Secretary of State. However, another design with a fourteen-storey hotel tower set back from the historic façade is to go ahead. The battle between developers and conservationists over the future of the Free Trade Hall is evidence that the remaking of the city centre has not gone uncontested.

Part of the process of city centre renewal is a bold attempt to repopulate the central area. A strategic objective of the master plan following the IRA Bomb was the creation of a 'living city'. This objective indicates recognition that what are regarded as exemplar cities, such as Barcelona, have at their core vibrant residential hearts. Thus the renewal programme, in its attempts to enhance the attractions of the city centre, sought to encourage housing investment and provide a physical infra-structure appealing to new residents. In fact the plan was knocking at an open door and tapping into one of the most striking, and unplanned, phenomena of city life at the turn of the millennium. The pattern of urban population movement over the last hundred and fifty years and more has been a migration from the central areas to the periphery. The chief result of this has been the growth of the suburb and a corresponding decline of the inner-city housing stock (see Chapter 11). As was also the case in other UK cities, a poor and often elderly population has occupied central Manchester's generally lower status rented properties. This process continued into the 1980s. Central Ward, which includes the city centre, experienced a 32% loss of population between the censuses of 1981 and 1991. Moreover, within that ward the population of the city centre itself had fallen to a mere 800 persons in 1991. Yet by the time of the city's local census of 1998 this figure had risen almost six-fold to 4,550. For the first time in 150 years the population of the city centre was increasing.[10]

The expansion of the residential sector has been a key feature of the urban renewal programme of the last twenty years and more. As early as the 1970s, 200 apartments were included in the Castlefield regeneration project. In the mid-1980s and early 1990s the 'village' concept took over with the construction of 125 town houses and apartments immediately north of the city centre alongside the Ashton Canal (Piccadilly Village) and Granby Village adjacent to the Rochdale Canal to the south. In the 1990s there were a plethora of schemes and a move towards building in the central area itself. This has involved the conversion of previous industrial buildings, especially warehouses, into apartment blocks by redevelopers such as Urban Splash. However, it is the composition of the incoming population that rents or buys these increasingly expensive apartments that is its most significant feature. The majority of the city centre's new population in the 1990s was young and either actually or potentially high earning. University students in a range of commercially provided lets, as well as halls of residence, make up part of this new influx. Others are high-income couples without children. A significant proportion is made up of young gay males attracted by the development in the city centre of a further residential village quarter located in the Bloom Street/Canal Street area known as the 'Gay Village'.

Manchester's Gay Village developed spontaneously in the 1980s as part of the property-led regeneration of the central district. However, the City Council was quick to realise its potential both economically and culturally. Since 1991 it has been treated as a separate planning district and supported as part of the strategy to bring jobs back into the core area, and to create a cosmopolitan 24-hour city. The area possesses two dozen gay bars and clubs, over a dozen gay businesses and its own community and health groups. The Gay Village symbolises the outward-looking confidence of the modern gay community, its culture not only tolerated but celebrated in the annual Mardi Gras Lesbian and Gay Festival which fills the city centre streets at the August Bank Holiday Weekend. The existence of Manchester's Gay Village contrasts markedly with the lack of a clearly identified gay quarter in London and the City Council thinks Manchester competes with Amsterdam rather than London for international gay tourism. However, it is not just gay males who make the young migrant population distinctive. In the late 1990s, a survey of single male households in the city centre revealed that gay males headed around 25%, a further quarter were headed by young heterosexual males. Such statistics make a marked contrast with the character of the surrounding population. Whilst almost half (45%) of the households in the city centre consisted of single males, the figure was only 11% for Greater Manchester as a whole.[11] These new residents are often high earners and their spending in the clubs and cafes, which have sprung up in the central areas, has done much to rejuvenate the economic fortunes of the city core and gives credence to the claim that Manchester possesses a vibrant urban culture.

The development of the 'Northern Quarter' is the most recent manifestation of this new cultural status. This is the name given by the City Council to that part of the central area located between Piccadilly, Ancoats and the Arndale Centre, including the former Smithfield Market and the run down shops of Oldham Street. Following the Northern Quarter Regeneration Study Report of 1994 it has been promoted as a cultural quarter, with the emphasis upon popular culture especially popular music. As with the Gay Village, commercial development preceded official status. By the end of the 1970s, this once-busy industrial, residential and shopping district was depopulated and in rapid decline. Its chief thoroughfare, Oldham Street, was particularly badly hit as the retail focus of the centre shifted after the completion of the Arndale Centre. In the 1980s the booming Manchester music scene and the availability of low rents encouraged musicians, eager to find valuable rehearsal space, and musical entrepreneurs keen to promote the many local bands, to find a base in the disused warehouses and factories off Great Ancoats Street and in the warren of back streets north of Piccadilly. Following the musicians came the cultural commentators. The listings magazine *City Life*, which began as a Manchester version of London's *Time Out*, was published from this quarter. Most important, the opening of Affleck's Palace in the former Affleck & Brown department store building in 1982 secured the district's status as a site for the consumption of popular youth culture. It was closely linked to the youth fashion phenomenon that gave Manchester a distinctive cultural identity in the late 1980s and early 1990s as 'Madchester'. Oldham Street itself was reborn as a site for the new cultural businesses, with shop signs and window displays that could be regarded as a form of informal public art.[12]

The Gay Village and the Northern Quarter exemplify an aspect of the cultural approach to urban regeneration, i.e. marketing Manchester as a 'lifestyle' for sections of the educated 25–40 age group. It is not just that the cultural industries are an important element in the local economy, or that the gay community is a focus for consumption and tourism, but that they both represent the young and the professional. This is precisely the segment of the population that has been identified as the focal group for economic production in the advanced economies of the 'Network Society'.[13] Manchester's 'cool' image with the young for most of the 1980s and 1990s has been part of its cultural identity and an element in its economic regeneration. The City Council's

Cultural Strategy Consultation Draft of June 2001 shows how far the city recognises this. The creative industries, the media, and the popular music industry, along with tourism, sport and leisure, are seen as the key components in the cultural economy.[14]

The prestige model of urban regeneration has gone some way towards rescuing central Manchester. But in the twenty-first century global cities face the challenge of achieving economic growth whilst also advancing the employment prospects, quality of life and full social inclusion of all their citizens. Few Western European cities face a more acute version of this challenge than Manchester. Since the 1960s the region's economy has faced a dramatic restructuring with the balance shifting from the industrial to the service sector (see Chapter 10). As industrial activity has declined, social inequality has grown. A 'poverty belt' more or less encircles the city core (a pattern of residential segregation Engels might still recognise) in which lives a predominantly low-income, low-skill population experiencing poor educational achievement, high levels of ill health and crime and a poor physical environment. Deprivation is more widespread than in any other UK city and many neighbourhoods display levels of social and economic deprivation substantially above the national averages. In 2000 the city as a whole was the sixth most deprived local authority area in the country on the Index of Multiple Deprivation and 27 of the 33 wards in the city featured in the top 10% of the National Index of Deprivation. Contrasting values in the housing market are a symptom of greater social inequality. Whilst city centre values soar, a collapse in the demand for pre-1919 terraced homes in parts of north and north-east Manchester, and in Ordsall and other parts of Salford, has rendered solid and viable houses in some districts virtually worthless.

The attempt to re-brand Manchester as an international city of commercial and cultural repute has to contend with facts like these. Cities are 'states of mind' as well as shapes on the ground. Historically entrenched images of industrialism, a dreary combination of pollution and poverty, are hard to dispel. Similarly, mid-1990s media constructions of inner-city districts, such as Moss Side, as sites of criminality and violence did little to help. For a moment 'Gunchester' replaced 'Madchester', putting at peril the city's recently earned 'cool' image, as Moss Side acquired national status as the archetypal inner-city 'problem area'.[15]

Business success at the centre needs to be translated into secure (and decently paid) jobs for local people. This is a question of social justice. It is also widely recognised as a matter of economic survival. The creation of a sustainable economic environment requires an improvement in the quality of life for all. The shift in local government priorities from 'welfare' in the 1980s to 'growth' in the 1990s has culminated in the recognition that these priorities are inter-dependent. If the

Manchester-led revival of the region is to be maintained, it must be underpinned by an attack on poverty and deprivation which displays the same degree of vigour and imagination as has been applied to the reinvention of the city centre.

The problem is recognised in Manchester City Council's area regeneration policy. Since the early to mid-1990s, this has focused on policies designed to promote economic development and investment in some of the city's most deprived areas. Area-based regeneration is designed to combine the efforts of public, private, voluntary and community organisations in strategies to promote economic revival and the quality of life. Thus, Area Regeneration Teams work with local businesses to stimulate job creation, improve the environment, enhance the existing housing stock and build new homes, tackle crime and vandalism and provide leisure and training facilities for the young. Area Regeneration Teams include the Moss Side and Hulme Partnership, Eastside Regeneration (Ancoats, Miles Platting and the Northern Quarter), the Cheetham and Broughton Partnership, North Manchester Regeneration (Newton Heath, Lightbowne, Harpurhey and Monsall), Beacons for a Brighter Future (East Manchester – Clayton, Beswick and Bradford) and the Stockport Road Corridor Initiative (Ardwick, Longsight and Levenshulme).

Regeneration initiatives have gone farthest and proved most innovative in Moss Side and Hulme. In 1992 Hulme Regeneration Ltd was established by the City Council in partnership with a range of public, private and community interests to develop and manage the City Challenge programme for Hulme. The programme that followed saw the demolition of some of the worst system-built high-rise housing remaining from the 1970s (including the unpopular Crescent flats). This was accompanied by an extensive rebuilding programme, one of the most ambitious exercises in community architecture ever undertaken in Britain. Tenant participation in choice of housing and estate layouts and the role of housing associations in the development has suggested a degree of community involvement which hopefully produces a more enduring solution to housing problems than its predecessor.[16] Since the completion of the City Challenge programme in 1997, the Moss Side and Hulme Partnership Team has overseen the area's various funding programmes. Further fruits of this investment include the improvement of the Princess Road approach to the city, the remodelling of Alexandra Park housing estate, the construction of a large business park (Birley Fields) and the continuing development of Hulme High Street. The future success of the city's revival strategy depends as much on progress in area regeneration initiatives like this as it does on successive city centre prestige projects.

There are signs that the attempt to promote Manchester as an international city of commerce and culture is yielding fruit. The City

Council's Community Strategy document of October 2001 claimed that Manchester is now in the top ten European cities for business location, in the world's top fifty as a conference centre and second only to London as the most visited city in England for overseas visitors.[17] This potential for economic regeneration is rooted in traditional strengths in financial and professional services plus success in heritage and tourism, the cultural and creative industries and knowledge-based information and technology sectors. However, the occasional re-branding of Manchester as 'post-industrial' has caused some concern amongst those who recognise the necessity to defend the declining industrial base of the city and region (although it must be said that the City Council has rarely deployed this kind of rhetoric). Employment statistics for the 1990s suggest a continuing shift from manufacturing to service jobs. There are, however, some brighter spots and a recently revived industrial and business core at Trafford Park Industrial Estate can be counted among them. Derelict and neglected after the collapse of trade at the Manchester Docks, this former industrial heartland of the city has undergone a transformation – a success story of the 1990s, in which the Trafford Park Development Corporation has played a major role. The World Freight Centre in Trafford Park is now the largest road/rail interchange complex outside London. More generally, Manchester's transport infrastructure as a whole is a major asset – notably the continued expansion of the Airport (second runway opened in 2001), the extension of the Metrolink light rail system to Salford Quays and Eccles in 2000, and the long-awaited completion of the M60 orbital motorway (2000). Future success also depends on educational

Metrolink trams pass the Central Library. (*Photograph: Ian Beesley*)

and technological institutions and the city benefits from the presence of the four local universities, creating the largest 'university campus' in Western Europe and one of its major centres of advanced teaching and research in science and technology.

Local confidence in the city's future remains high. The extent to which the devastation caused by the IRA bomb was turned to the city's own advantage and the ambition exemplified in the international games strategy both serve to demonstrate the ability of local forces to engineer an escape route from industrial decline. Part of this is the attempt to reinvent Manchester as a post-modern, cosmopolitan, international city. The extent to which the city and the region can adapt to the pressures of the twenty-first century will depend much upon the success of this re-branding. The process still has far to go. However, in negotiating the future under conditions of globalisation, Manchester is well served by its past history of economic and cultural connections with Europe and the wider world.

References

1. *Manchester Evening News*, 1 October 1993, quoted in A. Cochrane, J. Peck and A. Tickell, Manchester plays games: exploring the local politics of globalisation', *Urban Studies*, 33 (1996), p. 1327.

2. S. Quilley, 'Manchester first: from municipal socialism to the entrepreneurial city', *International Journal of Urban and Regional Research*, 24 (2000), pp. 601–15.

3. J. Borja and M. Castells, *Local and Global: Management of Cities in the Information Age*, United Nations Centre for Human Developments, 1997, pp. 93–108, esp. p. 98.

4. *Manchester 2000: Economic Benefits and Opportunities of the Olympic Games*, quoted in Cochrane *et al.*, 'Manchester plays games', p. 1329.

5. J. Peck and A. Tickell, 'Business goes local: dissecting the "business agenda" in Manchester', *International Journal of Urban and Regional Research*, 19 (1995).

6. P. Loftman and B. Nevin, 'Going for growth: prestige projects in three British cities', *Urban Studies*, 33 (1996), pp. 991–1019; M. Hebbert and I. Deas, 'Greater Manchester – "up and going"?', *Policy and Politics*, 28 (2000), pp. 79–92.

7. Sir David Trippier, 'Marketing Manchester: the promotion of the city region nationally and internationally', *Manchester Memoirs*, 135 (1996–7), pp. 47–54; I. Deas and K. Ward, 'From the "new localism" to the "new regionalism"? The implications of regional development agencies for city-regional relations', *Political Geography*, 19 (2000), 273–92; Hebbert and Deas, 'Greater Manchester – "up and going"?'.

8. P. Malone, 'The mending of Manchester', *Urban Design Quarterly*, 61 (1997); G. Williams, 'Rebuilding the entrepreneurial city: the master planning response to the bombing of Manchester city centre', *Environment and Planning B: Planning and Design*, 27 (2000), pp. 485–505.

9. Nikolaus Pevsner, *The Buildings of England: Lancashire I, The Industrial and Commercial South*, Penguin, 1969, p. 282. See also John Archer's assessment of the Hall and the current conversion plans in Clare Hartwell, *Manchester*, Pevsner Architectural Guides, Penguin, 2001, pp. 92–5.

10. The City Council expects the city centre population to be over 10,000 by 2002.

11. P. Hindle, 'The influence of the Gay Village on migration to central Manchester, *The North West Geographer*, 3 (2000), pp. 21–8.

12. K. Milestone, 'Sites of sounds: spaces of pop culture in Manchester's Northern Quarter', *The North West Geographer*, 2, (2000), pp. 31–9.

13. Manuel Castells, *The Rise of the Network Society*, Blackwell, 2nd edn, 2000.

14. Manchester City Council, *Cultural Strategy Consultation Draft*, June 2001.

15. For an assessment of the issues see Penny Fraser, 'Social and spatial relationships and the "problem" inner city: Moss Side in Manchester', *Critical Social Policy*, 49 (1996), pp. 43–65.

16. R. Ramwell and H. Saltburn, *Trick or Treat? City Challenge and the Regeneration of Hulme*, North British Housing Association, Preston, 1998.

17. Manchester City Council, *The Manchester Community Strategy: Competing in the Global Economy*, section 2:9, October 2001.

Further Reading

If this brief history has whetted the appetite for further reading or study then there is a plentiful supply of material. The following bibliography is merely a selection of the reading available for those who may wish to extend their knowledge of the topics touched on in this book. Much fuller coverage can be found in Terry Wyke's 'Nineteenth-century Manchester: a preliminary bibliography' in A. J. Kidd and K. W. Roberts (eds), *City, Class and Culture*, Manchester University Press, 1985, pp. 218–73. In 27 sections and running to 1,200 published items, this bibliography belies its title. However, it is confined to publications about the nineteenth century. There is no comparable listing for other periods, although the Joint Committee on the Lancashire Bibliography published several volumes which include references for Manchester chiefly relating to pre-1800. Since 1987 the *Manchester Region History Review* (published each May from the Manchester Metropolitan University) has included an annual Manchester bibliography covering all topics and periods. Beyond published material, the serious student may want to consult some of the numerous unpublished theses and dissertations listed and classified according to subject in U. R. E. Lawler, *North-West Theses and Dissertations 1950–1978: A Bibliography*, University of Lancaster Centre for North-West Regional Studies, 1981 and M. E. McClintock, W. R. Clark and L. C. Kirtley, *North-West Theses and Dissertations 1979–84*, University of Lancaster Centre for North-West Regional Studies, 1988.

Since the publication of the second edition of this book in 1996 there have been several important additions to the bibliography of Manchester's history. The twentieth century remains a somewhat neglected period and it is the 'heroic' era of the city's history in the nineteenth century that continues to attract most attention. In particular, a handful of valuable studies have acted as a corrective to the view that there is nothing more to say on the history of the cotton industry. Among these one must select Mary B. Rose (ed.), *The Lancashire Cotton Industry: A History since 1700* (Preston, 1996), and G. Timmins, *Made in Lancashire: A History of Regional Industrialisation* (Manchester University Press, 1998) for particular recommendation. Both of these include significant discussions of the origins of industrialisation in the North West and add further context to our knowledge of the role of Manchester in that momentous process. An invaluable tool for the researcher is Terry

Wyke's *Cotton: A Select Bibliography on Cotton in North West England* (Bibliography of North West England, Volume 17, Manchester, 1997). However, compared to the economic history of textiles, we know much less about the broader social and political history of the town in the seventeenth and eighteenth centuries. Instead, the great age of the Victorian bourgeoisie retains its power to fascinate. Michael Turner's *Reform and Respectability: The Making of a Middle-Class Liberalism in Early 19th-Century Manchester* (Manchester, 1995) casts light on the pre-history of that middle-class liberalism of Cobden and Bright with which mid-Victorian Manchester is forever associated. Meanwhile, Simon Gunn's *Public Culture of the Victorian Middle Class: Ritual and Authority in the English Industrial City 1840–1914* (Manchester, 2000) explores aspects of bourgeois public culture in a study using evidence from Birmingham and Leeds as well as Manchester. Like Simon Gunn, Martin Hewitt has interesting things to say about the contested use of public space in the nineteenth-century city using Manchester as a case study: see M. Hewitt, *The Emergence of Stability in the Industrial City: Manchester, 1832–67* (Scolar, 1996). His focus is on the post-Chartist history of the Manchester and Salford working class. Manchester's place in working-class history is clearer thanks to Paul Pickering's most readable *Chartism and the Chartists in Manchester and Salford* (London, 1995). Two other studies which have thrown light on important aspects of the history of the city are Peter Shapely, *Charity and Power in Victorian Manchester* (Manchester, 2000) and Rainer Liedtke, *Jewish Welfare in Hamburg and Manchester c. 1850–1914* (Oxford, 1998). Both examine aspects of civil society and issues of culture, authority and identity. Mervyn Busteed's research on the Manchester Irish parallels Liedtke's on the sense of identity among Manchester Jewry. Busteed's work appears in several articles and essays, but I can draw particular attention to M. A. Busteed and R. I. Hodgson, 'Irish Migrant responses to urban life in early industrial Manchester', *Geographical Journal*, 162 (1996), 139–53 and M. Busteed, 'Songs in a strange land – ambiguities of identity among Irish migrants in mid-Victorian Manchester', *Political Geography*, 17 (1998), 627–65.

In addition to the contributions to the bibliography identified above, the list of further reading appended to the second edition appears unaltered below. Items have been cited only once, even if they are of value for more than one of the sections into which the bibliography is divided.

General Histories

Carter, C. F. (ed.), *Manchester and Its Region*, Manchester University Press, 1962.

Farrer, W. *et al* (eds), *The Victoria History of the County of Lancashire*, Vol. 4, Constable, London, 1911, pp. 174–338.

Frangopulo, N.J. (ed.), *Rich Inheritance: A Guide to the History of Manchester*, Manchester Education Committee, 1962.

Kennedy, M., *A Portrait of Manchester*, Robert Hale, London, 1970.

Makepeace, C. F., *Manchester As It Was*, Vols 1–6, Hendon Publishing, Nelson, 1972–7.

Redford, A. and Russell, I., *The History of Local Government in Manchester, Vol. I, Manor and Township; Vol. II, Borough and City; vol. III, The Last Half Century*, Longmans, London, 1939–40.

Simon, S., *A Century of City Government: Manchester 1838–1938*, George Allen & Unwin, London, 1938.

Walton, J., *Lancashire: A Social History, 1558–1939*, Manchester University Press, 1987.

Before the Industrial Revolution

Bryant, S., *et al.*, *The Archaeological History of Greater Manchester, Vol. III, Roman Manchester: A Frontier Settlement*, Greater Manchester Archaeological Unit, Manchester, 1987.

Kenyon, D., *The Origins of Lancashire*, Manchester University Press, 1991.

Malet, H., *Bridgewater: The Canal Duke 1736–1803*, Manchester University Press, 1977.

Morris, M., *et al.*, *The Archaeological History of Greater Manchester, Vol. I, Medieval Manchester*, Greater Manchester Archaeological Unit, Manchester, 1983.

Tait, J., *Medieval Manchester and the Origins of Lancashire*, Manchester University Press, 1904.

Wadsworth, A. P. and Mann, J. de Lacy, *The Cotton Trade and Industrial Lancashire, 1600–1780*, Manchester University Press, 1931.

Walton, J., 'Proto-industrialisation and the first industrial revolution: the case of Lancashire' in P. Hudson (ed.), *Regions and Industries: A Perspective on the Industrial Revolution in Britain*, Cambridge University Press, 1989.

Willan, T. S., *Elizabethan Manchester*, Chetham Society, Manchester, 1980.

First Industrial City: 1780–1850

Bamford, S., *Autobiography, Vol. II, Passages in the Life of a Radical* (1841), Frank Cass, London, 1967.

Belchem, J., *'Orator' Hunt*, Oxford University Press, 1985.

Bohstedt, J., *Riots and Community Polities in England and Wales 1790–1810*, Harvard University Press, London, 1983.

Booth, A., 'Popular loyalism and public violence in the north-west of England 1790–1800', *Social History*, 8 (1983), pp. 295–313.

Bradshaw, L. D. (ed.), *Visitors to Manchester: A Selection of British and Foreign Visitors' Descriptions of Manchester from c. 1538 to 1865*, Neil Richardson, Swinton, 1987.

Briggs, A., *Victorian Cities*, Penguin, Harmondsworth, 1963.

Chalklin, C. W., *The Provincial Towns of Georgian England 1740–1820*, Edward Arnold, London, 1974.

Darcy, C. P., *The Encouragement of the Fine Arts in Lancashire 1760–1860*, Chetham Society, Manchester, 1976.

De Motte, 'The Dark Side of the Town: Crime in Manchester and Salford 1815–1872', Unpublished DPhil. Thesis, University of Kansas, 1977.

Dennis, R., *English Industrial Cities of the Nineteenth Century*, Cambridge University Press, 1984.

Edwards, M. M., *The Growth of the British Cotton Trade, 1780–1815*, Manchester University Press, 1967.

Fleischman, R. K., *Conditions of Life Among the Cotton Workers of Southeastern Lancashire, 1780–1850*, Garland, New York, 1985.

Fowler A., and Wyke T. (eds), *The Barefoot Aristocrats: A History of the Amalgamated Association of Operative Cotton Spinners*, George Kelsall, Littleborough, 1987.

Gaskell, E., *Mary Barton: A Tale of Manchester Life* (1848), edited by Angus Easson, Ryburn Publishing, Halifax, 1993.

Gatrell, V. A. C., 'Incorporation and the pursuit of Liberal hegemony in Manchester 1790–1839' in D. Fraser (ed.), *Municipal Reform and the Industrial City*, Leicester University Press, 1982.

Hadfield, C. and Biddle, G., *The Canals of North West England*, 2 vols, David and Charles, Newton Abbot, 1970.

Howe, A., *The Cotton Masters 1830–1860*, Oxford University Press, 1984.

Jones, D., *Crime, Protest, Community and Police in Nineteenth-century Britain*, London, 1982, ch. 6.

Kargon, R. H., *Science in Victorian Manchester: Enterprise and Expertise*, Manchester University Press, 1977.

Knight, F., *The Strange Case of Thomas Walker: Ten Years in the Life of a Manchester Radical*, Lawrence and Wishart, London, 1957.

Lloyd-Jones, R., and Lewis, M. J., *Manchester and the Age of the Factory*, Croom Helm, London, 1988.

Lowe, W. J., *The Irish in Mid-Victorian Lancashire*, Peter Lang, New York, 1989.

Manchester Region History Review, III:i (1989) (Special issue on Peterloo).

Marcus, S., *Engels, Manchester and the Working Class*, Random House, New York, 1974.

Musson, A. E., and Robinson, E., *Science and Technology in the Industrial Revolution*, Manchester University Press, 1969.

Prentice, A., *Historical Sketches and Personal Recollections of Manchester* (1851), Frank Cass, London, 1970.

Read, D., *Peterloo: The 'Massacre' and Its Background*, Manchester University Press, 1958.

Redford, A., *Manchester Merchants and Foreign Trade 1794–1858*, Manchester University Press, 1934.

Reid, R., *The Peterloo Massacre*, Heinemann, London, 1989.

Scola, R., *Feeding the Victorian City: The Food Supply of Manchester 1770–1870*, Manchester University Press, 1992.

Sykes, R., 'Early Chartism and trade unionism in south-east Lancashire', in

Epstein, J. and Thompson, D. (eds), *The Chartist Experience*, Macmillan, London, 1982.

Thackray, A., 'Natural knowledge in a cultural context: the Manchester model', *American Historical Review*, LXIX (1974), pp. 672–709.

Thomas, R. H. G., *The Liverpool and Manchester Railway*, Batsford, London, 1980.

Thompson, E. P., *The Making of the English Working Class*, Pelican edn, Harmondsworth, 1968.

Williams, B., *The Making of Manchester Jewry 1740–1875*, Manchester University Press, 1976.

Wolff, J. and Seed, J. (eds), *The Culture of Capital: Art, Power and the Nineteenth-century Middle Class*, Manchester University Press, 1988.

Commercial Metropolis: 1850–1914

Archer, J. (ed.), *Art and Architecture in Victorian Manchester*, Manchester University Press, 1986.

Ayerst, D., *Guardian: Biography of a Newspaper*, Collins, London, 1971.

Beesley, I., and de Figueiredo, P., *Victorian Manchester and Salford*, Ryburn Publishing, Halifax, 1988.

Briggs, A., *Friends of the People: The Centenary History of Lewis's*, Batsford, London, 1956.

Chorley, K., *Manchester Made Them*, Faber and Faber, London, 1950.

Cooper, A., 'The Manchester Commercial Textile Warehouse 1780–1914: A Study of its Typology and Practical Development', Unpublished PhD Thesis, University of Manchester, 1991.

Farnie, D. A., 'The commercial development of Manchester in the later nineteenth century', *Manchester Review*, 7 (1956), pp. 327–37.

Farnie, D. A., *The English Cotton Industry and the World Market, 1815–1896*, Oxford University Press, 1979.

Fielding, S., 'Irish politics in Manchester 1890–1914', *International Review of Social History*, XXXIII (1988), pp. 261–84.

Freeman, T. W., *The Conurbations of Great Britain*, Manchester University Press, 1966, ch. 5.

Harrison, M., 'Housing and town planning in Manchester before 1914' in Sutcliffe, A., *British Town Planning: The Formative Years*, Leicester University Press, 1981.

Henderson, W. O., *The Lancashire Cotton Famine 1861–1865*, 2nd edn, Manchester, 1969.

Holt, G. O., *A Regional History of the Railways in Great Britain, Vol. 10, The North West*, David and Charles, Newton Abbot, 1978.

Jones, D. R., *The Origins of Civic Universities: Manchester, Leeds and Liverpool*, Manchester University Press, 1988.

Kellett, J. R., *Railways and Victorian Cities*, Routledge & Kegan Paul, London, 1969, ch. 6.

Kidd, A. J., 'The Social Democratic Federation and popular agitation amongst the unemployed in Edwardian Manchester', *International Review of Social History*, XXIX (1984), pp. 336–58.

Kidd A. J. and Roberts K. W. (eds), City, *Class and Culture: Studies of Social Policy and Cultural Production in Victorian Manchester*, Manchester University Press, 1985.

Kirk, N., *The Growth of Working-Class Reformism in Mid-Victorian England*, Croom Helm, London, 1985.

Liddington, J. and Norris, J., *One Hand Tied Behind Us: The Rise of the Women's Suffrage Movement*, Virago, London, 1978.

Maltby, S. E., *Manchester and the Movement for National Elementary Education 1800–1870*, Manchester University Press, 1918.

Marr, T. R., *Housing Conditions in Manchester and Salford*, Sherratt & Hughes, Manchester, 1904.

Neal, F., 'The Manchester origins of the English Orange Order', *Manchester Region History Review*, IV:ii (1990–1), pp. 12–24.

Owen, D., *The Manchester Ship Canal*, Manchester University Press, 1983.

Pickstone, J. V., *Medicine and Industrial Society: A History of Hospital Development in Manchester and its Region 1752–1946*, Manchester University Press, 1985.

Pooley, M. and Pooley, C., 'Health, society and environment in Victorian Manchester' in R. Woods and J. Woodward (eds), *Urban Disease and Mortality in Nineteenth-century England*, Batsford, London, 1984.

Price, R., 'The other face of respectability: violence in the Manchester brick making trade, 1859–70', *Past and Present*, 66 (1975), pp. 110–32.

Redford, A., *Manchester Merchants and Foreign Trade, Vol. II, 1850–1939*, Manchester University Press, 1956.

Roberts, J., *Working-Class Housing in Nineteenth-Century Manchester*, Neil Richardson, Swinton, 1982.

Rodgers, H. B., 'The suburban growth of Victorian Manchester', *Journal of the Manchester Geographical Society*, 58 (1962), pp. 1–12.

Rose, M. E., 'Settlement of university men in great towns: university settlements in Manchester and Liverpool', *Transactions of the Historic Society of Lancashire and Cheshire*, 139 (1989), pp. 137–60.

Scott, R., *The Biggest Room in the World: A Short History of the Manchester Royal Exchange*, Royal Exchange Theatre Trust, Manchester, 1976.

Sharratt A. and Farrar, K. R., 'Sanitation and public health in nineteenth-century Manchester', *Memoirs and Proceedings of the Manchester Literary and Philosophical Society*, 114 (1971–2), pp. 50–69.

Simmons, J., *The Railway in Town and Country 1830–1914*, David and Charles, Newton Abbot, 1986, ch. 4.

Spiers, M., *Victoria Park, Manchester: A Nineteenth-Century Suburb in Its Social and Administrative Context*, Chetham Society, Manchester, 1976.

Stewart, C., *The Stones of Manchester*, Edward Arnold, London, 1956.

Within Living Memory: Manchester Since 1914

Bertenshaw, M., *Sunrise to Sunset: A Vivid Personal Account of Life in Manchester*, Printwise Publications, Bury, 1991.

Burke, M., *Ancoats Lad: The Recollections of Mick Burke*, Neil Richardson, Swinton, 1985.

Cardwell, D. S. L. (ed.), *Artisan to Graduate: Essays to Commemorate the Foundation of the Manchester Mechanics Institution, now U.M.I.S.T.*, Manchester University Press, 1974.

Charlton, H. B., *Portrait of a University 1851–1951*, Manchester University Press, 1951.

Clay, H. and Brady, K. Russell, *Manchester at Work*, Manchester Civic Week Committee, 1929.

Davies, A., *Leisure, Gender and Poverty: Working-Class Culture in Salford and Manchester 1900–1939*, Open University Press, Buckingham, 1992.

Davies, A. and Fielding, S. (eds), *Workers' Worlds: Cultures and Communities in Manchester and Salford 1880–1939*, Manchester University Press, 1992.

Davies, P., *A Northern School: Lancashire Artists of the Twentieth Century*, Redcliffe Press, Bristol, 1989.

Department of Economic Affairs, *The North West: A Regional Study*, H.M.S.O., London, 1965.

Deakin, D., *Wythenshawe: The Story of a Garden City*, Phillimore, Chichester, 1989.

Farnie, D. A., *The Manchester Ship Canal and the Rise of the Port of Manchester 1894–1975*, Manchester University Press, 1980.

Fleming, D., *The Manchester Fighters*, Neil Richardson, Swinton, 1986.

Fowler, A. and Wyke, T., *Many Arts. Many Skills. The Origins of the Manchester Metropolitan University*, Manchester Metropolitan University Press, 1993.

Gomes, M., *The Picture House*, North West Film Archive, Manchester Polytechnic, 1988.

Green, L. P., *Provincial Metropolis: The Future of Local Government in South-East Lancashire*, George Allen & Unwin, London, 1959.

Hardy, C., *Manchester Since 1900: Ninety Years of Photographs*, Archive Publications, Manchester, 1988.

Kennedy, M., *The Hallé Tradition: A Century of Music*, Manchester University Press, 1960.

Kennedy, M., *The History of Royal Manchester College of Music 1832–1972*, Manchester University Press, 1971.

Law, C. M. *et al.*, *Comparative Study of Conurbations Project: The Greater Manchester Area*, University of Salford, 1984.

Law, C. M., *The Redevelopment of Manchester Docks*, University of Salford, 1988.

Lloyd, P. E. and Mason, C. M., 'Manufacturing in the inner city: a case study of Greater Manchester', *Transactions of the Institute of British Geographers*, n.s. 3 (1978), pp. 66–90.

Manchester and District Joint Town Planning Advisory Committee, *Report on the Regional Scheme*, Manchester, 1926.

Manchester City Council, *Manchester City Centre Local Plan*, Manchester, 1984.

Manchester Employment Research Group Ltd, *Trends in Employment and Unemployment in Manchester*, Manchester Polytechnic, 1987.

Nicholas, R., *City of Manchester Plan*, Jarrold & Sons, Norwich and London, for Manchester Corporation, 1945.

Pritchard, F., *Dance Days Around Manchester*, Neil Richardson, Swinton, 1988.

Rodgers, B., 'Manchester: metropolitan planning by collaboration and consent or civic hope frustrated' in G. Gordon (ed.), *Regional Cities in the United Kingdom 1890–1980*, Harper and Row, London, 1986.

Sandberg, L., *Lancashire in Decline: A Study in Entrepreneurship, Technology and International Trade*, Ohio State University Press, Columbus, 1974.

Simon, E. D. and Inman, J., *The Rebuilding of Manchester*, Longmans, London, 1935.

Singleton, J., *Lancashire on the Scrapheap: The Cotton Industry 1945–1970*, Oxford University Press, 1991.

Smith, D. M., *Industrial Britain: The North West*, David and Charles, Newton Abbot, 1969.

Stocks, M., *Fifty Years in Every Street: The Story of the Manchester University Settlement*, Manchester University Press, 2nd edn, 1956.

White, H. P., *The Continuing Conurbation: Change and Development in Greater Manchester*, Gower, Farnborough, 1980.

Williams, P., *Chethams: Old and New in Harmony*, Manchester University Press, 1986.

Index